I0797663

# THE FAR EDGES OF THE KNOWN WORLD

# THE FAR EDGES OF THE KNOWN WORLD

Life Beyond the Borders of Ancient Civilization

OWEN REES

W. W. NORTON & COMPANY
*Independent Publishers Since 1923*

First published in Great Britain by Bloomsbury Publishing in 2025 under the title
*The Far Edges of the Known World: A New History of the Ancient Past*


Printed in the United States of America



Maps by Michael Athanson

Manufacturing by Versa Press

ISBN 978-1-324-03652-4

W. W. Norton & Company, Inc., 500 Fifth Avenue, New York, NY 10110
www.wwnorton.com

W. W. Norton & Company Ltd., 15 Carlisle Street, London W1D 3BS

1 2 3 4 5 6 7 8 9 0

# CONTENTS

# Introduction: Beyond the Known World

'All the Greeks consider you to be wise, and you are held in high regard. But if you still lived at the far edges of the world, there would be no talk of you.'[1]

So speaks the Greek hero Jason to his wife Medea, the woman he took from the distant lands of Colchis after she had given him all the tools with which he could complete his quest to capture the Golden Fleece from her father, the king Aeetes. In what amounts to a very short passage in the fifth century BCE Greek playwright Euripides' *Medea*, Jason articulates an enduring conception of life at the edge of the world.

According to many of the classical authors, the edge of the world was the domain of monstrous humanity. Libya was the land of Medusa and her gorgon sisters, India was filled with men who would eat their deceased fathers as a mark of respect and the northern lands like Gaul and Scythia were filled with head-hunters and cannibals. It was also where their world views were inverted, where women held power and fought in armies alongside the men. At its most extreme, it was on the edges of the known world where the Amazons lived, the female warriors who excluded men from their society.

The sentiment in Jason's words is clear: by taking Medea from Colchis, the edges of the known world, Jason had taken her away from a barbarian life. No matter what hardship she was now facing as a single mother of Jason's two sons, abandoned by her husband who had taken a new wife; these could not diminish the great benefits he had given her all those years ago when he whisked her away from her father's palace. The land of Colchis sat on the eastern coast of the Euxine Sea, which means the Friendly Sea, today better known as the Black Sea. Jason's description of Medea's homeland being at the edges of the world is not simply poetic hyperbole, but actually reflects a wider Greek view of the region. Colchis was situated just south of the Caucasus Mountains, where the mighty god Zeus tied the poor Titan Prometheus to a rock for stealing fire from the gods and giving it to humanity, having his liver feasted on every day by an eagle. The land of Colchis was a boundary between worlds. Through it ran the River Phasis, which ancient writers considered the natural landmark that separated Europe and Asia, akin to the River Nile, which separated Asia and Libya (what we would now consider the rest of Africa).

The people of Colchis were themselves a thing of legend. The fifth-century BCE Greek poet Pindar described the Colchians as 'dark-skinned', and his contemporary, the 'father of history' Herodotus of Halicarnassus, comments on the resemblance between the Colchians and the Egyptians.[2] Herodotus goes as far as to invent a story whereby some soldiers from the army of the Egyptian pharaoh Sesostris, who it is claimed campaigned as far north as Scythia and Thrace, stayed in the region and became the people of Colchis. Herodotus uses this fake story to explain certain traits and customs of the Colchian people: their dark skin, their 'woolly' hair and their practice of circumcision. Historians do not credit any of what Herodotus says on the matter.

Centuries later, the first-century BCE/CE Roman geographer Strabo described the people of the Black Sea in vague Roman terms, but the picture he paints is a clear one. The 'Scythians' are a people who will be discussed in more detail later in the book, but for now it is important to note that Greek and Roman writers were very inconsistent in their labelling of tribes and peoples. They would regularly group people together who would not necessarily consider themselves to share a cultural or ethnic identity, as we understand those terms. Strabo describes the Black Sea, before Greek colonisation:

> [It] was called Axenus [or the Unfriendly Sea] because of its stormy waters and the savage nature of the peoples who live around it; in particular, the Scythians who sacrificed strangers, eating their flesh and using their skulls as drinking cups.[3]

To Strabo, the Scythians were just one of the many groups of people living around the Black Sea. While he stereotypes the Scythians as the most barbaric of these inhabitants, he is no kinder to the other tribal groups. Similarly, the second-century CE historian Appian describes the Colchians as a 'war-like people', often a coded description for barbarian societies, especially in the north.[4]

The irony is that there were Greek people living in Colchis. No doubt the Greek inhabitants were not in the minds of the writers describing the region, but it raises the question: if the land was so isolated, and the people so barbaric, what were the Greeks doing there? And, more importantly, what did they make of their neighbours? Colchis, like much of the Black Sea, witnessed the appearance of Greek merchants and settlers throughout the seventh to sixth centuries BCE. The name for the major river in the region, Phasis, was likewise the name of a

Greek town established to exploit the interconnected river networks that snaked through Colchis. The area might not have been Greek, but there were certainly settlements filled with Greek people calling it home.

At the turn of the fourth century BCE, a Greek army of mercenaries known as the Ten Thousand entered Colchian lands as part of their long retreat from Babylonia following their defeat at the Battle of Cunaxa (401 BCE). Like any army at that time, the Greeks took to raiding the local area for food and loot. They were based at the small Greek town of Trapezus, whose citizens attempted to offer a market for the mercenaries to acquire food and provisions. For the Ten Thousand, the raiding of Colchian lands, barbarian lands, was second nature, so the actions of the Greek people of Trapezus are particularly enlightening:

> And the Trapezuntians supplied a market for the army, received the Greeks kindly, and gave them oxen, barley-meal, and wine as gifts of hospitality. They likewise took part in negotiations with the Greeks on behalf of the near-by Colchians, who dwelt for the most part on the plain, and from these people also the Greeks received hospitable gifts of oxen.[5]

By acting as negotiators, middlemen as it were, between the Greek army and the non-Greek inhabitants, the people of Trapezus highlight the need for local cooperation. For Greeks to survive this far away from the Greek mainland, and to be able to thrive through trade, it was important to get along with other local groups. The mercenary army was unsettling that local balance. They were treating the region as if it was on the edge of the world, and the people were barbarians and of no real value. But the people of Trapezus knew differently, and by treating the

Colchians with a little dignity, the Greeks, Xenophon tells us, received the reward – gifts of oxen.

* * *

To cultures that strongly believed in their own cultural superiority, such as the ancient Egyptians, the Athenians and the Romans, the further away you were from the core of that society, the further away you were from civilisation itself. To a member of the Roman elite, Rome was the beating heart of their world, a beacon of Roman ideals and cultural normality. While it rarely lived up to these standards in practice, there is a clear impression that to be sent away from Rome was in itself a horrible punishment, especially for a member of the Roman social elite. Much like in classical Athens, where individuals could be sent into exile for ten years from the city (ostracism), Roman emperors would likewise punish people who had fallen from grace with exile.

The most renowned exile is undoubtedly that of the poet Ovid, sent to the Black Sea by the Emperor Augustus in 8 CE. To this day we do not know what caused his fall from grace in the eyes of the emperor. Perhaps it was his erotic poetry, which flew in the face of Augustus' moral reforms. In 18 or 17 BCE, Augustus passed the *Lex Iulia de Adulteriis Coercendis*, which made adultery a crime – a crime for which he would later have to punish his own daughter. Considering that the publication of Ovid's first collection of love poetry *Amores* was in 16 BCE, his timing was perhaps a little off; while his later collection, *Ars Amatoria* (the Art of Love), reads more like a guide to seduction for the higher social classes. We cannot be sure that these were in any way responsible for his falling out with Augustus, but it is fair to assume that 'when he [Ovid] committed his fatal error, he could expect no margin of compassion whatsoever'.[6]

While in exile, Ovid wrote numerous poems and letters often focused on his experiences at the edge of the world. What they tell us about the town where he had been sent, and the people he was surrounded by, is minimal. Ovid was from a long-standing provincial equestrian family in Rome and was set up for a successful career in politics or law. But he had little interest in this life plan and, as a young writer, he had acquired his own wealthy patron called Messalla Corvinus. This offered him a leisurely life and the status such an existence bestows upon people. To the dismay of his father, Ovid did not pursue traditional Roman values. He avoided standing for political offices for which he was eligible, and even managed to avoid obligatory military service. It was his secure financial position, from both his family finances and his patron's, that allowed him to live the life he wanted: one of literature.[7]

Ovid's Rome was the Rome of the old history books, a Rome for the elite; something that in exile he sorely missed. To him, it was normal to have seen the great poet Virgil and to have listened to Horace reciting his *Odes*. The contrast between this and his new home of Tomis, on the west coast of the Black Sea in modern Romania, could not have been clearer to Ovid. Thus, he had a decision to make. He could embrace the situation he was in, soak in the undiluted beauty of the Black Sea coast and explore the peaks and valleys that guide the mighty Danube to the west; or become the victim in his own self-pitying narrative. He picked the latter, and at times his writings read like the petulant protestations of a spoiled teenager. He considered his exile as a brutal punishment, and his views of Tomis were particularly scathing: 'This bitter place than which there can be nothing more sad in all the world'.[8]

In one particular letter, Ovid describes the difficulties he was facing in Tomis. He paints the people as aggressive and warlike, dressed in animal skins, which served as a marker of their barbarousness. He describes the freezing winters which froze wine in the jar and turned the Black Sea into solid ice, preventing ships from sailing and dolphins from jumping. This was a land where peace was only ever temporary, and war inevitable. It was a place where grapes would not grow, and the land was barren.[9] It was a place entirely of Ovid's bigoted imagination.

In reality, Tomis was a Greek settlement most probably established in the sixth century BCE, according to the archaeological evidence. It also had a mythological pedigree of its own. For, long before the settlement was founded, this area was traditionally considered the place where Jason and Medea paused in their escape from Colchis. With the Golden Fleece on board, the famous *Argo* was in a race against the pursuing king Aeetes; but Medea had also taken one other valuable item from her father: her young brother Apsyrtus. When a lookout spotted the ship of Aeetes closing in while the *Argo* was beached, Medea knew they were on the verge of capture. Her eyes looked to the horizon in front, then to the lands behind them; they darted in all directions until they finally settled on the young Apsyrtus. Suspecting nothing of his sister, Apsyrtus was swiftly killed by a sword through the heart. Medea then ripped his body limb from limb, scattering the remains throughout the surrounding fields except for his head and hands. These she placed in plain view on a nearby prominent rock, certain as they were to attract her father's attention. Her gruesome plan worked, and her father stopped to collect the body parts and give them a proper burial. He buried them there and, according to Apollodorus, named the place Tomis, from the Greek word *tomous*, meaning cutting. To Ovid, this was the story of how the town received its name, borne from the barbarous act of a foreign woman who lived at the edge of the world.[10]

We know from epigraphical evidence (inscriptions) that the settlement was part of a large Greek network of towns and trading posts throughout the Black Sea and Asia Minor to the south. Archaeologists have discovered remnants of Attic pottery, showing that the cultural and financial exchanges extended beyond the Black Sea and Ionian coast. There is also evidence of non-Greek pottery, most likely traded with the local population, who would have served as valuable trading partners. We know that around the third century BCE, the town underwent a transformation, possibly as a result of a local conflict, and then expanded from a trading settlement into a fully fledged city-state (*polis*).[11] This was a thriving and bustling trading town, with all the hallmarks of an urbanised, orderly political landscape, and that is evidenced even before the Roman annexation of the region in the first century BCE. This was no backwater town, and it was certainly not a lawless and barbaric home for Ovid.

The fact of the matter is that Ovid was not doing anything out of the ordinary by portraying Tomis in such a way. Part of Ovid's indignation draws from his own expectations. Tomis was a Greek town, and part of the Roman Empire, so he should have felt at least a small sense of continuity. Of course, towns throughout the empire held their own customs, languages and systems in place, but Ovid's experience of travelling as a young man meant he had visited similarly affluent centres of learning and culture: Athens and the cities of Asia Minor. Tomis should have been filled with civilised intellectual people, in Ovid's mind, like Athens, or Alexandria in Egypt, but instead he found himself baulking at the lack of Latin spoken, and the strange Greek dialect that jarred with the classical Greek he would have learned as a young boy.[12] It was a place where Romans, Greeks and indigenous people regularly mixed, where trade with locals was a prized asset and indigenous cults sat side by side with Greek and Roman ones.

Tomis was also a place where Ovid's privileged upbringing no longer protected him from his duties. Military service was a responsibility he had avoided his entire adult life while in Rome, but out on the periphery he had to serve just like everybody else.

As he complains on more than one occasion, Tomis was often under threat from raiding tribes, and in his early fifties Ovid finally donned the weapons of war to help defend the town:

> The rough contests of military service I shunned even as a youth and touched arms only with a hand intending to play; but now that I am growing old I fit a sword to my side, a shield to my left arm, and I place a helmet upon my grey head. For when the guard from the lookout has given the signal for a raid, forthwith I don my armour with shaking hands.[13]

Ovid's writings are not particularly useful for understanding life on the edges of the ancient world, but they are pivotal to our understanding of how the edges of the world were perceived by ancient writers, historians and philosophers – the majority of whom were wealthy men living in urban centres of culture. What we do not have, for instance, is an impression of what the people of Tomis thought of him. How would they have reacted to this spoilt aristocrat sent to live in their town? The clues we have in his writing suggests they were not very impressed, but we have nothing from the people themselves. Alas, we do not know, but we should not make the mistake of believing Ovid's exaggerations of what life was like for everyone else at the edge of the Roman Empire.

* * *

There is a fundamental problem when considering the edges of the world: the edges are determined by where we think the centre is. There are, in effect, an infinite number of possible peripheries that can be explored, peripheries that are determined by the culture we are relating them to. Through our emphasis on the ancient history of particular cultures, we are conditioned to consider the edges of the world as those described by the Greeks and Romans. This would include the lands of modern Germany, Scotland, 'Sub-Saharan' Africa and Pakistan; places these cultures knew of but considered beyond their boundaries. Such an approach is especially defined in Roman history by the lines of the empire. This makes a delineation of the edges of the Roman world easy to visualise, but it ignores the fact that these lines on the map were prone to moving as societies explored the world around them.

There is a second problem borne not from the history itself, but from the modern history writer. There are elements of the ancient world that simply do not get discussed, especially outside academic circles. Our obsession with Greek and Roman cultures, and their perceptions of the world, means that we explore the ancient world from their perspective. This drives us to misunderstand other cultures, to explore them almost exclusively through their interactions with Greece and Rome, and to ignore cultures that our sources do not mention. There is no perfect solution to this problem, which is driven by various practical as well as ideological factors. Greece and Rome offer the largest evidence base of all the ancient cultures in and around the Mediterranean Basin, so it is understandable that they have formed the basis of most ancient historical exploration in the European tradition, but this should not distract us from looking at the ancient world as a global environment.

To be fair, this is changing, and changing fast. We are now seeing an explosion in studies exploring the links and comparisons between ancient Rome and China, and the study of Greco-Indian exchanges has a long-standing tradition. Similarly, ancient Africa, beyond Egypt, is becoming a more prominent field of study and in turn is unveiling an amazing cache of cultural histories that have been too long ignored. As a result, we are seeing this more global approach permeate the public sphere, with works exploring the interconnected nature of the ancient world through trade along the Silk Road and through intellectual exchanges. This is surely the way ancient history should be going, by trying to understand the wider global context of some amazing cultures that have enthralled readers for centuries. Yet it comes with its own set of issues.

By studying the connections between ancient societies, such as Rome and China or Greece and India, we are often reinforcing separate cultural identities where the interchange is rather formal. It is as if we are examining how two cultures interacted based on the letters exchanged between imperial courts. This tells us nothing about normal people, or the day-to-day reality of these cultures intermingling. Similarly, such an approach prioritises those cultures and locations for which we have the most written evidence, to the detriment of places where the interactions mostly took place – at the borders.

We often visualise the ancient world as one filled with boundaries and borders, but those borders were not empty places. They were filled with life, families and culture, but it does not always look the way we may expect. As Ovid discovered to his disgust, away from the prying eyes of their fellow countrymen, people living at the edge of their civilisation were able to adapt and change their ways in keeping with the environment around them. The firm lines between culture and identity are blurred, and ideological zealotry often gives way to pragmatism and compromise. There would be violence and conflict, of course, but this is not the only thing we find on the edges of the known world. There we find the impossible become the norm, where the boundaries of 'civilised' and 'barbarians' begin to dissipate, where normally juxtaposed cultures intermarry, where nomadic tribes build their own cities and where the rules don't always apply.

Now, thanks to extensive archaeological excavations that have been ongoing for over a century, we are able to step away from our reliance on textual evidence and find something new: cultures that most of us have never heard of. Sifting through the everyday items of ancient people's lives, we can relate the experiences, the relationships, and at times even the written word of ordinary people living their ordinary lives. We do not find the fictional humanoid monsters invented by ancient writers, but actual societies that thrived beyond the realm of the classical world.

To explore these boundaries, and life at them, this book hopes not only to shed light on some lesser known ancient histories of the world, but also to soften our perspective on the seemingly homogeneous classical cultures like those of Greece and Rome. We will embark on a journey from northern England to as far south as Kenya, from the western regions of Morocco to the eastern reaches of Vietnam, all with the sole aim of exploring the boundaries, the points of most regular interaction.

This book does not – indeed it cannot – follow a strict historical narrative, but is instead split into historical spheres of influence. Section I looks at pre-history, the boundless world before the advent of historical writing. Going beyond the usual limitations of ancient history, our story begins south of the Sahara, first with the early pastoralists in Kenya and then with the urbanised kingdom of Kush in Sudan, before exploring life at the borderline between Kush and Egypt, between Egypt and Libya (the name the Greeks gave to the rest of Africa). Finally, it moves to the Levant, the pivotal fulcrum between Mesopotamia and the Mediterranean Basin. Here we see, in contrast to the Egyptian frontiers with southern African kingdoms, the intrinsic value in international cooperation and the truly interconnected nature of the ancient world at the site of Megiddo.

Section II moves into the Greek world, a world of migration, the expansion of trade networks and the fundamental urge to colonise the outreaches of the known world. This section follows the founding and unique developments of three cities at very different points in the Greek world. To the north we have Olbia, on the northern peninsula of the Black Sea, where we see Greeks living shoulder to shoulder with supposedly the most barbarous of peoples, the nomadic, head-hunting Scythians. To the south, in the city of Naucratis in the Nile Delta, the Greeks had a solitary inroad to the vast riches and cultural knowledge of ancient Egypt. To the west is the city of Massalia (Marseille), a vital trading point with northern Europe that would become the location for one of the most important works of geography in the ancient world, based on the voyages of Pytheas of Massalia. The success of Massalia is self-evident in its claim to being one of the longest continuously inhabited cities in Europe.

Section III explores the very firm boundaries of the Roman Empire, defined by its military outposts and defensive monuments. At the farthest reaches of northern England, the impact of multiculturalism is observed as foreign troops interact with the local population around Hadrian's Wall. In the south-west corner of the empire lies the Moroccan site of Volubilis which offers a unique blend of Punic, Roman and Berber culture in the everyday life of its people. And we move finally to the south-east, to the poor town of Karanis in Egypt where Roman veterans struggled to fit into a world they did not understand. This section not only explores these unique expressions of Roman culture, but also highlights the impact that central politics in Rome had at the periphery, especially during the Crisis of the Third Century CE when the empire witnessed twenty-six new emperors in just fifty years.

Section IV takes us, once again, beyond the boundaries of the traditional 'ancient world' which is so often limited to the lands and cultures which surround the Mediterranean Sea. In turn, this section offers a reversal of our common understanding of antiquity: not one built on Greek and Roman observations of different cultures, but, rather, on those cultures' own histories. Further north than Olbia, we find the Scythians' semi-mythical city of Gelonus identified in the remains of the wooden city of Bilsk, the footprint of which is four times larger than Babylon – an impressive feat for a supposedly nomadic people. From here we move south-east, to the furthest extent of the Greco-Roman cultural sphere, in the valley of the Indus River, examining the region from the Indian perspective, as they had to adapt to this new Greco-Roman presence. By land, the peoples of the ancient Mediterranean were beginning to connect to eastern Asia in the first millennium CE, but by sea those networks were already firmly established. Following the route of Roman traders, we enter Vietnam, to the city of Co Loa where the heart of the Vietnamese nation was forged. Finally, we return to Africa, where this story began. In the kingdom of the Aksumites, the global nature of the ancient world can be best understood as the ancient epoch came to an end in the seventh century CE.

Unlike the Greek hero Jason, we no longer want to threaten the people who lived at the edge of the world with anonymity and the curse of being forgotten. These are the stories of everyday people: men and women, adults and children, soldiers and civilians, freemen and the enslaved, citizens and foreigners. Stories that are linked by the unique circumstances that are created by supposedly living on the edge of civilisation. Instead of ignoring them, we will discover just how amazing these communities were.

# Section I

# PRE-HISTORY

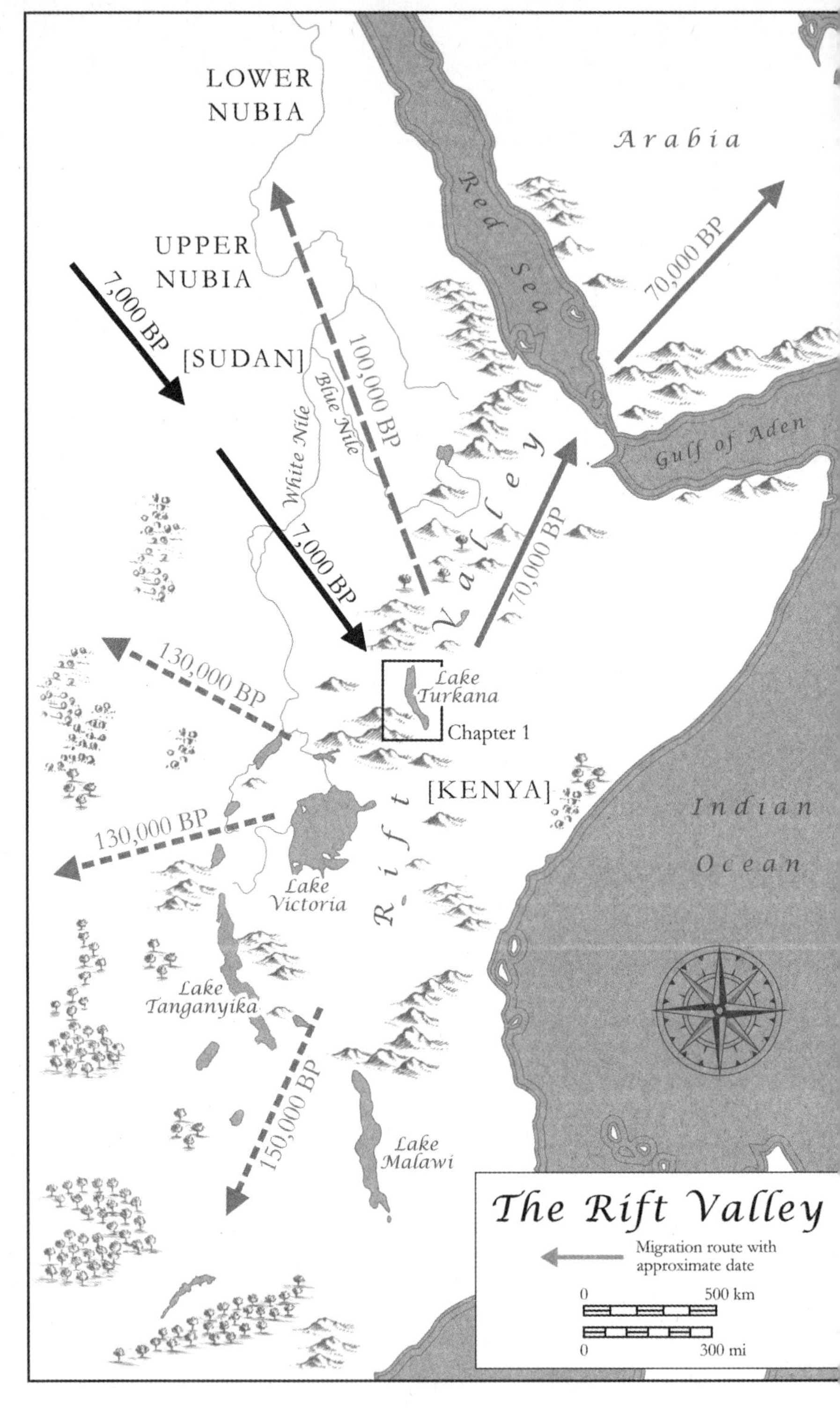

LOWER NUBIA
UPPER NUBIA
[SUDAN]
Arabia
Red Sea
Gulf of Aden
White Nile
Blue Nile
Rift Valley
7,000 BP
7,000 BP
100,000 BP
70,000 BP
70,000 BP
130,000 BP
130,000 BP
150,000 BP
Lake Turkana
Chapter 1
[KENYA]
Lake Victoria
Lake Tanganyika
Lake Malawi
Indian Ocean
The Rift Valley
Migration route with approximate date
0
500 km
0
300 mi

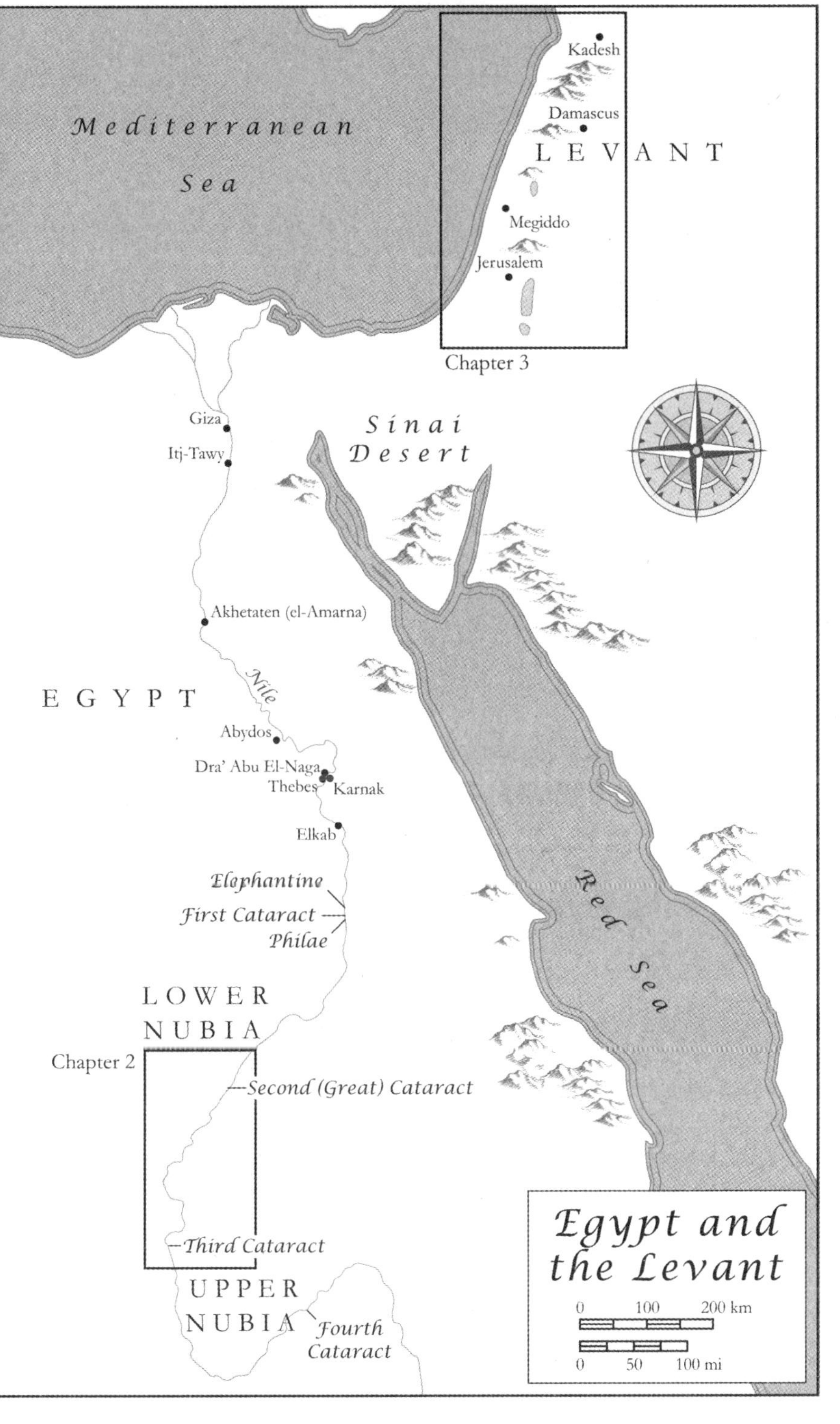
Mediterranean
Sea
Kadesh
Damascus
LEVANT
Megiddo
Jerusalem
Chapter 3
Sinai
Desert
Giza
Itj-Tawy
Akhetaten (el-Amarna)
Nile
EGYPT
Abydos
Dra' Abu El-Naga
Thebes
Karnak
Elkab
Elephantine
First Cataract
Philae
Red Sea
LOWER
NUBIA
Chapter 2
Second (Great) Cataract
Third Cataract
UPPER
NUBIA
Fourth
Cataract
Egypt and
the Levant
0
100
200 km
0
50
100 mi

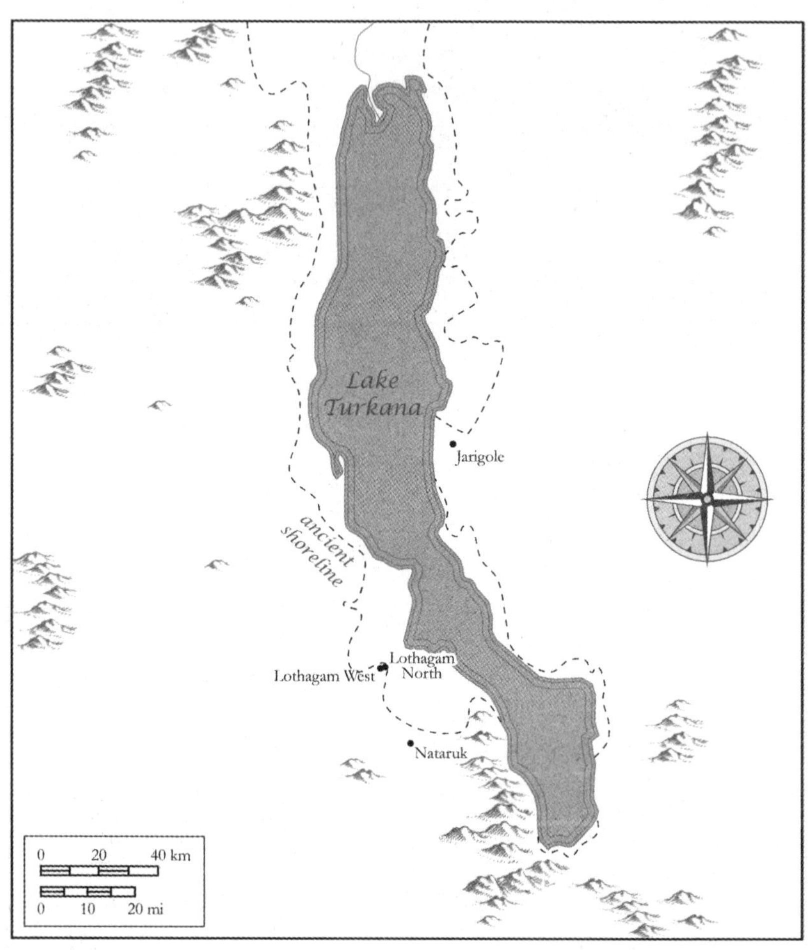

Lake Turkana
Jarigole
ancient shoreline
Lothagam North
Lothagam West
Nataruk
0 20 40 km
0 10 20 mi

I

# Lake Turkana, Kenya

When does history begin? It may seem a silly question, but if we think for a moment then its answer can reveal a lot about our own assumptions of the historical narratives that we tell ourselves. Conventionally, we focus on one of two stages of human development as the beginning of 'history': the invention of the written word, which allows us to read narratives and accounts from those time periods, or the advent of 'civilisation', a notoriously tricky concept to define that is usually associated with the urbanisation of cultures in the land between the rivers Tigris and Euphrates known as Mesopotamia (literally meaning 'between rivers'). But are either of these appropriate starting points for the 'historic' period?

By focusing on writing, we favour those cultures who recorded their world view to the detriment of those who did not. While focusing on the development of civilisation, we find that a problem comes from the idea of 'civilisation' itself. Without getting into the issue of definitions, we have to ask ourselves if basing our understanding of history on an innate hierarchy of culture is a useful thing. Put these two problems together and we are left with a final question: who gets left out and what does this omit from our historical narratives?

My solution is not perfect; indeed, it is innately flawed. I have chosen to define pre-history loosely: the period before the first works of historical inquiry, i.e. the works of Herodotus of Halicarnassus and his contemporaries in fifth-century BCE Greece. My reasoning is that before the Greeks our ability to reconstruct historical narratives is very limited and this innovation forms a watershed moment in the study of the ancient world.

Over these next three chapters, the cultural centres of particular interest are those of Egypt and the west Asian civilisations such as the Assyrians and Babylonians, the influence of which cannot be denied. But theirs are not the stories we are interested in. We are more interested in those living at the edges of their spheres of influence, the nomads and pastoralists of north-eastern Africa, and the small, autonomous kingships in the Levant. For these stories reveal much about how cultures adapt and survive in the wake of growing political and military powers. They also show how our traditional narratives of cultural domination and technological superiority winning the day are somewhat oversimplified. But before we can explore these subjects in detail, let us start with a story that goes to the heart of all these themes.

* * *

In the north-west of modern Kenya, ever so gently straddling the border into southern Ethiopia, sits the largest desert lake in the world. At roughly 7,000 square miles, Lake Turkana is a spectacular sight to behold in the relentless heat of the Kenyan Rift Valley. The lake is a geological marvel, fed predominantly by the Omo River to the north, and while it is technically a fresh-water lake, it is also salty. The lake was once an even larger, lush oasis, offering fertile land sheltered all around by mountains. It still plays host to an array of animal species, including Nile perch, crocodiles and hippopotamus, while archaeological evidence shows the long-term presence of large mammals that evolved over the millennia such as giraffes, rhinoceroses and elephants.

Lake Turkana serves as a unique microcosm of mammalian evolution. Its position as a large body of permanent water that attracts wildlife, combined with the fluctuation of water levels that have willingly revealed its amazing archaeological secrets, have allowed scientists to find some of the oldest remains of our humanoid ancestors ever to be discovered. The lake has given evidence for many hominid species including the stone-tool-using *Homo habilis* (c.1.9 million years ago), and *Homo erectus* in the specimen known as the 'Turkana boy' (c.1.5 million years ago). In the 1990s, researchers uncovered even older species, *Australopithecus anamensis* and *Kenyanthropus platyops*, which were two-legged hominids from much further back in the human evolutionary story. Of course, there are also remains of more modern man: Neanderthals and *Homo sapiens*. Lake Turkana is in many ways the cradle of human history, or at least the story of humanity. In fact, researchers at the Turkana Basin Institute believe that *all* modern humans share DNA inherited from ancestors living in or around Lake Turkana approximately 60,000 or 70,000 years ago.[1]

The story of humanity, then, so often leaves Kenya behind. As humans spread throughout Eurasia, history follows them to Mesopotamia, between the rivers Tigris and Euphrates, and the so-called cradle of civilisation. Similarly, we move west to Egypt and bear witness to the growing urbanisation of humans, bringing with it the iconic monuments at Giza or the temples at sites such as Karnak. Within Egypt and Mesopotamia, we seem to leave the human-animal behind and embrace the civilised human cultures of history, the ones we are most accustomed to reading and learning about. We see the mastery of writing and agriculture, of large-scale building techniques, and even sea exploration. But what about Lake Turkana? Did humans simply abandon it without a cause? Does it serve no further purpose in our history?

While many *Homo sapiens* migrated out of Africa around 60,000 years ago, many others chose to stay. The abundant life that inhabited the waters allowed Lake Turkana to play host to a substantial population of hunter-gatherer groups, or perhaps more accurately fisher-gatherer-hunters. Lying over 2,000 miles away from Mesopotamia and the traditional starting point of ancient history, Lake Turkana sat well outside the boundaries of what we think of as the 'civilised world' during this period. But the concentration of extended family groups living in the region for many generations offers us just as important an insight into our shared human past. While it is the urban societies that receive the most focus in history, Lake Turkana offers us the highs and lows of human nature, from cooperation and artistry to the darker aspects of our instincts.

Numerous family groups vying for resources and, of course, the best hunting and fishing spots around the vast lake, inevitably brought them into conflict with one another. The gruesome reality of this conflict is brought to the fore at the site of Nataruk, to the south-west of the lake. Today the innocuous site appears thirty kilometres from the south-western coast of Lake Turkana, but 10,000 years ago it was on the edge of the lake's shoreline. Nataruk is also fortuitously placed on the eastern edge of a small depression in the ground, which would form a lagoon during periods of heavy rainfall, a common occurrence during the African Humid Period. Such a location was prime real estate for fisher-gatherer-hunters, surrounded as it would have been by marshes and even woodland, attracting many animals to an isolated area and still providing access to the fishing stock within Lake Turkana.

Perhaps it comes as little surprise, then, that such a coveted area of land became the site of one of humanity's first known massacres, bearing so many of the hallmarks that we associate with war and combat. This lagoon bore witness to a very dark moment in human history, when an extended family was attacked and killed. Some were even bound before they were executed in cold blood.

In 2012, a palaeoanthropology team from the University of Cambridge, led by Dr Marta Mirazón Lahr, discovered the remains of some twenty-seven individuals, including at least eight women and six children.[2] Of the twelve skeletons that were still intact, ten showed clear signs of a violent death from blunt-force trauma to the skull. At least five remains showed evidence of damage caused by a sharp object, maybe one of the obsidian arrow or spear heads discovered at the site. At least four remains showed signs of having been bound before they were killed. This was not a fight, it was a slaughter.

The significance of Nataruk is not in the carnage on display, but on what it possibly means for our understanding of human conflict. We know from more contemporary history that hunter-gatherer groups would often kill the men in scuffles over hunting grounds, but would then absorb the women and children into their fold. The presence of women and children among the dead, including the heart-rending remains of a pregnant woman who was near to term – the remains of the unborn child take the unofficial body count to twenty-eight – show that this was not a normal clash of social groups. Researchers are not certain what the cause of the massacre was: perhaps it was over resources and stored food supplies, as the remains of pottery found at the site seem to suggest; or perhaps it was a classic example of an external group coming into conflict with a local one as they migrated towards the lake, as evidenced by the presence of non-local obsidian stone weapon heads.[3]

The events at Nataruk are not unique for this time period. A site in Jebel Sahaba, Sudan, shows similar evidence of violence, but what makes Nataruk so exceptional is the aftermath of the massacre.[4] In Jebel Sahaba, the remains were found in a cemetery, with the bodies showing signs of ritual burial. Presumably these burials were performed by other members of the community, suggesting a static and sedentary society – the beginnings of urbanisation. The family group at Nataruk shows no such reverence. The bodies were left where they fell, including one male who plunged into the lagoon face first. He had been struck by two weapons: the first was a superficial blow from an obsidian edge that ended up embedded in the skull, the second was swung with such force that it smashed most of the right-hand side of his face and head. The pregnant mother was left bound and seated where she had been killed, which is how the research team discovered her ten millennia later.

* * *

Approximately 5,000 years ago (c.3000 BCE), while the peoples of Mesopotamia were founding their urban societies, and Egypt was unifying into its first dynasty (the Early Dynastic Period), the African continent was undergoing a monumental shift in climate. The so-called African Humid Period was coming to an end, and the once lush lands of northern Africa were swiftly turning to desert. The Sahara Desert would reach its current point of desertification at approximately this same time period. Such a fundamental change to the world around them forced humans to react and adapt in order to survive.

At Lake Turkana the most dramatic change was the depleting water levels. The lake shrank to almost half its original depth; in some areas the original beaches now sit ten miles west of the lake's edge today.[5] As the levels fell, the lake lost the vast supply of fresh water that came through the complex river networks that once linked it to the Nile, causing the lake to take on its now high levels of salt. The receding of the lake offered a remarkably different landscape for the people living around it. Of course, the shrinking lake and increased salinity also saw the fishing stock decrease, putting pressure on the local fisher-gatherer-hunter groups. As the water receded it exposed fertile lands that were perfect for grazing animals. As a result of the changing landscape around them, the people living beside the lake did what humans do best: they adapted. They began to use domesticated animals, such as cattle and sheep, to form the basis of a new diet and new way of life.

Scholars are not sure how this change actually happened. Either the locals of Lake Turkana arranged an exchange market with pastoral groups to the north, or those pastoral groups migrated into the region. It seems it could have been a little bit of both but, either way, archaeological evidence shows a distinct migration of pastoralism as a way of life from the Sahara about 8,000 years ago, down through Sudan 8–7,000 years ago, and into the Turkana Basin approximately 5,000 years ago.[6]

Pastoralism is by its very nature a nomadic way of life, something that is usually contrasted with 'civilisation' and urban life. This has meant that nomadic groups, throughout time, have regularly been 'othered' and considered separate from our stories, often reduced to playing the antagonist to the history of urbanised societies as cultures in need of subjugation, or as marauding hordes upsetting the balance of powerful empires.

Pastoralist societies, like all nomadic societies, have their own motivations and purposes behind their actions, while their need to move often put them in conflict with static societies less willing to share land. Of course, luscious feeding grounds were the goal, but if you stayed on those grounds for too long you would deplete the grass supplies. Overfeed your animals in one place and you risked ruining the pastureland over the long term. These animals would normally need to be moved from one feeding ground to another, which requires an enduring knowledge of reliable feeding pastures and seasonal weather patterns. Usually, this knowledge is collated over years of experience, passed from generation to generation, which in turn forges an ancestral route of nomadic migrations based on the seasons.

For the pastoralists around Lake Turkana, they had to achieve this knowledge base with the added complication that the climate was still drastically changing around them. This means that what may once have been a perfect grazing pasture could quickly become an arid and barren piece of land no longer suitable for their animals. This perpetual process of learning and relearning the natural cycles around the lake forced people to find security and stability, something that remained unchanged against a world of constant fluctuation and change. The introduction of pastoralism brought with it another interesting change to Lake Turkana: the building of monuments.

At a time for ever lost to history, an unknown group of pastoral nomads stopped on the western coast of the lake and made a decision that would influence the actions of their descendants for the next 700 years.[7] First, they planned their site and cleared the beach-like sand on the ground surface. Covering a space of almost 120 square metres, they dug down a few feet until they hit the hard sandstone below. Next, they needed to cut more sandstone and use these slabs to shore up the sides of the hole they had dug. With the site no longer in danger of collapsing, they began to dig smaller, more specific holes deeper into the sandstone floor. These were burial pits.

Lothagam North Pillar Site, named after the local term for the geological formation where it is found, stands as a poignant memorial to an unknown society. For hundreds of years these men, women and children came to bury their dead, showing them love, care and attention. Such a monument for the dead was once considered the remit of static, urbanised societies: cultures that accumulated excess resources and of course time, two things often not associated with nomadic pastoralism.

This site was not a spontaneous or ad hoc burial site: it was planned and designed. The surrounding ground was paved with more sandstone, and then ringed with boulders. Over time, the original site was expanded to the east with nine stone circles built as well as six raised cairns. By the time it was abandoned this was a substantial space of sacred ground. The original burial platform was 700 square metres, the additional stone circles and cairns contributing a further 700 square metres.

The evidence for planning can be seen in the finer details. The platform was cleared and dug out in one go; it was never expanded over time as more bodies were buried. More tellingly, when it was filled and capped in its final state, there was still a lot of room left for further burials if needed. The site was then marked with basalt columns, no taller than 1.5 metres, sourced from up to a kilometre away from the site. When we consider the time, the resources available, then the labour hours required – especially during the initial digging and final capping of the site – and the distances travelled to make sure they used the materials they deemed most important, this was a monumental undertaking for these pastoralists.

* * *

All monuments share certain functions. No matter how large or small, permanent or ephemeral, monumental building projects require a clear level of social complexity. They require a large group of people to hold a shared set of beliefs: beliefs held so strongly that people feel driven to build a memorial – a rather time-consuming endeavour that serves no purpose beyond those shared beliefs. Objectively, burying the dead serves little survival function for a nomadic society. It does not aid their production of food, nor serve to protect them against wild animals or aggressive neighbours, nor does it ensure water supplies or pasturelands – but Lothagam North clearly shows the importance of a shared belief that people should be buried and in a particular place.

Funeral monuments serve numerous purposes. First and foremost they honour the dead, providing them with a resting place for eternity and bestowing due care and honours upon them. They also serve the living, as a place to go and honour those community members that have been lost over time; much like our modern forms of communal commemoration surrounding the war dead, for instance. It is in this interaction with monuments and commemorations that we can better understand a culture, or cultures, and their shared beliefs.

So, what do we learn about the pastoralists who used the Lothagam North Pillar Site? First and foremost, we learn that they were not alone. The Lothagam North site is by far the largest, but by no means the only, monumental structure around Lake Turkana.[8] There are at least six other major sites, which look very similar in design. On the surface of it, this would suggest various nomadic groups with a shared culture building numerous monuments, but the artefacts that have been found in each of the sites do not match. The nearest site to Lothagam North, in both location and chronology, is the creatively named Lothagam West. These two sites have been dated within forty years of each other, but the artefacts uncovered do not suggest a shared material culture. Oddly enough, the site that most closely matches the material culture of Lothagam North can be found nearly 100 kilometres away, on the far side of the lake at Jarigole. Rather unexpectedly, many of the pillar sites do not actually have any human remains interred, suggesting that they are not burial sites.[9] So, the same sort of monument was being built but for different reasons. Maybe it was a case of one group trying to upstage another, or perhaps these sites were claims to a location, like sticking a rather elaborate flag in the ground, providing a permanent marker for any other group to see and recognise that this land was spoken for.

The second thing we learn from the Lothagam North Pillar Site is a rather harsh lesson about our own assumptions. It has long been assumed that a society which builds large monuments would be urbanised, or at the least non-nomadic, and that the building of the monument was often a show of power and wealth from a hierarchical society. We would expect to see monuments such as these in the cultural and urban centres of Mesopotamia, for instance. But at Lothagam North, the sparse evidence we do have suggests an altogether different approach.

The mortuary site holds fewer than 580 bodies, bodies that were carefully tended to and deposited over hundreds of years by new generations of this pastoralist community. The burials beneath the large platform are quite unusual in that nowhere is there a clear indication of a social hierarchy. No bodies have been found separated from the rest, with a larger grave or more notably ornate grave goods. There is no distinction between the genders, levels of affluence, or even age, with children and elders buried next to each other. There is no rich area, no poor area; no clear leader burials. As it stands, this seems to be a communal grave monument, built by a community that considered everyone within it to be equal.[10] It would be a little idealistic to claim this was an egalitarian society of some sort. The entire site has yet to be excavated, so a clearly prestigious area with more ornate burial goods could yet be discovered – but the finds so far make this unlikely.

Although the people are all buried together as one, we do see individuality in the items found with them. Most of the people were buried with, or wearing, ornaments, including hippo-ivory rings and beads. A beautifully colourful array of worked stone and minerals were found, some worn as pendants and others as earrings, revealing that there was leisure time available for crafts to be worked. Ostrich eggs and hippo tusks were used for larger items; twelve pierced hippo tusks, most likely strung together and worn as an adornment, evidence the level of detail involved in crafting some of these.

But it was not just the items made from large animals, like hippo and ostrich, that catch the eye. One burial revealed the most exquisite headdress, formed from the patiently worked material of a rather overlooked animal. Four hundred and five teeth have been identified, from some 113 individual animals, small enough to create an intricate, almost scale-like texture which would have shone brightly as the sun hit the enamel: they were gerbils' teeth.[11] Gerbils were not domesticated at this time, and while it is enticing to imagine the little pets we now house in cages being harvested for their teeth, in reality these wild speed demons would have had to be chased as they raced for their burrows. Less dangerous than a hippo, but no less worthy of proper planning.

Here, at Lothagam North, we see yet another side of the human story; one which offers us familiarity in the need to remember the dead, the desire to decorate our bodies with beautiful objects, and the clear passing of traditions down through the generations. It shows us that large monuments are not just objects of power and hierarchy, but can be the product of co-operation and shared belief. It also reminds us of the importance of identity, and how acts of remembrance help to forge a shared sense of belonging.

Nomadic and pastoralist groups are often omitted from the conventional narratives of the history of civilisation, but this removes a vibrant and colourful aspect of our human story. The nomadic groups around Lake Turkana were dealing with cataclysmic changes to their environment. Their migration from the far north is testament to their commitment to each other and to their way of life. But of course they were just one group, there were countless others. Some did not venture so far south as modern Kenya. In the region of modern Sudan, at about the same time as Lothagam North was being built, there is evidence of what has been described as a 'pastoralist state' being formed, in many ways offering a similar level of stability and continuity as the Pillar sites to the south, but for a much larger population.[12] This state would survive for nearly 2,000 years in one form or another, interacting with powerful empires such as that of Egypt, Persia and even Rome. The kingdom of Kush embodies all that there was to life at the edges of the world. Situated on the southern border of ancient Egypt, we know most of the kingdom's early history from archaeological excavations and the writings of their Egyptian enemies. Kush is presented by its enemies as a barbaric place, one of disorder and untrustworthy people, but this portrayal is clearly a caricature that reflects Egyptian fears more than it does reality.

Kush is the Egyptian name given to the lands and people further south, up the Nile, in Upper Egypt and northern Sudan. At its heart, Kush sat between the Third and Fourth Cataracts of the Nile. Cataracts are sections of a river where the water level is very low, and the river's flow is obstructed by small islands and boulders. The Nile has six numbered cataracts, and they were dangerous to navigate due to the obstacles and the subsequently fast rapids that grew around them. Through much of Pharaonic Egypt, the First Cataract formed the natural boundary of southern Egypt. Later Greek writers would refer to the stretch between the Third and Fourth Cataracts as part of the wider region of Nubia, which is perhaps how it is better known today, but Kush is the earliest attested name and one that may have come from their people's own indigenous language.

The main settlement for the Kush was called Kerma, which nestled beside a small tributary of the Nile in the north of Sudan. Evidence at the site shows that people had lived there since approximately 3000 BCE, in an age known to researchers as the pre-Kerma period. The original town, which would later be built over by future generations, was at least 1.5 hectares in size but perhaps even eight times that. This space was mostly filled with small, round houses with walls of wattle and daub. The majority of these houses were somewhere between 3 and 5 metres in diameter, but four larger huts stand out, with diameters between 6 and 7.5 metres – possibly signifying a higher status in the society, or perhaps simply that the inhabitant had a larger family. These houses were enclosed by a large defensive wall, made from the same building materials, which had various entrances.[13]

Even within this small town the pre-Kerma people maintained their pastoralist traditions. Researchers have identified what they believe to be an animal pen inside the enclosure, and the remarkable discovery of bovine footprints proves that these pens were for their cattle.[14] We also have scant evidence for temporary campsites in the wider region, where cattle were moved between grazing pastures. Perhaps Kerma was used as a permanent base to which they returned in winter.

Researchers have also discovered a large number of storage pits, which were probably used by the whole community for storing food surplus like a type of granary. Similar pits have been found in another pre-Kerma site further north, at Sai Island, which stored imported grains from Egypt such as barley and wheat.[15] So, the pastoralists were beginning to embrace agriculture as well, but notably not at the expense of their pastoralist traditions. Agriculture brings with it a need to be sedentary, which in itself requires more infrastructure for the community. As a result, there are two large rectangular buildings whose purpose has not been conclusively identified – the leading hypothesis that they were used for administrative purposes highlights the way archaeologists think about this culture.[16]

As it was a non-literate society, it is hard to fill in all the historical gaps at Kerma. However, within 500 years of this settlement being built, we know that it was abandoned. A new town was built by the people, roughly four kilometres to the west, on the edge of the Nile. The exact reasons for this move are not certain, but it seems that the original tributary that the site was next to had dried up, so, much like the pastoralists around Lake Turkana, the people of Kush needed to adapt.

The site of Kerma became the foreground for a new, cohesive, cultural identity. The clearest evidence for this is in their burial practices which they placed, rather poetically, over the old, abandoned site of their ancestors. In their graves we see the care and attention they paid to their dead; we also see the central importance that cattle and pastoralism still had in their society. The dead were placed in a round pit, on top of a cowhide. The bodies themselves were positioned to lie on their right side, with their bodies curled up and their hands resting up to or even under their heads. In a few instances, the impression of the dead being in bed or asleep is capped by another cowhide that they laid on top, like a blanket. They would often be buried with small items, such as pottery, and the horns from cows, sheep or goats. One man has even been found with a bow, an important marker of status and masculinity. The graves themselves were sometimes decorated or adorned with standing stones serving as grave markers.[17]

By the Kerma middle period (2000 BCE–1750 BCE), the spread of this new culture and the reach of its influence had grown exponentially. What began as a small town to protect their cattle had become the centre of a growing civilisation. By tracking burial patterns along the Upper Nile, along with settlement designs, we can see the true extent of their growth covering a distance of 600 kilometres. Kerma itself was also growing. Fortification walls enveloped an area of three hectares that was now beginning to fill with large buildings, halls and even a temple, built no longer from wattle and daub, but from mud bricks. But even during this period of growth and cultural change we still see the central importance of cattle to their identity.

The presence of painted cow figurines in the town, and large murals decorating the large funeral chapels in the cemetery, shows that the pastoral roots still held great social significance. They could also be used to mark out someone of very high status in society. For, as Kerma grew, so too did the power of the social elites. One particular mark of respect found at graves most abundantly during this period is what archaeologists call 'bucrania': the horns of cattle which have part of the skull still attached. It was common for a person to be buried with one or two bucrania, but of course the more important you were the more bucrania you could expect. One study identified twenty-seven graves with a total of 6,082 bucrania between them, and yet one of those graves dating from this middle period possessed 80 per cent of those – a staggering 4,899 for one person, presumably a sovereign or leader of some sort.[18]

Perhaps even more startling is that an analysis of the horns has shown that these cattle were not all grazing from the same pasturelands, meaning that they came from different herds most likely herded by different people.[19] Five thousand cows is an astronomical number. To put it into a real-life context, 5,000 cows would produce roughly 600,000 kilograms of meat, which, according to one archaeologist's calculations, would feed 1.2 million people in a single day, or 240,000 people over a week.[20] The population of Kerma was big, but it was nowhere near that big. So, these bucrania were most likely sent as offerings by people who were herding their cattle over a large and varied area of land.

It was during this period of growth, both culturally and physically, that the Kerma people were assigned their official name in the historical record. During the rule of the pharaoh Senusret I (r.1961–1917 BCE), a powerful king who reigned during a period known as the Middle Kingdom (c.2000–1650 BCE) in Egyptian history, the Egyptians continued a policy of expansion south of the First Cataract. Lower Nubia had borne the brunt of Egyptian aggression, but the lure of lands further south was too much to resist for Senusret. At the site of what would become the great fortress of Buhen, just north of the Second Cataract, archaeologists discovered a rather harrowing stone inscription.

The sandstone monument, known as a stela, is just under two metres in height, and just over one metre wide. It was erected by Senusret I's military commander in the south, a man called Mentuhotep.[21] On it, the pharaoh is depicted to the left-hand side, originally being fanned by a man behind him, but this was later reworked to have Senusret holding the hand of the god Horus behind him instead. The pharaoh is facing another falcon-headed god, the war god Montu. Behind the god and beneath his feet are ten men, almost identical in appearance, who are roped together, and the ends are held in Montu's left hand. The inscription at the top has Senusret speaking: 'I have brought for you all the countries that are in Nubia, beneath your feet, Good God.'[22]

Each one of the enslaved men is depicted from their heads down to the bottom of their chests, followed by a defined oval outline that contains the names of either the lands they represented or maybe the people. The first of these bears the name *kAs*, or as it became known – Kush.

According to Mentuhotep, he had successfully subdued or defeated ten regions, including Kush, in the name of the pharaoh. The glee with which he pronounces the terror and devastation he had caused is apparent, even with the heavy erosion and damage on the sandstone:

> Their life is finished, slain, ... fire in the tents ... Her grain cast to the Nile ... I myself swear, this happened in very truth; I, the general of the army, Amu's son, Mentuhotep.[23]

The Egyptian plans to push south were driven by their desire for riches. On the boundary between Egypt to the north and the non-urbanised, often nomadic or pastoralist societies to the south, the Kushite kingdom was an intermediary between two trade markets. They would facilitate the trade of luxury items such as ivory, ebony and animal skins. The lands of Kush themselves were highly productive, with good stretches of fertile land and pastures. But, perhaps most important of all, Kush and the wider region of Nubia was rich in natural minerals like diorite, an igneous rock the Egyptians used to made statues, or precious and semi-precious stones such as gold, copper and amethyst.[24]

Like so many cultures at the edges of the known world, Kush would be defined by its enemies living at the 'centre' – the Egyptians. From its first appearance in the written record, Kush was a supposed enemy of civilisation. This reputation would grow over the years, and the name of Kush would frequently be accompanied by an epithet that translates as 'wretched Kush'. Yet, the reason why the Egyptian pharaohs wanted to extend their control into the south was precisely the reason the Kushite kingdom was thriving and, as a result, presenting a veritable threat to Egyptian power along the Nile. The town of Kerma was growing ever larger. The Kushite people were becoming more and more distinguishable from other Nubian cultures to the north, cultures that held on to their pastoralist roots as the Kushites blended their old traditions with their growing appetite for urbanisation. Kerma was filling with temples and chapels, bakeries and administrative buildings. It was a hive of trade and of industry, something that the Egyptians could not ignore even if they had wanted to.

Kush would finally succumb to Egyptian authority, but not for long. Later Nubian rulers would embrace the Kushite name and, while the city of Kerma would be replaced with new centres further south, the Kushite people would continue to expand their cultural influence and interact with the Egyptians. Indeed, after a thousand years, Sudan would bear witness to a pyramid-building project that would put the Egyptians to shame. But for now, during the Kerma middle period, Kush would be a concern that would consume not only Senusret I, but also his great-grandson Senusret III, who would continue his predecessor's attempts to control Lower Nubia. Within the ensuing conflicts it would be easy to pit culture against culture and assume that they were diametrically opposed in almost every way, Kush having perhaps more in common with the pastoralists at Lake Turkana than they did with the Egyptians to the north, but this would be a gross oversimplification. Instead, we need to look at where the two cultures of Kush and Egypt interacted most – at the frontier.

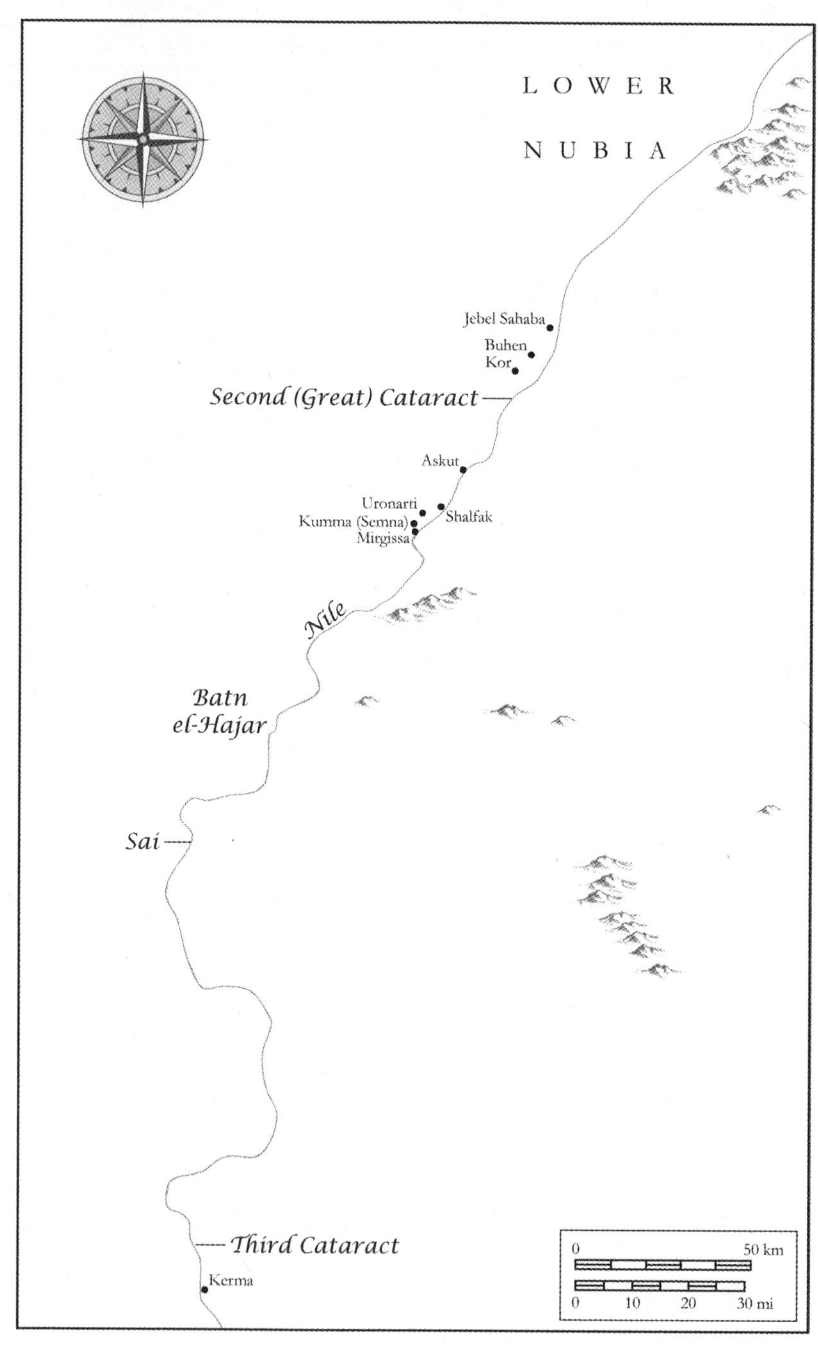

LOWER
NUBIA
Jebel Sahaba
Buhen
Kor
Second (Great) Cataract
Askut
Uronarti
Shalfak
Kumma (Semna)
Mirgissa
Nile
Batn
el-Hajar
Sai
Third Cataract
Kerma
0
50 km
0
10
20
30 mi

# 2

# The Great Cataract, Sudan

The mighty Egyptian fortress of Buhen must have been a formidable sight. Sitting on the west bank of the Nile, Buhen's outer walls measured 150 metres by 450 metres, enclosing an area of 67,500 square metres. Its thick, mud-brick walls measured five metres in depth and were given extra strength with the use of reed matting and wooden beams. This long stretch of perimeter walling was broken up by protruding bastions, giving a strong vantage point for archers or other members of the garrison force. The main entrance was through a heavily fortified gate in the western wall, itself a forbidding sight for any enemy force. All of this was encircled by a dry moat, three metres deep and roughly six metres wide.[1]

If, by some miracle, an attacking force could penetrate these defences, they would then enter the grounds to find yet another monumental defensive structure awaiting them. The inner fortification of Buhen was 150 metres by 138 metres, with walls that were nine metres high. These were encircled by another, much shorter, wall that was broken up by semicircular towers with numerous arrow loopholes. All of this overlooked a ditch of its own, which matched the external moat in both width and depth. It was inside this inner fortress that the administrative buildings and living quarters were to be found.

To build such a fortress would, at a conservative estimate, have required approximately 13 million bricks, accounting only for the fortifications themselves.[2] The sheer scale of Buhen highlights its critical importance to the two Middle Kingdom pharaohs who invested most heavily in it: Senusret I, who we met previously, and his great-grandson Senusret III (r.1887–1848 BCE).[3] For the elder Senusret, the fortress's position at the northern end of the Second Cataract, near to the smaller fort of Kor, enabled him to create a fixed and heavily defended frontier with the growing power of Kush to the south. It also allowed him to solidify his control over the newly acquired area of Lower Nubia, which could now be exploited for its rich mineral reserves. What he had not anticipated, however, was that this frontier would become a home not only to the Egyptian garrison but also to local Nubian communities living in the vicinity. Inadvertently, Senusret I had laid the groundwork for a unique environment where Egyptian and Nubian culture would intermingle.

Senusret I was succeeded by his son, Amenemhat II, who in turn was succeeded by his own son, Senusret II. During the reign of these two pharaohs, Egypt was able to maintain a relative level of stability and prosperity. Under Senusret II in particular, we do not have any records of foreign expansion or military activity. But all this changed under Senusret III, who came to hold sole rule during the 1870s BCE.

Senusret III was driven by a powerful sense of ambition and purpose. His primary goal as pharaoh was to build on the legacy of his predecessors, chiefly that of his great-grandfather. This ambition was in part fostered by his upbringing and education. However, it is perhaps no surprise that the young pharaoh's actions duly emulated the advice found in the contemporary instructional literature regarding kingship:

> Equip your border against the lands to the south,
> For they are aliens who take up the panoply of war.[4]

Or perhaps he was more motivated by the instruction written in the guise of his great-great-grandfather Amenemhat I's teachings to his son, Senusret I. Most likely written during the reign of Senusret I himself, the *Teaching of Amenemhat I* offers a clear example by which an impressionable ruler could measure himself:

> I tamed lions and I captured crocodiles.
> I subdued the people of Nubia, and I captured the Medjay.
> I made the Asiatics do the dog walk.[5]

The territorial expansion of the two pharaohs brought the region of Lower Nubia under Egyptian control, but this large stretch of land was not empty. It was filled with a variety of Nubian cultures who would have identified neither with the Egyptians nor with the Kush further south. One group, a semi-nomadic people living in the deserts to the east of the Nile, was given the name Medjay by the Egyptians. Nomadic cultures can be hard to identify in the archaeological record, but some archaeologists think they may align with a material culture in the region known as the Pan Grave culture, named after the oval shapes of their graves.[6] We also know of a less nomadic, pastoralist culture in the region, known by archaeologists as the C-Group, but they do not correlate as well with the descriptions given of the Medjay. In effect, the Medjay were an Egyptian invention, one name among many given to various Nubian people who lived in the space between the Second and Third Cataracts and between the Nile and the Red Sea.[7]

Where Senusret I had expanded Egyptian control into Lower Nubia, Senusret III intended to push further still – going beyond the beginning of the Second Cataract, which itself was not a single hindrance but a series of rapids and obstacles that continued for kilometres down the Nile. In pursuit of his goal,

Senusret III invested in the pre-existing fortresses to the south including Buhen, the description of which at the start of this chapter reflects the secondary phase of building work. In addition, he financed the building of at least seven more forts and extended the frontier to Semna. Mirgissa was located just a little further down the cataract from Kor and built to a similar size and scale as Buhen. Next, after a long stretch of river, was Askut, which was built on a small island on the Nile. After another long stretch, the fortresses come thick and fast: Shalfak, followed by Uronarti, and then came the final three, Semna and Semna south on the western side of the river, and Kumma on the eastern side, forming the frontier line.

The building of such fortresses was deliberate and motivated as much by ideological as by practical reasons. A large section of the river which had now been claimed is known today as Batn el-Hajar, 'Belly of the Rock'. It was a barren stretch of the Nile that was rich in granite, but it was very poor for arable farming. The new frontier's greatest contribution was to increase the buffer zone between Egypt and the Kushite heartland further south, and to secure the rich mining opportunities in the area. Beyond this, Senusret III completed his fortress system that now spanned the Second Cataract. In so doing, he had created a fortified frontier the likes of which would not be matched until the height of the Roman Empire (see Chapter 8). The forts were interconnected and reliant on one another for supplies, trade access, reinforcements and storage. While the distance between Buhen to the north and Semna at the most southern point was sizeable (around forty kilometres), the fortresses could use a relay system of fire signals to call for help. So, if there was trouble at the frontier, the commander at Semna could shut the gates and signal to Uronarti for help, who in turn could signal Shalfak, through Askut; up the river this signal would be transferred until it reached the larger garrisoned fortresses of Mirgissa and Buhen.[8]

It would be easy to speculate as to why this frontier was built; maybe it was driven by fear, or simply ambition. But we do not need to speculate; conveniently for us, Senusret III had an inscription erected at his frontier in Semna, telling us exactly why he established it:

> The southern frontier made in year 8 under the majesty of the King of Upper and Lower Egypt *Khakaure* [Senusret III] (may he live for ever and ever) in order to prevent it being passed by any Nubian journeying north by land or in a *kai*-boat as well as any livestock belonging to the Nubians . . .[9]

But was there more to it than simply controlling the movement of Nubians north up the Nile?

Senusret III left behind two further clues regarding his motivation. The first comes from a separate inscription found in Semna, which was erected eight years later. In it he boasts that he has stretched his boundaries further south than his predecessors, adding to the kingdom that he had inherited. But more so, he defines how he will be remembered:

> I am a king who speaks and acts,
> What my heart plans is done by my arm.
> One who attacks to conquer, who is swift to succeed ...

He has aggressively expanded south as a way to legitimise his rule as pharaoh and to live up to the standards of kingship that his forebears had set down for him. For one of the pharaoh's most important roles was his creation of order in a world of chaos. The Egyptians referred to this cosmic order as *maat*, and it was the pharaoh's job not only to maintain it through upholding law and justice, but also to ensure the correct rituals are being performed. The pharaoh was the guardian against chaos, the sword arm for *maat*, and Senusret III did what was expected of him – he expanded the borders of Egypt, the lands of order.

It worked, because his story became a thing of legend. Over 1,000 years later, the Greek historian Herodotus tells the story of a great king of Egypt, Sesostris (the Greek form of Senusret) who conquered all of Asia and also ruled over Ethiopia.[10] Herodotus gets many of the details wrong, but historians believe the central story he is telling is that of Senusret III, mixed with various other pharaohs that followed him.

Senusret also wanted to target the Nubian people themselves. On a superficial level, the naming of the new fortresses betrays the pharaoh's intent: fortresses were given names such as 'Destroying the Nubians' and 'Repressing the Medjay'. Clearly there was no room for subtlety within the nomenclature of this fortress network.

As many anthropologists and historians have noted over the years, a sense of ethnic or cultural identity is often forged when one group is in conflict with another. For the Egyptians, they had three groups surrounding their lands which they used to define themselves and their place in the world: to the west were the Libyans, to the north and east were the Asiatics (people from Mesopotamia and the Levant region) and to the south were the Nubians. Each race was caricatured and stereotyped, each was looked down upon and derided.[11] Being Egyptian generally could mean looking a certain way, dressing and speaking a certain way, of course; but there was always variation within this, and this sense of identity could change. What did not change was that they could not be considered to be from anywhere else. Being Egyptian was as much about not being Libyan or Nubian as it was about what you wore or ate.

In Egyptian art, the Nubians were painted with the darkest skin colour of the four groups, after only the Egyptians themselves, who were normally portrayed with a reddish skin colour for the men and a paler, yellowish brown for the women. The colour of Nubian skin was not a specific point of derision, or anything akin to more modern racist ideologies, but it was used as a clear indication of 'otherness' compared to an Egyptian standard. The Nubian was often compared to an animal, much like their Libyan and Asiatic counterparts. He was also a coward who could not be trusted. But it was not enough simply to portray him in an exaggerated style and stereotypical dress; it was important to elite Egyptian identity that people were reminded of these supposed truths:

> Since the Nubian listens to rumours,
> To answer him is to make him retreat.
> Attack him, he will turn his back,
> Retreat, he will start attacking.
> They are not people one respects,
> They are wretches, craven hearted.[12]

On the surface of it, the Egyptians hated the Nubians to the south. The growing power of Kush, allied with the exploitable resources in Lower Nubia, prompted the rulers of Egypt to expand their boundaries to Semna and establish a clear demarcation of power and control. A person from Nubia was below contempt, not to be trusted or relied upon – the very antithesis of a civilised people.

We may expect, then, that life on the frontier was a difficult one for the Egyptian garrison. Far from their homes in Egypt, they were charged with protecting Egypt from this wretched enemy to the south. They were surrounded by people they looked down on, people they couldn't trust or rely on. That, of course, is if we believe all that we read.

* * *

Visualising human interaction through the concept of national borders on a map has the potential to reduce the human experience merely to the political interaction between states. It creates the impression of firm lines in the sand between 'us' and 'them', where one culture stops and another begins. This impression is often reinforced by the political rhetoric of the groups involved, such as Senusret's claims discussed above. Realistically, if the only evidence we had surviving from this period was the written records and the shells of these fortresses, we would be forced to accept this narrative. But the surviving archaeology offers a slightly different picture.

However, trying to use the archaeological evidence to understand the lives and experiences on the Egyptian–Nubian frontier is made all the more complicated by more contemporary historical developments, namely, the filling of the Aswan High Dam in 1970, which flooded the stretch of the Nile where these fortresses stood. All are now under water. As part of the UNESCO Campaign to Save the Monuments of Nubia, a large international team of Egyptologists and archaeologists worked tirelessly to catalogue as much as they could before the flooding occurred, leaving us with an amazing cache of physical evidence but no real opportunity to conduct new excavations or surveys at most of the sites.

This leaves us, at times, with conundrums that cannot be fully explored. One such conundrum concerns the most modest of material evidence, the cooking pot. In the small fortress of Askut, slightly less than twenty kilometres north of Semna, researchers found a large number of vessels, pots and pans all used for either the serving, the storage or the cooking of food. Of these, it is possible to discern those that are of an Egyptian style and those of a Nubian style. The very presence of Nubian pottery is in itself intriguing. The garrison had no need to use local craftsmen: their supply network included larger fortresses such as Mirgissa which were home to pottery-making industries. In fact, there is even evidence to suggest that Askut itself had a moderate level of pottery production on-site, so the use of Nubian pots must have been a deliberate choice rather than as a result of the pressures of circumstance.[13]

The majority of the remains are Egyptian in design and make, with some estimates suggesting Nubian vessels account for 3.6 per cent of the overall pottery at the site, or 5 per cent if you only consider the food-related ones. What is surprising is that this number jumps quite considerably if you look specifically at pots used solely for cooking. Within the collection of cooking pots, the Nubian style accounts for a remarkable 45.5 per cent, and this increases exponentially during the later periods.[14] The interesting element here is that a cooking pot is a very normal, day-to-day item. If we had found that fine tableware formed the majority of the remains, we could explain this as a prestige item from a foreign culture and therefore only really relevant to the elite; or if it was storage vessels that made up the majority, this could be explained by the increase in trade with Nubian merchants. But it is not, and this is both strange and revealing.[15]

Askut stood in one form or another for approximately 800 years, and in that time it saw great changes and flux. Throughout its lifespan it transformed from a settlement to a fortress and finally into a fortified settlement. It had a rotating garrison to start with, but this changed to a permanent settled garrison before too long. Control over the fortress was Egyptian; it then pledged allegiance to the rulers of Kush during the so-called Second Intermediate Period (c.1650–1550 BCE) before it was retaken by the Egyptians during the New Kingdom (c.1550–1070 BCE). It witnessed periods of raiding and warfare, but also long periods of peace and relative quiet. Through all of this, the one constant seen in the fortress is the steady, uninterrupted increase of Nubian cooking pots. But what are they doing there in such abundance?

Unlike fine tableware or storage vessels, cooking pots are used daily by all elements of society, and in Egyptian homes cooking took place towards the backs of houses, away in a private space. The pervading explanation for these Nubian pots is that they suggest a growing presence of Nubian cuisine inside the Egyptian homes along the frontier. Analysis of the residue of fats that remain on the pottery shows a distinct culinary difference in the food being cooked in Egyptian-style and Nubian-style pots.[16] So Nubian food was being cooked in what seem to be Egyptian homes and the dominance of this cuisine in the archaeological record increased over time.

This idea jars somewhat with the cultural ideology in central Egypt and their perception of Nubians as barbaric and untrustworthy. Indeed, the original name for Askut itself translated as 'Destroyer of the Nubians'. Why would the Egyptians living there adopt the cuisine of a culture they despised? Well, the presence of Nubian cooking pots also, indirectly, proves the presence of another key to Nubian culture and society – women. In Egyptian culture, as in others, women were very much expected to do the cooking in the household. In fact, the simplest explanation for this continuity at Askut is the presence of Nubian women inside the homes of garrison soldiers as wives and partners. This is interesting for two crucial reasons: first, it shows two supposedly opposing cultures intermarrying; and second, it shows that the Nubian women were never forced, nor indeed inclined, to abandon their cultural food traditions. If anything, the opposite is true: Egyptian men were moving away from their own food cultures.

The presence of Nubian women in the fortress is no stretch of the imagination. We know that an earlier pharaoh, Mentuhotep II, had at least one wife of Nubian descent named Ashayet.[17] We also know that there were many more Nubian women in Egypt, not least as performers of religious rites and even priestesses of Hathor who, according to Egyptian myth, had been collected from Nubia by the gods Shu and Thoth. In her form as the lion goddess Tefnut, Hathor had set out to devour all humanity for daring to rebel against her father Re while he was king of Egypt. Shu and Thoth approached her, having transformed themselves into monkeys; they got her drunk, danced and used magic spells to subdue her and bring her home. Near the island of Philae, at the First Cataract of the Nile, her temperament was soothed in the cool waters, and she transformed into Hathor, goddess of love, music, dance and intoxication.

It has more recently been argued that perhaps the Nubians had adopted Hathor and merged her with their own cow goddess.[18] Considering the strong pastoralist roots in Lower Nubia, and the regular presentation of Hathor with bovine ears, horns, the head of a cow, or in some instances as a cow herself, this is a realistic possibility. The Nile Valley was a place where cultures merged and interacted with one another. Nubian women were possibly chosen for their distinctive dance forms, which are often displayed in Egyptian art that depicts the rites and celebrations for Hathor. We also see Nubian tattooing on the mummified remains of some of the priestesses of Hathor, a form of body art most likely introduced to Egypt by the inhabitants of Lower Nubia.[19]

Perhaps it was Hathor who was the subject of veneration at a modestly subdued chapel discovered in Askut. The design of the mud-brick chapel, with its east–west orientation, certainly suggests an Egyptian building associated with a solar cult, and the presence of some Nubian-style jewellery goes some way to support Hathor's identification, but it is impossible to know for sure. The mixture of Egyptian and Nubian religious traditions can also be seen in a few of the houses, where figurines and idols used in private ancestor worship have been found.

The increase in female Nubian items at Askut may reflect a shift in Egyptian policies on the borders. Originally, the forts were manned by garrisons that were regularly rotated. It was not their home, simply their posting. This changed during the later Middle Kingdom as the garrisons became permanent and the men brought with them their wives and families. For young unmarried men living there, the local Nubian communities clearly offered a place to look for a potential partner.

For this to be possible there must have been a degree of cordiality between the forts and the Nubian communities living in the neighbouring areas, and our limited written evidence suggests that this was the case. In 1895–6, Egyptologists unearthed a cache of paperwork in the Mortuary Temple of Ramesses II that included dispatches originally written at the fortress at Semna at the southernmost point of the frontier. What the dispatches make clear is that the frontier was a place where trade took place regularly between the garrison and the Nubian locals who were known as the Nehesy:

> [The Nehesy arrive at a specific time] to do trade
> What they brought was traded,
> A payment for it was given to them,
> They went south to the place that they came from
> after bread and beer were given to them.[20]

The giving of bread and beer in this instance was not part of the trade, but most likely a sign of hospitality on the part of the Egyptians.

These tradespeople were not only men. A couple of the dispatches specifically mention both male and female Nehesy traders, but they don't specify what was being traded. All we do know is that the men would come to trade and then depart on the same day, while the women would stay the night and leave the following day.[21] Once again, the reason for this is not explained, but it is not uncommon in colonial contexts such as this for a sexual trade to be taking place in tandem with a material one.[22]

Of course, it would be very misleading to think of life on this frontier as idyllic. The close proximity of garrisoned fortresses and local Nubian settlements always allowed for the prospect of friction. Equally, the intermarrying of Nubians and Egyptians did not change the underlying sense of Egyptian superiority that formed military policies on the border; policies made and influenced by the central powers in Egypt, who did not live on the frontier. As a result, we have scouting reports which highlight the mistrust the Egyptians had for their neighbours:

> Two Egyptian-Medjay patrols who went following that track in month 4 of prōyet, day 4, came to report to me on this day at the time of evening, having brought three Medjay-men ... saying, 'We found them on the south of the desert-edge, below the Inscription of Shōmu, likewise three women' – so said they. Then I questioned these Medjay-people, saying, 'From where have you come?' Then they said, 'We have come from the Well of Ibhet.'[23]

Here we see what was, no doubt, a regular occurrence along the frontier. A group of Medjay men and women, perhaps an extended family, were somewhere that the Egyptians did not think suitable and they were swiftly intercepted. This monitoring of Medjay movements went beyond a simple scouting mission: the Medjay were rounded up and taken to the fortress of Mirgissa, where they were questioned by an official. In this instance, the Medjay group was small, but in another dispatch we see the monitoring of thirty-two men who may have been Nubians or perhaps Egyptian outlaws.[24]

It is tempting to ask how the Medjay who formed part of the Egyptian patrol may have felt about their part in this quasi-police state they were helping to form, but that would be to assume that they were part of the same Medjay community, or indeed that they felt any closer affinity to other Nubian nomadic groups than they did to the Egyptians in the forts. What it does show is, once again, the Egyptian desire to assimilate Nubians into their own system, and that the use of Nubian men within Egyptian armies was well established before these events. For the Medjay members of the patrol, the trade-off was a simple one – the Egyptian garrisons offered regular work and in turn paid with vital food staples. Life in the desert was hard, and one dispatch describes another small Medjay group of men and women being questioned in Elephantine about the state of the desert. Their response was clear: 'The desert is dying of hunger.'[25] In such a situation, the food payments on offer at the fortresses must have been enticing to many.

Considering the inconvenience and sheer harassment undergone by these small Medjay groups, their situation could have been a lot worse. A surviving graffito from Semna records an Egyptian official claiming to have put down a small uprising in the region. He states that he did not capture them, but instead 'destroyed and slew these rebels of his'.[26] If he had decided on not killing them, Nubian captives were regularly pressganged into manual labour, often in the mines. An example of this can be seen in the bragging of one Sihathor, a high official during the reign of Amenemhat II, who commissioned a shrine to be placed in the sacred city of Abydos, on which he details certain personal achievements. Among them is his claim that, as a young man, he forced 'tribal chiefs to wash gold'.[27]

A discovery at Mirgissa highlights the harrowing forms that Egyptian persecution of the Nubians could take. Researchers found evidence of an execration ritual – a ritual-magic process designed to help resist or destroy one's enemies – including nearly 200 broken vases inscribed with the names of enemies, as well as human models made of clay and limestone to represent the intended victims. Alongside these was a ritual knife used for sacrifice, the blade of which was crafted from flint. Next to the knife was a human skull, turned upside down in the ground and missing its jaw. The body itself was discarded and not present in the execration pits. The presence of the skull and the ritual knife buried alongside it very strongly suggests that this poor man was executed as part of the ritual. Not content with the use of small models to represent their victims, the Egyptian practitioners chose to magnify the power of their magic by killing a human being at the same time. As for the man, we know nothing about him. Could he have been a prisoner of war, or a criminal? Perhaps he led a rebellion against the Egyptians? We do not know. All we do know is that he was of Nubian descent, and that he is one of the few, clear instances of the Egyptian practice of human sacrifice.[28]

The frontier fortresses at Semna, then, had a clear and simple aim: to stop the free movement of non-Egyptians into Egyptian-held lands. The inscription erected by Senusret III and the evidence for the monitoring of the Medjay could not make this clearer. But that does not mean that people did not move between Nubia and Egypt.

* * *

We have already seen the presence of Nubians in Egypt, whether it was the women present in Egyptian rituals to

Hathor, or male soldiers acting as mercenaries. Being Nubian did not actually stop everyone from being able to cross the frontier, no matter how aggressively the stela of Senusret III is worded. But it was not easy. The men were only allowed north to serve a function the Egyptians deemed acceptable. Likewise, many of the women would have been of elite status, or else specifically chosen by the Egyptians for a purpose. We do have one example of a woman by the name of Geheset who it is presumed crossed through the frontier zone during the eighteenth century BCE.

Geheset is known to Egyptologists thanks to a remarkable discovery in 2004 at the necropolis of Dra' Abu El-Naga in western Thebes. Her body was found inside two coffins. The ornate outer coffin was originally made for her husband, Imeni, who was a high court judge, but he rededicated it to his wife for her burial when she was between fifty and sixty years old. Inside this larger coffin was placed a smaller, less decorated coffin made specifically for Geheset herself. The nature of the burial, the design of the two coffins and the position of the tomb all point to the simple conclusion that Geheset was an elite woman married to an elite man; something that is confirmed by Imeni's position as a judge.

Since her discovery, it has been conjectured that she was of Nubian descent due to some shared genetic markers. If this is the case, Geheset serves as yet another example of the thriving presence of Nubians in Egypt during the Middle Kingdom. Her story is all the more unique to the historical record because her remains show the wearing of teeth in the left-hand side of her jaw, along with the left jaw hinge, which suggests she favoured the left side when chewing. Add to this her hands which show a hyper-flexibility around the wrist joint, and a reduced density in the fingers, suggesting limited use during her life, and Geheset has convincingly been argued to present the first known historical example of cerebral palsy, a motor disability that can affect a person's muscle movement, mobility and balance.[29]

During her life, Geheset would have lived further north than Thebes, in the original royal city of Itj-Tawy. But she lived during a period of great flux in Egypt during the Second Intermediate Period. Gone were the days of political stability and military expansion, when the Egyptians could reconcile their sense of cultural superiority with the chaos of the world outside their lands. This was a time of political decline and instability for the Egyptians, one that would culminate in a foreign power from the Levant region known as the Hyksos taking control of northern Egypt, while the ever-growing power of Kush in Kerma began to push their influence into Lower Nubia. This forced the Egyptian pharaohs to move from Itj-Tawy and, instead, to base themselves in Thebes in central Egypt. One would expect such a seismic shift in political stability, and its obvious repercussions on military organisation at the frontier, to result in conflict, war and destruction along the fortress network. After all, the forts beyond the Second Cataract were designed specifically to resist an invading force from Upper Nubia. And yet, the archaeological evidence does not suggest that this was the case. There is no evidence, at any of the forts, of a siege or some level of destruction dating to this period of their history.[30]

The story of a man called Ka and his family may go some way to explain how this was possible. Towards the final stages of the seventeenth century BCE, an Egyptian administrator at Buhen by the name of Iah-User erected a stela to honour his grandfather Ka, who had likewise held an official role in the fortress:

> The nobleman Ka … says: I was a valiant servant of the ruler of Kush. I washed my feet in the waters of Kush among the retainers of the ruler Nedjehm and I returned home safe and sound to my family.[31]

Much, it seems, had changed from the days of Senusret III.

The Kush did not aggressively expand north, but seem to have utilised the Egyptian infrastructure in place to their own advantage. We do not know how this took place, but it seems to have been amicable. The monument to Ka clearly demonstrates that the allegiance of both himself and the fortress was with the ruler of Kush. We know that he was the third in a direct line of five generations of administrators at Buhen. His father, Sobekemhab II, is likely to have been the man who witnessed the transfer of allegiance from the pharoah to the rulers of Kush. We also know that Ka's brother, Sopedhor, built a temple to Horus at Buhen, to the 'satisfaction of the ruler of Kush'. And, of course, we have his grandson who erected the stela with the clear intention of memorialising Ka's steadfast loyalty to the Kush rulers.[32] So how did this happen?

When Iah-User was commissioning this inscription, his family had lived on the frontier for at least five generations. Their daily life necessitated that they befriended various Nubian people from a variety of cultures, both inside and outside the fortress. No doubt they learned to speak the local language as well. To thrive on the frontier it was necessary to have strong relationships with Nubian communities, perhaps stronger than those with Egyptian communities further afield.[33] When the Egyptian authorities abandoned the fort system and pulled their resources back up the Nile, this was not simply a matter of extracting military garrisons; it would have uprooted families and people who considered Lower Nubia their home. When the rulers of Kush did exert their influence in the region, it was not done with violence (although we cannot discount the possibility of threats and a show of force). They did not attempt to micromanage the forts in any way, or to overturn the way things were working. In fact, many of the forts seem to show a certain degree of continuity during the Second Intermediate Period. For this family, and many like them, the answer was an easy one: stay put, pledge a new allegiance and carry on as usual.

Things looked little different in central Egypt. A few decades after Iah-User raised his stela, the ruler of Egypt, Kamose, declared that he sat 'united with an Asiatic and a Nubian, each man with his slice of Egypt'.[34] The Hyksos rulers controlled much of Upper Egypt and the Nile Delta, while the Kush had reached as far as the First Cataract. So, while there is no evidence for violence along the Second Cataract forts during this period, that does not mean there was no violence across the new frontier at the First Cataract. As the frontier moved so too did the cause of friction between Egyptians and Nubians.

According to the biographical writings found in the tomb of Sobeknakht, an official in the town of Elkab which lay just south of the Egyptian capital of Thebes, the armies of Kush did push north beyond the First Cataract.[35] He describes an allied force from Kush, the tribes of Lower Nubia (perhaps C-group communities), the Medjay, and the people from the land of Punt (to the far east of Nubia and possibly stretching down into the Horn of Africa). They are described as raiders, but their reach so far into Egyptian-held land was a major cause for alarm. An unnamed Egyptian ruler mustered a force to repel the Nubian alliance and pushed them back over the frontier. According to Sobeknakht, the Nubians were resoundingly defeated with the help of Nekhbet, the vulture-headed deity of Elkab who was 'powerful of heart against the Nubians'.[36] Archaeological evidence in Kerma dating from the so-called Kerma Classical Period – which coincides with the Second Intermediate Period of Egypt – strongly suggests that these raids were not only occurring, but that they were very successful. Loot from these raids has been found in the royal burials of Kerma, including sculptures connected to sites as far north as Abydos, which sits even further up the Nile than Thebes.

Kushite control of the frontier was not to last. The Second Intermediate Period soon came to an end, and the 18th Dynasty of Egypt ushered in a new era of control of the Nile during the New Kingdom Period. The first pharaoh of the dynasty, Ahmose, regained control of the frontier at the Second Cataract and revitalised the fortresses once more. His intention was clear: he wanted to re-establish Egypt's former boundaries and show that he had restored Egypt to its former glory. His successors were not as short-sighted in their ambitions. Soon, the armies of Egypt passed through the Second Cataract and established control as far south as the Fourth Cataract and the heartland of Upper Nubia, taking control of all the land and sacking the city of Kerma itself in the process. In the words of Thutmose I, the Egyptians were 'like a panther among the fleeing cattle'.[37]

With the movement of the borderlands to the south, many of the Second Cataract fortresses became obsolete and while some were repurposed with religious buildings, many were seemingly abandoned. By the time of Thutmose III and his mother Hatshepsut, with whom he co-ruled for fifteen years (c.1473–1458 BCE), Nubia was being forced into a more Egyptian model of social, bureaucratic and economic structure.[38] What is important to remember here is that during such a period of Egyptian military aggression, social change in Lower Nubia and political shifts, those small cooking pots at Askut tell a slightly different tale: during the New Kingdom Period, Nubian wares accounted for 83 per cent. So it was not wholescale change on the Nubian frontier.

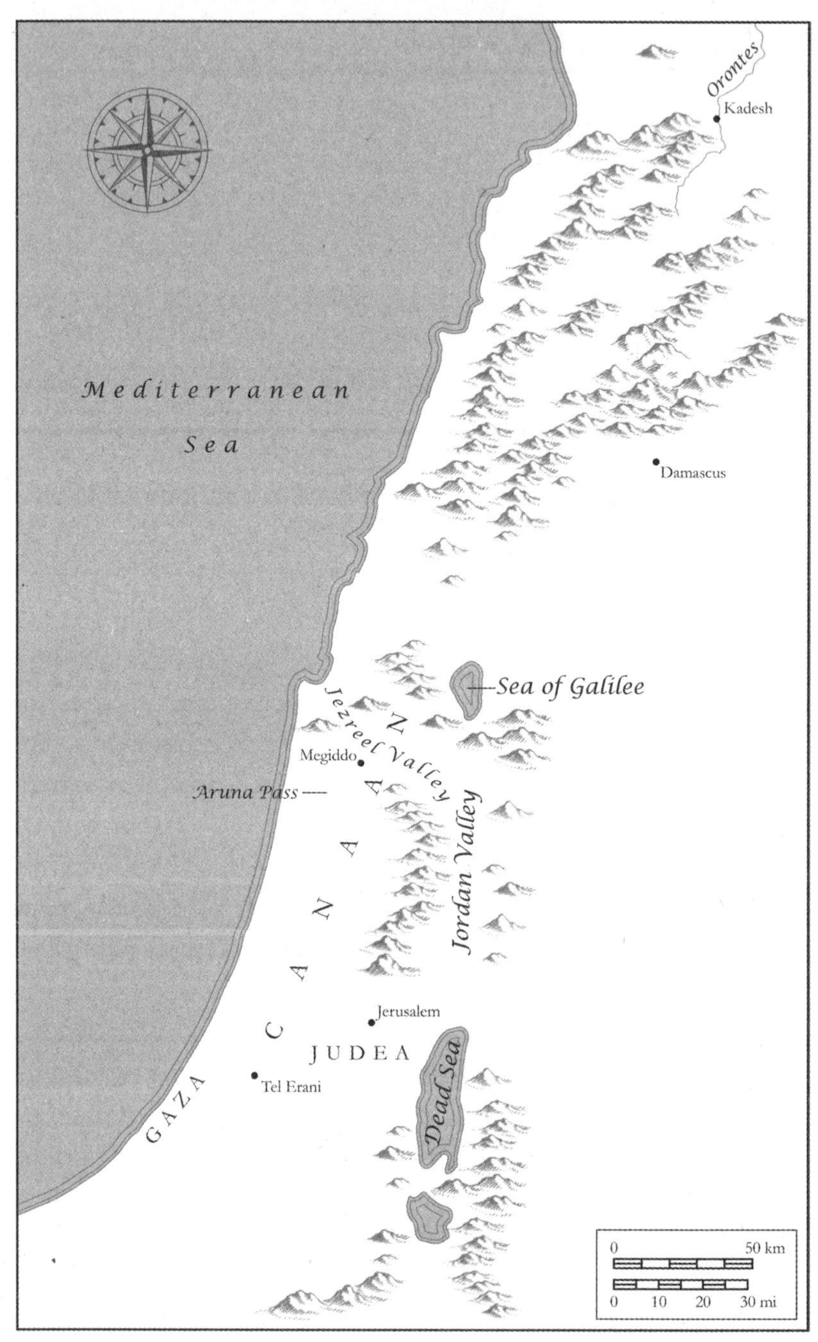
Orontes
Kadesh
Mediterranean
Sea
Damascus
Sea of Galilee
Jezreel Valley
Megiddo
Aruna Pass
CANAAN
Jordan Valley
Jerusalem
JUDEA
Dead Sea
Tel Erani
GAZA
0
50 km
0
10
20
30 mi

3

# Megiddo, Israel

Sometimes, the motivations of a historical figure are as clear to read as the words on a page. For the young pharaoh Thutmose III, fresh from his many victories in Nubia, it is not hard to discern the reasoning behind his decision to invade Canaan, in the heart of the Levant, and quell a major uprising of Canaanite kings against his influence in the region. It was officially the twenty-second year of his reign (c.1457 BCE), but until a few months earlier he had been a co-ruler alongside his stepmother, and aunt, Hatshepsut, one of the few women to rule Egypt as pharaoh. Thutmose was only a young child when his father died; his mother was a royal concubine, so when it came to announcing an appropriate regent to help rule the kingdom until Thutmose came of age, it was his father's wife who was chosen. What began as a standard regency soon changed when Hatshepsut pronounced herself pharaoh, ruling with the title and regalia that went with it.

The relationship between Hatshepsut and Thutmose III is hard to assess with any accuracy. She ensured he had a good education, prepared him to rule and even made him the commander of her army, paving the way for Thutmose to earn his later reputation as the 'Napoleon of Egypt'. When Thutmose came of age, he took on the title of pharaoh as well and ruled alongside Hatshepsut. His actions, however, suggest that he was not happy with co-ruling. Much is hidden in the silence of the historical record, however Thutmose would later scratch Hatshepsut's name from the king's lists and other monuments, as well as vandalise her statues in a sustained campaign of *damnatio memoriae*, literally, condemnation of memory (of her rule). Considering what we know about his later actions, we can see that his invasion of Canaan was an important start to his sole rule. It was his emergence from what he perceived to be the shadow of his stepmother – the point at which he made a name for himself and reaffirmed his right to rule Egypt alone.

This moment was so important to Thutmose that almost twenty years later he would have the campaign committed to stone. Inscribed on the walls of the temple of Amun in the holy city of Karnak are the so-called 'Annals of Thutmose III', which record each of Thutmose's military victories and the booty that was claimed. These annals are a fascinating insight into the man as well as the history. They don't report on all of Thutmose's military victories, such as his early campaigns in Nubia and up around Gaza, but, rather, they start with his first victory as the sole ruler of Egypt against a loose alliance of autonomous Canaanite kings led by the most powerful of them, the ruler of Kadesh.

This entry in the annals, the first of sixteen campaigns listed, is by far the longest and the most detailed. Indeed, the account of this campaign constitutes the first detailed military narrative found anywhere in history. It would have no rival to this claim until the classical Greek period and the work of Herodotus of Halicarnassus (fifth century BCE). While it does, of course, embellish parts of the narrative and no doubt omits any errors or setbacks that may have been experienced along the way, it also offers us a no-nonsense account based on seemingly factual information. One historian argues that the detail is so specific that it may have even drawn on the official war diaries of the army itself.[1]

The subsequent battle was fought just outside the city of Megiddo in the Jezreel Valley, which cuts across the north of modern Israel and offers an important passage from the Mediterranean coast in the west to the Jordan Valley to the east. The valley is intersected by the Via Maris, the most direct route from the south, in Egypt, taking you north along the coast of Canaan before passing through the Jezreel Valley, entering near Megiddo, towards the Sea of Galilee and up to Damascus. The historical importance of the valley is hard to overstate. Over 3,500 years, it witnessed the passing of almost every single military force that marched through the region led by great commanders such as Vespasian, Saladin and even Napoleon Bonaparte. Indeed, we know of at least thirty-four major battles fought in the valley, making it potentially one of the most fought-over strips of land in human history.[2]

The Megiddo that bore the brunt of Thutmose's ire was actually the latest of numerous settlements on the site, which had been occupied in one way or another since the eighth millennium BCE. The modern-day site of the city is an artificial mound, something called a 'tell' in both Hebrew and Arabic, giving the site its other name, Tel Megiddo. This tell is borne from settlements being built on top of settlements for thousands of years. It would have grown slowly, but the accumulation of building foundations, debris and other remains has left archaeologists with a wonderful treasure trove resembling something akin to a multi-layered cake. As they dig down, each layer of settlement (called a stratum) can be identified and roughly dated, allowing researchers to focus in on specific periods of the site's history and development. In total, there are twenty identifiable periods of settlement spanning from prehistory right through to the end of the first millennium BCE, which highlights just how important a site Megiddo really was.[3]

By the twentieth century BCE, Megiddo's position along the Via Maris had already drawn the attention of the growing power of Egypt. We have Egyptian artefacts in the form of small statuettes with hieroglyphs, one of which refers to an Egyptian official we know from other inscriptions from Egypt itself. These examples suggest a close tie between Egypt and Megiddo and have been used to suggest not only some form of Egyptian oversight of the town, but that it may indicate a strong Egyptian grip over the important Via Maris trade route through the Levant.[4] Equally important for Megiddo, they do not suggest a close, overbearing level of control and influence. The city was fortunate to be so far away from the lands of Egypt; it was not in the best interests of any pharaoh to try and take Canaan into their direct control.

This grip inevitably waned as Egyptian stability was challenged by a series of dynastic changes, including the Hyksos, a ruling Egyptian dynasty who most probably originated from Canaan. But when the 18th Dynasty took control of the Egyptian throne, Egypt entered a golden age in its history, one of prosperity, stability and affluence, where the arts and architecture flourished once more. This era known as the New Kingdom is the period of Egypt we most often imagine, the time of Akhenaten and his son Tutankhamun (fourteenth century BCE), and of Rameses II and his war with the Sea People (thirteenth century BCE). It was in this time of Egyptian cultural ascendancy that the land of Canaan became a target for subjugation once more. The dynastic founder Ahmose initially brought Canaan back into the Egyptian fold; but, eighty years later, Thutmose III was facing a new form of resistance:

> That wretched enemy of Kadesh has come and has entered into Megiddo. He is there at this very moment. He has gathered to him the princes of every foreign country which had been loyal to Egypt, as well as those as far as Naharin and Mitanni, them of Hurru, them of Kode, their horses, their

> armies, and their people, for he says – so it is reported – 'I shall wait here in Megiddo to fight against his majesty'.[5]

The ruler of Kadesh was no fool. His city was located a few hundred kilometres north of Megiddo, but he knew that the Egyptians' army would have to pass through the Jezreel Valley to reach him, so it was a good position to try and amass his allies. This task alone would have been challenging. Canaan may be our name for the region, but it was not a united country, nor were the Canaanites a united ethnic group. How closely related they felt to each other is hard to qualify, but the ruler of Kadesh would have had to make some big promises or some big concessions to bring together as many rulers as he did.

The Egyptians had a choice of three paths ahead: one that entered the valley a few miles north of Megiddo; one that entered a few miles to the south; or the most direct route through the Aruna Pass, which emerged into the valley plain next to the city. Of the three, Thutmose was warned against taking the Aruna Pass. This was the narrowest pass his army would have to march through and, due to its length, he would have some of his forces emerging next to Megiddo while others were still waiting at the other end of the pass. The threat of ambush and total annihilation was very real, even though he held a numerical advantage over the rebels. Thutmose disregarded his advisers' caution and chose the Aruna Pass, in a bold move that was either a stroke of strategic genius or simply a result of his own hubris. His gamble paid off: the king of Kadesh had not prepared for anyone to be so foolish and take such a risk, so the Egyptian army made it through safely and set up camp.[6]

On the day of battle, the two armies lined up to face one another. All of the strategic trickery and predictions were complete the moment Thutmose was able to camp inside the valley.

It was no longer a tactical battle, but one of brawn and bronze. The account of the combat itself is notably short and concise:

> His majesty set forth in a chariot of fine gold, adorned with his accoutrements of combat ... prevail[ing] over them at the head of his army. Then they [the Canaanites] saw his majesty prevailing over them, and they fled headlong to Megiddo with faces of fear. They abandoned their horses and their chariots of gold and silver ...[7]

Any excitement about victory would have quickly subsided with the growing realisation that the enemy had retreated inside the walled city of Megiddo, and the pharaoh now faced a long siege to douse any embers of rebellion. One source claims that the siege lasted over half a year, but the Egyptians were finally victorious and effectively brought the lands of Canaan under their rule. While the king of Kadesh was able to escape, and Thutmose would wage numerous campaigns further north in an attempt to cement his control over the region, this victory at Megiddo firmly placed Egypt as the great powerhouse in the region. We know that as a result of his campaign, the pharaoh received gifts from other political powers such as the ruler of Babylonia, Assyria and the Hittites, which he rather cheekily and somewhat untruthfully recorded in his annals as foreign tribute.[8]

Megiddo remained semi-autonomous; the Egyptians had no interest in directly ruling over the city but ensured whoever was ruling was beholden to them. It was sitting in a rather precarious position, between the powers of Egypt to the south, the Assyrians and Hittites to the north, and the Babylonians to the east. It had no power to exert itself against these dominant societies, so it became a thoroughfare for different trends and ideas coming from all directions.

Even closer to home, Megiddo was not particularly safe from local intervention, being only one of a number of independent Canaanite city-states, each vying for their own slice of power in the region. Thanks to a remarkable discovery in the city of Akhetaten (modern-day el-Amarna), the royal capital of the pharaoh Akhenaten (r.1353–1336 BCE), we have surviving clay tablets with letters written in cuneiform that lay out the complaints made by local rulers in west Asia to the Egyptian pharaoh. The letters only cover a small period of less than thirty years, giving us an amazing snapshot of the political ecosystem in which Megiddo sat.

Among the El-Amarna letters are a handful written by a man called Biridiya, who refers to himself as the ruler of Megiddo. His letters show reverence to the pharaoh, who he refers to as 'the king, my lord and my Sun', and are also self-deprecating: in one instance he presents himself as a lowly dog in comparison to the Egyptian ruler. The power dynamic is clear and predictable. One letter in particular is the most revealing, in which he complains about the military aggression of another local ruler called Labayu. In his petition, Biridiya cannot help but portray a sense of betrayal and abandonment due to the lack of Egyptian support:

> Say to the king, my lord and my Sun: Message of Biridiya, the loyal servant of the king. I fall at the feet of the king, my lord and my Sun, 7 times and 7 times. May the king, my lord, know that since the return [to Egypt] of the archers, Labayu has waged war against me. We are thus unable to do the plucking [harvesting], and we are unable to go out of the city gate because of Labayu. When he learned that archers were not coming out, he immediately determined to take Megiddo. May the king save his city lest Labayu seize it.[9]

What Biridiya makes clear is his reliance on a modest Egyptian military presence; a unit of archers is no great army, but their placement at Megiddo had been enough to prevent Labayu from attacking. While Megiddo was not under constant siege, it was not safe for the people to harvest their crops and the cramped urban conditions created a pestilential environment which is described later in the letter. Biridiya also suggests that Megiddo did not have the military power necessary to defend itself from this assault. His reliance on Egyptian support was both a strength and a weakness, leaving him at the whim of the wider military needs of the pharaoh's empire.

News of Labayu's actions would not have come as much of a surprise in the royal court. His name appears in fourteen separate letters, only three of which he sent himself. Biridiya's complaint was not unique and Labayu was forced to defend himself against accusations of harbouring rebellious ambitions.[10] In one letter he shows his desperation by, on the one hand, arguing that any military activity he was undertaking was in direct response to the orders of the pharaoh, and on the other, that he was given no choice by his rivals:

> Moreover, when an ant is struck, does it not fight back and bite the hand of the man that struck it? How *at this time* can I show deference and then another city of mine will be seized?[11]

Akhenaten finally had enough and ordered Labayu's capture and transportation into Egypt. We know about this because Biridiya had the unfortunate role of sending the pharaoh a letter explaining why this order had not been fulfilled. Biridiya had been part of the entourage chosen to transport Labayu south by land, but Surata of Akka (Acre) took command and assured Biridiya that he would send Labayu to Egypt by boat. This was a lie: Labayu had bribed Surata with a large ransom and bought his freedom.[12] He was eventually killed by the local populace, but Labayu's sons continued his violent approach to local diplomatic relations.

This was the world in which Megiddo not only existed, but actually thrived as a city: far enough away from the larger political powers around it to assert its own clear identity, but close enough to be influenced by cultural and technological transformations in the Eastern Mediterranean. During this period of the late Bronze Age, the city flourished not only as a hub of Canaanite culture but also as a cultural melting pot of art, knowledge and literature that was befitting of its position as a crossroads in the ancient world.

* * *

In our modern, interconnected and highly globalised society we sometimes lose sight of just how fortunate we are when it comes to food choices. Before the advent of such things as refrigeration, the transportation of food over long distances was reduced to items that keep easily (such as grain) or that could be cured and preserved (such as salted fish). Fresh, soft fruit does not keep particularly well over long journeys. Bananas, for instance, need to be picked when they are large enough but still unripe, cooled immediately and kept cold for a long period. They also need to be packaged in a way that stops them from beginning to ripen – usually in a plastic bag – and stored in a controlled environment to begin the ripening process. In the ancient world, none of this was possible. So what should we make of a recent discovery of banana proteins found in a burial in Bronze Age Canaan?

During the late Bronze Age, bananas had not yet reached western Asia or Africa. First cultivated in New Guinea sometime during the fifth millennium BCE, the western spread of the banana took a very long time, not reaching West Africa until the first millennium BCE. However, researchers have discovered the presence of a banana protein in the teeth of an individual who died in Tel Erani, in south Canaan, towards the end of the second millennium BCE – around the same period as Thutmose

III's successful invasion. Even with the growing influence of Egyptian trade in the Mediterranean and beyond, and the central position of Canaan within the land networks to the north and east, the appearance of banana in the dental calculus – the calcified plaque on the teeth – is rather surprising. There is no evidence that the fruit was being grown in or around Canaan during this period, and it is not a food that is commonly found in western Asia during the ancient period more generally. What is it doing there?[13]

There are two possible explanations, neither of which have any positive evidence to support them but might best explain this anomaly. The first is perhaps the more obvious: our historical models are wrong and cultivated bananas had arrived in the region earlier than first thought. The only problem with this explanation, plausible though it is, is that there is no other contemporary evidence of banana cultivation. After this so far isolated find, the next time period in which bananas have been securely identified in the region date to the fifth century CE, more than 1,500 years later.

The second possible explanation is that this banana was grown in south, or maybe even south-east, Asia, and the person found at Tel Erani was some sort of merchant or traveller. The second explanation cannot yet be verified, but is at least supported by the overall impression we get of ancient Canaan – that this was a place connected to a much wider global trade, perfectly situated as a nexus between east and west, Europe and Asia, as well as between north and south, Asia Minor and Africa.

The finds at Megiddo confirm this impression. Similar studies of dental calculus have identified inhabitants of the city eating exotic foods for the region during this time period. Alongside mainstay crops such as wheat and dates, researchers found evidence of turmeric and soybeans. The discovery of turmeric pushes back our understanding of the spice's presence in the region by at least 500 years, the earliest written evidence coming from seventh-century BCE Assyria; but archaeologically there was no evidence before now until the Islamic period of the twelfth century CE. Turmeric had a multitude of uses, as it still does, in the culinary arts, medicine, colour dyes and perfumes.

Soybeans on the other hand have no known ancient precedence in the region at all. According to present archaeological study, they were never cultivated in the region. Since their earliest domestication near the Yellow River in China, they were not grown in the lands of Canaan until the twentieth century CE. The soybean was most likely transported long distances as an oil that, much like turmeric, could be used in a variety of different ways.

Similarly, a separate tomb has been excavated in which three small jugs have been found to contain the remnants of vanilla, the flowers of which were not domesticated outside the Americas until the sixteenth century CE. The tomb belonged to nine wealthy, elite individuals, perhaps from a single family or household. One middle-aged man was found wearing a golden headband and bracelet; next to him was a younger woman wearing a golden pin and a rather exquisite silver pin shaped like the head of a duck; there was also a young child about ten years old, wearing two silver rings. Even with the obvious wealth on display, it is still somewhat of a surprise to find vanilla in those jugs, the rarity of which must have made it inordinately expensive. The vanilla most probably originated from the same region of the world where fruit from south Asia, beans from China and spices such as turmeric could be readily traded and transported: India.[14]

It seems the ancient world of the Bronze Age was not as closed as it so often appears. Life in Megiddo may have focused predominantly on external forces from Egypt to the south, Anatolia to the north and Judea in its immediate vicinity, but it tapped into a much wider world, the scope of which was no doubt beyond their understanding. The Canaanites may have known about India, or at least certain Canaanites may have done through trade and travel, but they had no knowledge of China or Indonesia. So, it is quite amazing to consider that innovations and experimentations in lands beyond their world map were having an impact and an influence on the small city of Megiddo.

It was not only food items that were travelling such long distances. The Bronze Age is so named due to the predominance of bronze as the metal alloy of choice for making anything from weaponry and jewellery to a whole host of everyday objects. The importance of bronze does not preclude the use of other metals. We do sometimes find the odd iron object in Bronze Age sites, for instance, but bronze is so omnipresent that scholars have used it as a means of defining an entire epoch of human development. So, it may come as a surprise to realise that, of the two core metals required for bronze (copper and tin), tin in particular was in very short supply – especially in the Mediterranean Basin. In reality, the origin of the tin, and, at a wider view, the bronze of the Bronze Age itself, has been somewhat of an archaeological mystery. There are some small deposits in Egypt and Anatolia which could have been used in Canaan, but nowhere near enough for how much bronze was produced over several millennia. So where did it come from?

A recent attempt to analyse the geological age of tin ingots discovered in various shipwrecks off the coast of Israel has revealed some amazing results. In the first study of its kind, a research team led by Dr Daniel Berger of the Curt-Engelhorn Center for Archaeometry in Germany analysed the tin and lead isotopes present in the ingots to offer an approximate age of the metal. Tin deposits around the world have formed at different times, so if we know the age of the natural formation then we can compare that with the age of the metal in the ingot. This is not perfect, of course; it is not a fingerprint as such, but it does allow researchers to dismiss potential sources for being either too old or too young. At one wreckage site off the coast of Haifa, the tin ingots found gave an especially fascinating age approximation of 291 million years ago, give or take 17 million. This age range allowed the archaeologists to discount a number of presumed sources – Egypt, Anatolia, Central Asia. In fact, based on this dating, the most likely source of the tin is not the east side of the Mediterranean, but, rather, the far north-west of Europe. It would seem that the most likely source of tin for Bronze Age Canaan was Cornwall, England.[15] If this is true, then Megiddo was centrally located in a trade network that spanned both land and sea, stretching from modern England to perhaps as far east as Indonesia and China.

While these finds are exciting and give us an amazing insight into just how interconnected the ancient world actually was, it is fair to say that greater cultural influences were coming from societies nearer to Megiddo itself. We have already seen the presence of small Egyptian statues in the city dating from before the time of Thutmose III, and Egyptian items such as distinctive vases and the like only become more prevalent through the late Bronze Age. Perhaps the most extravagant items have been found in the palace that was built in the northern part of Megiddo during this period of prosperity. Excavators have uncovered around 400 ivory objects, the material for which must have come from Africa, India or possibly Babylon where we know elephants were being bred during this period.[16] The ivory alone would have been very expensive, but what is equally important is what appears as decoration on the ivory itself.

Many of these objects were made to adorn and decorate wooden furniture, so the ivory is often carved to depict beautiful scenes either of cultural relevance or as art in its own right. These scenes, and these styles of art, reveal an extended network of artistic influences that were entering Megiddo, by way of trade, plunder, or as gifts. Artistic styles and motifs show Egyptian and Hittite influences; others clearly show local Canaanite styles, and one particularly striking example depicts a griffin – with the body of a lion and the head and wings of an eagle – in a form strongly associated with a Greek or Aegean style of art.[17]

* * *

The city of Megiddo is most famous as a religious site, and considering what we have seen so far this should not come as much of a surprise. Its appearance in the Jewish and later Christian scripture is not simply a geographical coincidence; it is indicative of a city that found itself attracting different cultures inside its walls and, as a result, different deities and religious trends.

Megiddo is best known as a city of the Canaanites in the middle to late Bronze Age, a period which rather notably sees the receding of Egyptian influence, to be replaced by more local matters, not least of which was the emergence of the Israelites. Megiddo appears in Old Testament scripture as one of many cities targeted by the sons of Israel and is the scene of a battle in the Song of Deborah.[18] But the site had already seen its own share of important religious developments before this. By about 3000 BCE, Megiddo had its own Great Temple, the size of which was unprecedented in the region. This monument did not appear out of thin air: it was the third sacred building built on the tell, each new temple sitting on the remains of the previous one. But this one was special; its architectural footprint was 1,100 square metres, a phenomenal size when we consider the second largest in the region at this time measured only 360 square metres. This grand monumental construction came with an intricate level of design and expert execution that makes it really stand out as an unsung wonder of the early Bronze Age.[19]

The Great Temple's central room was a long rectangular shape, maybe forty metres wide, with twelve columns running centrally through it to hold up a roof no doubt made of degradable material such as wood, straw and clay. The entrance was perfectly aligned with the basalt altar found at the rear of the room, and the dimensions of the room are determined by a precise grid using an identifiable measuring standard used in Egypt as well, one cubit (52.5 centimetres). Behind this main room are two separated corridors, which both open out into another external corridor but have no entrances from the sanctuary itself. The exact purpose of these corridors is so far unknown, but many remains of sacrificial victims have been discovered in them, highlighting their cultic importance. The precision of the design goes one step further: researchers have noticed that if you find the central point of the Temple, drawing diagonal lines from the four outer corners, the cross passes through the middle of the altar itself.[20]

The builders of this temple would have needed the requisite skill in design and stonework as well as the necessary manpower to complete the task. Labourers would have needed feeding and compensating for their work. In addition to the architectural design and geometrical understanding we can add an assumed input from priests, who no doubt helped create the ritual space and ensure its suitability for them to perform their sacred duties. But even beyond the human element, the resources required for this single structure were astonishing. Its foundations alone required 1,100 cubic metres of stone, which would have needed quarrying and transporting to site. Researchers estimate that the temple used an estimated volume of 2,200 cubic metres of mud bricks. Straw was a vital ingredient in mud bricks and a conservative estimate suggests that they would have needed fifty-eight tonnes, which would have been grown over 250 acres.[21]

Remarkably, researchers still know very little about the people who built this amazing structure. To date, no corresponding settlement has been found, so it has been suggested that it may have served as a pilgrimage site for local pastoral communities living in the wider region.[22] We may be tempted to presume a level of hierarchical authority was involved, a state-like political structure that would be capable of managing the logistics behind such a building project, but we know that this does not need to have been the case.

The Temple was abandoned, maybe as a result of an earthquake wreaking havoc in the region, and Megiddo underwent various transitions as it stopped becoming a place of pilgrimage and transformed into the urban settlement we have encountered so far.[23] But there is a small sense of continuity in this sacred area of the city, for the evidence shows that it consistently held a temple of worship in one form or another until the tenth century BCE.

Canaanite religion is easy to discern at Megiddo, if not always easy to pin down specifically. The presence of animal bones and a large round altar all point to a reliance on animal sacrifice as a way to communicate and interact with the gods. Animal sacrifice may not be the most pleasant of images to many, but for most ancient cultures it was an essential way of communicating with the divine, a gift given in the hope of either placating or thanking the gods. There is not, however, any evidence for a later practice strongly associated with the Canaanites and their cultural ancestors the Phoenicians: child sacrifice.

Equally as intriguing, excavations at Megiddo uncovered two clay models of an animal liver. These models were a reference guide for the priests as they attempted to divine the future by reading the liver of a sacrificial animal. The practice originated in Mesopotamia rather than in Canaan itself, and some examples from that region reveal a very intricate and sophisticated breakdown of the liver into discernible areas. Any abnormality or feature worthy of note could be assigned to a specific region on the liver map, which in turn allowed the reader to identify what the divine message was referring to, based on an appropriate annotation. This practice of hepatoscopy (divination by the liver) would later spread out of western Asia and throughout the Mediterranean, to be used by Greeks and Romans alike.

The question of which gods were the object of worship at Megiddo is, however, a little harder to distinguish. Finds in the later so-called 'Tower Temple', a tall rectangular temple with two towers flanking the entrance, include figurines of Canaanite gods. We cannot be certain which of the pantheons is depicted. There may have been as many as 240 divine entities worshipped within the polytheistic religion, but a particularly ornate gold statuette most likely depicts one of the more powerful male gods such as El, the creator, or maybe Ba'al Hadad, the Lord of Thunder and bringer of rain.[24]

We also have evidence for a cult that was prominent in the Jezreel Valley dedicated to the mother goddess Asherah. Asherah was the wife-consort of El and she is often depicted either in human form or as a sacred tree that is the object of worship. Her presence at Megiddo is confirmed by statuettes and pottery that portray her symbol of the tree. Her cult was practised both privately in the home and publicly in temples, by both men and women.[25] Asherah's importance must have been deeply embedded in local identity, because it managed to survive one of the largest cultural shifts in Canaan with the expansion of the kingdom of Israel.

Egyptian influence in the area had waned by the end of the twelfth century BCE, leaving Megiddo at the whim of the growing power of the Israelites to the south. Its swift and brutal destruction at the turn of the tenth century BCE indicates the hostility and resistance that characterises Canaanite and Israelite relations. In its place, an Israelite settlement was built that would survive with a general level of continuity for its inhabitants until it was conquered by the Assyrians in the eighth century BCE.

During this period of early Israelite history, religion was obviously a focal point of cultural adaptation, but it was not yet fully monotheistic in its dedication to Yahweh. For instance, King Solomon, the son of David, erected temples to foreign goddesses, and the Hebrew Bible comments with disapproval on the regular presence of the cult of Asherah in the kingdoms of Israel and Judah.[26] We may cynically view this now as religious zealotry, assuming it to be an over-exaggeration of idolatry and sacrilege on the parts of the writers, but archaeological evidence suggests they were not wrong.

The discovery of an inscription found in the Sinai Desert dating from the eighth century BCE is important here. On broken potsherds, scholars have identified a number of clear blessings from 'Yahweh and his Asherah'. It would appear that, to some believers, Yahweh had a wife beside him. Similarly, an inscription was found by tomb robbers in a tomb in what was the kingdom of Judah which suggests that Yahweh and Asherah were closely connected:

> Uriyahu the rich wrote it.
> Blessed be Uriyahu by Yahweh [and] by his Asherah
> For from his enemies he has saved him.[27]

The Book of Jeremiah paints a vivid picture when it describes the people of Judah and Jerusalem: men and children gathering wood and making sacred fires, while the women are kneading the dough to make cakes as offerings to the Queen of Heaven.[28] Whether this Queen of Heaven is Asherah or another female deity from the Canaanite pantheon is unknown, but it clearly shows that in outlying cities such as Megiddo the coming of the Israelites did not result in the absolute abandonment of local customs and beliefs. It would take many centuries before Yahweh was worshipped in isolation as the one true god.

* * *

The history of Megiddo does not end with its absorption into the Israelite kingdom, but its position as a crucial crossroads at the edges between worlds does. That said, the legacy of the city goes well beyond its eventual collapse in the sixth century BCE while under Assyrian rule and reflects its long history of religious and military importance.

In the late first century CE, a man known to history simply as John found himself banished to the island of Patmos, just off the western coast of Asia Minor. The reason for his banishment is not known, but his position as a seer or prophet in a new and growing religious movement may well have played its part. John was what you might call a Jewish Christian, someone who believed that Jesus had embodied the messianic figure in Jewish scripture. While on Patmos, he claims to have heard a booming, trumpet-like voice behind him telling him to write down in a book everything he was about to see. His visions were both shocking and apocalyptic. He bears witness to the throne of God, encircled by a rainbow and emanating thunder and lightning; and to the Lamb, with its seven horns and seven eyes. He watches as the Lamb opens the seven seals and releases the Four Horsemen: the Conqueror, the Bringer of War, the Bringer of Famine and Death.

John's vision was of the last battle, between the forces of evil and Heaven above. He watches the seven-headed Dragon battle with the angel Michael; he witnesses the Beast of the Sea win his war against the saints; finally, he stands by as the Beast of the Earth appears – the false prophet who has his followers wear the mark of the Beast, 666.

The final battle is quick but no less dramatic. The heavens pull open and out comes a rider on a white horse, his eyes aflame, his clothes already decked in blood. Named only as the Word of God, King of Kings and Lord of Lords, the rider's mouth shoots forth a double-edged sword with which to strike the nations of Earth. As he descends onto the plains below, leading the army of Heaven, an Angel calls upon the birds to join them and feast on the flesh of kings, of mighty men and horses, indeed the flesh of all men whether free or enslaved. The Beast and his forces had all amassed in one place, but they were no match for the heavenly forces.

The Beast and his prophet were captured and thrown into a lake of fire and sulphur, while their followers were all killed to a man. The birds had their fill that day. For this was the final battle, the end of one world and the beginning of a new. It is a battle that resonates with so many people up to this very day, one that embodies the title that John would give his book: *Apokalypsis*. This would give us our word apocalypse, but also translates as the title *Revelation*. The name for this far-off, symbolic battle between good and evil comes to us from Greek, but this time it is a Greek transliteration of a Hebrew phrase, Armageddon – the hill of Megiddo.

# Section II

# THE GREEK WORLD

North Sea
Britain
Rhine
Elbe
Oder
Vix
Atlantic Ocean
Alps
Rhône
LIGURIA
Massalia
(Marseilles)
Chapter 6
Veii (396 BCE)
Rome
Tagus
Iberia
Mallorca
Sicily
Syracus
Carthage
Pillars of Hercules
[TUNISIA]
Lixos
(Drâa)
The Greek World
0
500
1,000 km
0
500 mi

Byzantium (Istanbul)
MACEDON
Granicus (334 BCE)
Cyzicus
0 50 100 km
Troy
THESSALY
Aegean
0 25 50 mi
Lesbos
Mytilene
Sea
Phocaea
Delphi
Athens
IONIA
Samos
Miletus
Sparta
CARIA
Vistula
Don
Olbia
Chapter 4
Danube
Black Sea
THRACE
Byzantium (Istanbul)
PONTUS
GREECE
Anatolia
Athens
Issus (333 BCE)
Inset
Euphrates
Tigris
Mediterranean Sea
LEVANT
Babylon
Naucratis
Pelusium
(525 BCE)
Siwa
Nile
Red Sea
EGYPT
Chapter 5

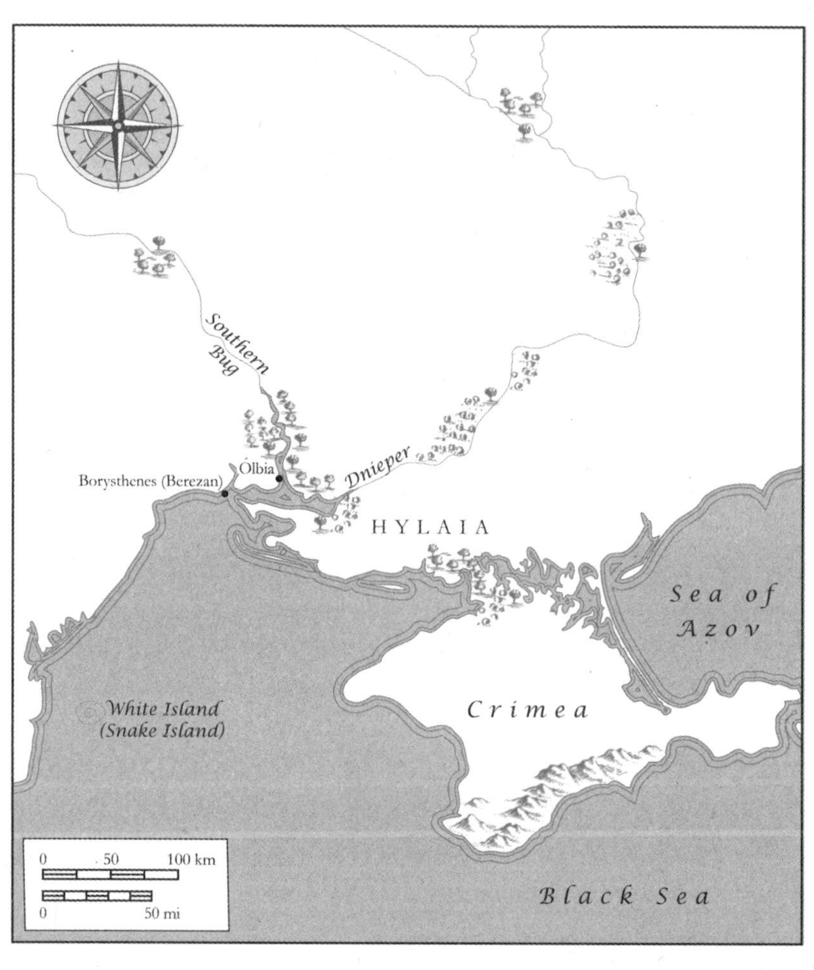

Southern Bug
Olbia
Borysthenes (Berezan)
Dnieper
HYLAIA
Sea of Azov
Crimea
White Island (Snake Island)
0 50 100 km
0 50 mi
Black Sea

# 4

# Olbia, Ukraine

From the fifth century BCE we have a new form of evidence that we can use to reconstruct our narratives: the writing of history itself. Herodotus of Halicarnassus was famously dubbed the father of history by the Roman writer and politician Cicero, and with good reason. His *Historia*, his inquiry, was the first of its kind. He was not simply trying to recount an event in the past, something that can more accurately be described as chronicling, but was more interested in *why* these events had occurred. For Herodotus, his interest lay in the most important event in living Greek memory: the invasion of Greece by the Persians in 490 and again in 480–479 BCE. But he does not actually start that narrative until over halfway through his work. He spent more time writing about the cultural differences and similarities between the Greeks and Persians, and indeed every society he could find out about. As we shall see in this chapter, this did lead him astray at times, relying on mythical stories and tall tales to supplement his analysis, but it also gives us as historians a treasure trove of information with which to work, alongside the ever-growing cache of archaeological evidence being uncovered every year.

Yet it is thanks to the works of Herodotus and his successors Thucydides and Xenophon that we look to this period between the sixth and fourth centuries BCE as one of Greek cultural dominance, especially in the Mediterranean. It is not just that the Greeks wrote the history of the period, and offered their perspectives on different cultures that can rarely be balanced out with others, but they did it with a clear sense of cultural superiority. The Greeks believed themselves to be better than everyone else, much like the Egyptians did before them and the Romans after them. But the Greek world was ever-growing and ever-changing. It was made up of over a thousand autonomous city-states called *poleis* (singular: *polis*) that, thanks to a period of colonisation throughout the Mediterranean, were spread far and wide. Our written sources, however, normally come from the Greek mainland or were heavily influenced by intellectual developments in classical Athens (fifth–fourth centuries BCE) in particular. This means that many of our assumptions about Greek life and Greek attitudes are skewed by a very narrow focus. When we talk about 'the Greeks' or 'Greek evidence', we are usually referring to a small handful of city-states, though to be frank we often just mean Athens. To understand the Greek world in its entirety, it is necessary to look far away from the mainland and Athens. It is also necessary to look at periods in which the Greek city-states were not so overbearing, such as the Hellenistic period (fourth–first centuries BCE) and the Roman Imperial period (first–fifth centuries CE). There we find a different perspective on the Greeks and their period of historical influence.

* * *

The northern shores of the Black Sea were at the outermost reach of the Greek world. To the north-west of Crimea, where both the mighty Dnieper and Bug rivers meet the sea, a small group of Greek men decided to establish a colony. What began as a settlement on Berezan, a small peninsula in the mouth of the Dnieper (Borysthenes as it was known in Greek), soon moved thirty kilometres inland along the bank of the River Bug and became the town of Olbia. To the Greeks, this really was the last point of Greek civilisation. To the east and north of the city were the territories of the Scythians, nomadic tribal groups who shared cultural traits but little else. Scythians were stereotyped as a savage society that was the complete opposite of the Greeks. While the Greeks lived in settled towns, the Scythians were nomads who carried their homes on wagons; the Greeks tilled the land, while the Scythians raised livestock; the Greeks drank diluted wine, the Scythians mare's milk and undiluted wine; the Greek warrior was a hoplite (heavy infantryman), but the Scythian was a superior horse-archer.

To the Greek mind, the Scythians sat somewhere between myth and reality. According to Herodotus, a group of young Scythian men encountered the remnants of the Amazons, a female warrior society which excluded men from their community.[1] These women were a mainstay of Greek myth, facing off against great heroes such as Heracles, Theseus and Bellerophon. Following a brief battle and reconciliation, the Scythian and Amazon groups established a new society living around the Caspian Sea; in the time of Herodotus, they were called Sauromatians. The Hippocratic text *On Airs, Waters, and Places* adds further details, including that the Sauromatian women would fight on horseback with bow and javelin until they took a husband and lost their virginity – something they should not do until they had killed at least three enemies in battle.[2]

Our evidence also speaks of the Neuroi, a Scythian tribe whose men would turn themselves into wolves for a few days before turning back into their human form.[3] Our source, the ever-dutiful Herodotus, informs us that he does not believe these claims of werewolves to be accurate, but he does make the point that the Greek and Scythian people who tell these stories clearly did believe them. Stories of lycanthropy were not unique to the Scythians. According to myth the Arcadian king Lykaon offered a dead baby as tribute to Zeus, either at an altar or, in some versions, Lykaon served the baby to Zeus during a meal. When Zeus realised what he had been fed he transformed Lykaon into a wolf as punishment.[4] The difference here, of course, is that the Scythians were not people living in a mythical past like Lykaon: they were very much of the here and now.

If you were brave enough to journey through Scythian lands, eleven days' travel took you beyond the Scythians into what Herodotus describes simply as 'desolate lands'. Beyond this was the country of the Androphagoi, a nomadic cannibalistic society whose name means man-eaters. Then came the one-eyed Arimaspians and the gold-hoarding griffins with their leonine bodies, and the head and wings of an eagle. Beyond them were the Hyperboreans, a blessed people who suffered no disease and never grew old.[5] Theirs was a land, according to the poet Pindar, where the hero Perseus overcame the gorgon Medusa. This is where Olbia sat, at the boundary between Greek and barbarian, between civilisation and chaos, between reality and myth.

As a result, the city almost absorbed that mythical mystique, that sense of unknown truths, rumours and misunderstandings. Olbia itself was so anonymous to the wider Greek world that ancient writers rarely give it its proper name. Most of our sources call it Borysthenes, after the nearest major river, the Dnieper, which was not even the river it sat on. We are told by Herodotus that other Greeks in the region knew the inhabitants as Borysthenites, even though they called themselves Olbiopolitai, 'citizens of Olbia'.[6] This confusion was evident nearly 500 years later, as the Greek orator and philosopher Dio Chrysostom (first–second centuries CE) still felt the need to explain the name:

> I should explain that, although the city has taken its name from the Borysthenes because of the beauty and the size of that river, the actual position, not only of the present city,

> but also of its predecessor, is on the bank of the Hypanis [the Bug] . . . [7]

His explanation is correct as to why people called it Borysthenes, but at the same time it is incorrect – the name of the town was Olbia. It is somewhat ironic that Dio Chrysostom also notes that the city he visited did not correspond to its 'ancient fame'.[8]

Olbia was no backwater town: it was a thriving city founded by the people of Miletus, a Greek city-state on the western coast of modern Turkey, in the sixth century BCE. Its location was surely chosen by the Milesian colonists to help establish and then control important trade routes across the Black Sea and upriver into mainland Europe. Yet, equally, the allure of the land itself is easy to see:

> [T]he Borysthenes is the most productive; it provides the finest and best-nurturing pasture lands for beasts, and the fish in it are beyond all in their excellence and abundance. Its water is most sweet to drink, flowing with a clear current, whereas the other rivers are turbid. There is excellent soil on its banks, and very rich grass where the land is not planted; and self-formed crusts of salt abound at its mouth; it provides great spineless fish, called sturgeons, for salting, and many other wonderful things besides.[9]

The most common trade item we hear about is salted fish, which could be transported throughout the Greek world as a luxury food item. But they also exported leather, salt, grain and enslaved people, possibly supplied by the surrounding Scythian communities. In exchange, Olbia imported wine, olive oil and fine pottery from further south. We even see evidence of trade from as far afield as Egypt, with the discovery of faience vessels made in the Nile Delta dating from the archaic period (pre-fifth century BCE). These include amulets and perfume bottles in various shapes and sizes, as well as items we associate more distinctly with Egyptian culture such as scarabs and a pendant to the god Horus.[10] By the fifth and fourth centuries BCE, substantial trade had also been established with the surrounding Scythian people. This was a city that was deeply connected to the wider ancient world.

The archaeological site of Olbia has been positively identified by researchers since the eighteenth century. Unfortunately, the earliest phases of the city's development are less understood than the more prominent remains from the Hellenistic period (fourth–first centuries BCE). The city was capped to its north and west by large ravines, with the river forming a barrier to its east. Over the years, the eastern part of the city has eroded away, but a rough estimate suggests it covered an area of 120 acres, roughly a mile long and half a mile wide. The lower layers of the city, from the archaic and early classical periods, suggest that the inhabitants lived in earth dugouts carved into the ground, but towards the end of the sixth century BCE stone houses standing above ground began to appear. It was around this time that the *agora* (marketplace) began to take shape, as did the sacred landscape of the city with its temples and ritual spaces. Yet this was not a planned city from the outset, designed like many new towns and cities are today.[11] The town may have been encircled by a wall made from stone and mud bricks, the remains of which have been cautiously dated to the fourth century BCE, but Herodotus does also mention Olbia having city walls so perhaps these are older still or replaced an older version.[12]

By the end of the fourth century BCE, the city had all the hallmarks of a Greek city-state. It had its bustling *agora*, its beating heart. It had its harbour and fish market, a great source of income for the inhabitants. It also had its *ecclesiasteria*, where the assembly of male citizens would meet and deliberate on public matters. It also had many public temples dedicated to central cults of Apollo, Zeus and the Mother Goddess. There are inscriptions which mention a theatre in the city, although the remains have yet to be uncovered, and a regular *Dionysia*, a festival dedicated to Dionysus. Other inscriptions which mention Olbia, found at sites all along the Black Sea coast as far south as Byzantium (modern Istanbul), show the reach of Olbian influence through trade and diplomacy.

But, if we were to listen to some of our ancient authors, you would think nothing interesting ever happened in the Black Sea, let alone around Olbia. For instance, the second-century BCE Greek historian Polybius claims that Byzantium, which sits at the mouth of the Black Sea, was beyond those parts of the world people generally visited.[13] He was quite wrong; there were people who travelled beyond Byzantium and went as far as Olbia. There were also Olbians who travelled south and saw what other Greek cities had to offer. These were not just traders or migrants but also learned men whose renown grew over the centuries.

Olbia was home to one Greek philosopher of particular note, Bion (fourth–third centuries BCE). Not a great deal is known about him for certain, but what we are told paints a colourful picture indeed. His father was previously enslaved but was freed and went on to trade in salted fish.[14] His earlier enslavement was never a secret he could hide: the punitive tattoo that his enslaver marked on his face was there for all to see many years later. Most likely he was branded as punishment for an attempted escape, and may have had the word *pheugo* ('I flee!') tattooed on his skin.[15] Bion's mother worked in a brothel in Olbia, most likely as an enslaved sex worker from Lacedaemonia, the lands of Sparta in the south Peloponnese.[16] His father fell into some financial difficulties – our evidence suggests he may have been cheating on his taxes – and the entire family was sold into slavery. Here,

Bion parted ways with his parents and was purchased by an unnamed orator who, on his deathbed, left Bion to inherit all that he owned and, in turn, Bion would have claimed his freedom. After burning the orator's entire library – the reason for which we are never told – he was able to scrape together what he could and travelled south to Athens where he became a philosopher.

Bion's writings straddled various philosophical schools, influenced as he was by the successors of Plato at the Academy, and Aristotle, as well as the Cynics. He even dabbled with atheism, but we are told he abandoned this after he had once fallen gravely ill and feared death.[17] He was known for his wit and would greatly influence the later satires of the Roman writer Horace. But in his own day his reputation was formidable enough to allow him to forge a close connection with Antigonus II, king of Macedonia, as his court philosopher. This was a phenomenal achievement for the young child from the far north, who was ripped from his parents and forced into slavery, before finding freedom and fame in Athens.

* * *

Considering the clear ideological boundaries in Greek thought between themselves and barbarians, we might expect to see a clear *cultural* separation between the Greeks at Olbia and their Scythian neighbours. So ingrained was this idea of two antithetical cultures that the Greeks told stories showing that even the Scythians enforced this separation. Take the story of another important philosopher from this region who predates Bion by roughly 200 years. His name was Anacharsis the Scythian.

Anacharsis was a Scythian prince who was able to travel widely through the Greek world, learning from their various branches of knowledge: philosophy, politics and even religion. He became the archetypal 'noble savage' in Greek and Roman writings, one who criticised Greek customs in favour of the simple life in Scythia. He was said even to have questioned the wisdom of some of the greatest thinkers of the Greek world. When Solon, the sixth-century BCE lawmaker of Athens, explained to him his plan to use new laws as a way of stemming injustice and greed, laws that would become the foundation of Athenian democracy, Anacharsis was characteristically blunt and critically incisive. He described these laws as being like spiders' webs:

> [T]hey would hold the weak and delicate who might be caught in them, but they would be ripped apart by those with power and money.[18]

His words are as relevant today as they ever were. But, in truth, we have no surviving work of Anacharsis, if indeed he even existed. All we have are quotes, claims and anecdotes from other writers infatuated with his story. Nevertheless, his position in the Greek world was well established by the fifth century BCE. His penchant for philosophy and his own innate wisdom were lauded, and he is sometimes named as one of the Seven Sages alongside other wise men such as his friend Solon and the renowned philosopher/mathematician Thales of Miletus. It is perhaps of little surprise, then, that later Greek traditions assert that Anacharsis was not fully Scythian but was in fact half-Greek – no doubt an attempt by the Greeks to claim this wise man as one of their own.[19]

His story, however, was not a happy one. Following his travels around the Aegean he headed home up through the Hellespont. While moored in the town of Cyzicus, he watched Greek locals celebrate their festival of Cybele, the Mother Goddess. The celebrations would have been loud, with music and frenetic dancing, with the worshippers whipped up into an orgiastic stupor similar to the bacchanalia associated with Dionysus. Whatever he saw made quite the impression on Anacharsis. He vowed to the goddess that, following his safe return home, he would worship her in the same fashion and dedicate an entire night-long festival in her honour. On his return to Hylaia, just across the River Bug from Olbia, Anacharsis made good his promise and privately performed the rites he had witnessed in Cyzicus. Unfortunately for him, he was spotted by a local Scythian who reported what he had seen to the king of Scythia, Anarchasis' brother Saulios. Saulios raced to the secluded spot and when he saw his brother dancing and banging his drum, raised his bow and shot him down with an arrow.[20]

This story served as an example of Scythian conservatism and their supposed rejection of all Greek cultural influence. Interestingly, we are told that, when asked, the Scythians would claim to have no knowledge of Anacharsis, raising the question of whether this was just a cautionary tale invented by the Greeks or if the Scythians had forgotten him. His was not the only story the Greeks told. Similarly, a later fifth-century BCE Scythian king called Skyles was killed for behaving too much like a Greek. In his defence, he was only half-Scythian on his father's side, but his mother was a Greek from Histria, on the west coast of the Black Sea. She raised him in the Greek manner and taught him everything he needed to know to survive in the Greek world.

Many wealthy Greek women were able to read and write and Skyles' mother was no exception. Skyles was brought up multilingual, so as well as his father's Scythian language he was also able both to speak and read Greek. After he reached adulthood, Skyles married a Greek woman and built a large house in Olbia that he decorated with statues of mythical beasts such as griffins and sphinxes. He is said often to have abandoned the nomadic lifestyle of the Scythians, leaving his men outside the gates of Olbia while he lived in the city for weeks on end, dressed as a Greek man. Only when Skyles decided to leave Olbia would he once again don his Scythian clothing and return to his men in the fields outside the city.[21]

The Scythians found this behaviour very odd, but they endured their king's eccentricities. The final straw, however, was his initiation into the mystery cult of Dionysus, of which the Scythians greatly disapproved. Rather sensibly, they believed that the pursuit of a god who instilled madness in his initiates was somewhat foolish. So, when rumours began to circulate that Skyles had joined the cult, his men did not react too kindly. When a citizen of Olbia brought some Scythians into the city to bear witness to the secret bacchanalian revelry, and Skyles' participation in it, his fate was sealed. By the time he returned to his Scythian homeland, the region was in revolt and the people had chosen a new leader, Skyles' half-brother Octamasades. Skyles fled west to Thrace, but he was soon returned to his brother and beheaded for the betrayal of his Scythian identity.[22]

The historicity of Skyles' story is, similarly to Anacharsis, highly suspect, but there is a tantalising possibility that there may be some truth to this tale. First, we have numerous archaeological finds from Olbia that suggest mystery cults were prominent in the city. Mystery cults were not open to all: you needed to become an initiate and were sworn to secrecy about the sacred rites that took place. In Olbia, we have inscribed mirrors and writing on pots that confirm the presence of the Orphic mystery cult, which had strong associations with the god Dionysus.[23] Second, regarding the figure of Skyles himself, we have numerous coins and rings discovered in the northern Black Sea region that bear the Greek letters SKYL, suggesting that either the king did really exist, or at least that it was a relevant dynastic name in the region.

What we can begin to see in the stories of Anacharsis and Skyles is that the boundary between Greek and barbarian was perhaps not as clear cut as is often imagined. Indeed, the Greek construction of the barbarian 'other' – as opposed simply to those who do not speak Greek – dates to the fifth century BCE, following the Persian Wars of 490–479 BCE.[24] As the founding of Olbia predates this intellectual movement, it is perhaps less of a surprise that the lines are not so clearly demarcated. In particular, the story of Skyles – or more specifically those of his mother and his wife – suggests that intermarriage was, as we saw between Egyptians and Nubians along the frontier, also a real possibility between Greeks and Scythians in the region. Such an idea is not only found in these stories being told, but also in the ancient descriptions of people living in the lands around Olbia.

Near the city lived the Callipidae, an otherwise unknown society who Herodotus tells us lived like Scythians but also farmed and consumed grains such as millet, and onions, garlic and lentils.[25] In his description he even refers to them as Greek-Scythians, a term that has caused no end of debate in scholarly circles.[26] North of them lived Scythian farmers, the Alazones, who grew grain for trade but did not actually eat it; and north of the farmers lived the shapeshifting Neuroi. In this description of the Callipidae we may be witnessing a literary device in action: Herodotus' attempt to illustrate the Greek world morphing into the unknown, fantastical periphery. We go from the 'normal' Greek life in Olbia, to the mix of Greek and Scythian customs in the Callipidae, and then the even more Scythian Alazones, and so on. With each step away from Olbia, the Greek world becomes further inverted. This is certainly a possibility, but we have more concrete evidence that perhaps Herodotus did *not* invent this Greek-Scythian mixed society.

In the late third century BCE, the people of Olbia erected a decree on a stela to honour one of their own, a wealthy and powerful man by the name of Protogenes.[27] The list of his achievements is remarkably long, but one section describes his investment in the defences of the city when they were under serious threat from various armed forces in the surrounding region. It states that the enslaved workers living in the countryside had been lost, as had the *mixellenes* – the half-Greeks. Fifteen hundred in number, the *mixellenes* were not simply lower-class inhabitants of Olbia. The inscription emphasises the loss of these men, for they had fought as allies of the city in a previous war. In turn, this suggests that the *mixellenes* lived in some way separately from Olbia, possibly as Herodotus describes.

The intermarrying of Greeks and non-Greeks was not well received by those living in the heartland of Greek culture. In his *Menexenus*, the philosopher Plato describes the Athenian mentality in no uncertain terms:

> So firmly rooted and so sound is the noble and liberal character of our city, and endowed also with such a hatred of the barbarian, because we are pure-blooded Greeks, unadulterated by barbarian stock . . . our people are pure Greeks and not a barbarian blend.[28]

The term he uses to describe the barbarian mix is *mixobarbaroi*, which, in this context, contrasts starkly with the pure-blooded Athenians. No matter what Plato may have thought, intermarriage was an absolute necessity at sites such as Olbia, not least because new Greek settlements were most commonly established by boatloads of men.[29] Women would have formed a small minority of early settlers, meaning that intermarriage with local women was critical to the survival of the new town.

As a result of this close interaction between Greek and non-Greek, life at Olbia was not simply a carbon copy of that in their *metropolis* (literally: mother city) Miletus. It acquired a slightly local flair all of its own. As we have seen, the first generation of houses were pit dwellings or dugouts, rather than stand-alone buildings above ground, an adaptation we see at various new

Greek settlements in the Mediterranean. We also see a local identity expressed in religion. Prominent cults included those of Apollo, the primary deity for Olbia, and also one for the hero of the Trojan War, Achilles. While cults of Apollo were widespread throughout the Greek world, those of Achilles were not normally so central to community life.

Achilles was from the northern Greek region of Thessaly, born to a mortal father, Peleus, and a sea-nymph mother, Thetis. According to the epic poem *Aethiopis*, Achilles was whisked away from the battlefield at Troy by Thetis just as he was about to die. She took him to the White Island (modern Snake Island) in the Black Sea, where he is said to have become immortal. Perhaps this version of his tale explains a short fragment of a hymn written at the turn of the sixth century BCE by Alcaeus, which describes the hero as Lord of Scythia.[30] On the island was a temple dedicated to Achilles, and a statue of the hero either alone or with Helen of Sparta as his lover.[31] These are not the stories of Homer, but other versions of myth that are less well known. Yet it seems that for the settling Milesians this story became something of a 'charter myth'.[32]

We also see an interesting reflection of identities in the money used at Olbia. Before the striking of conventional coins, they commonly used two rather unusual forms. The first were coins shaped like dolphins, perhaps a symbol of Apollo who was closely associated with the creature, or perhaps simply reflecting the presence of dolphins in the Black Sea. The second form of early coinage has come to be known as 'arrowhead money' due to their rather unique shape. It has been argued that both the arrowhead and the dolphin shapes may have been an attempt to promote the cult of Apollo, who was after all an archer.[33] But it cannot be ignored that the introduction of coinage to the region by the Greeks required the Scythian producers and traders to accept and adopt it. After all, a coin is only of value if all sides of the trade are in agreement. The use of a prominent local animal, and the head of a weapon that the Scythians held most dear, rather suggests that the people of Olbia had the local inhabitants firmly in mind.

It comes as little surprise that when Olbia did begin to mint its own coinage in the fifth century BCE, the images on the coins reflected both Greek and Scythian cultural values. We see headshots of the local, now Greek, river god Borysthenes. There are many delightful pictures of eagles clasping a dolphin in their talons – the meaning of which is somewhat of a mystery. And we also see specifically Scythian imagery, such as long-handled axes called a *sagaris*, and an archer's bow in its case (the *gorytus*). This is a far cry from the rhetoric of Greek identity and superiority. More tantalising still, there is evidence that suggests that the people of Olbia began to adopt parts of Scythian culture.

Scythian clothing was very different from the Greek way of dressing. Their clothes were made from animal skins, and they wore a greater number of layers due to the cold. But to the Greeks the true symbol of the barbarian was most definitely his choice in legwear – trousers were not suitable clothing for a man:

> [The Scythians] are the most impotent of men ... because they always wear trousers and spend most of the time on their horses, so that they do not handle the parts, but owing to cold and fatigue forget about sexual passion, losing their virility before any impulse is felt.[34]

If we were to look for a clear sign of Greeks 'going native', for want of a better term, it would be the adoption of clothing they considered emasculating; but, in the first century CE, we see exactly that. Dio Chrysostom's account of his visit to Olbia is predominantly given through a recounted conversation between himself and a local citizen called Callistratus. Callistratus was about eighteen, tall and good-looking. He was already an experienced warrior even at such a tender age, indicative no doubt of the incessant violence in the region. We are also told that he had many male lovers, some of whom Dio postulates could have been Scythian. In this description, Callistratus is characteristically very Greek. He studies rhetoric and philosophy, and he has an intimate knowledge of Homer, his favourite poet. What stands out in an otherwise quite positive portrayal of a young, Olbia-based Greek man is his clothing:

> Callistratus at first came riding by us on horseback … suspended from his girdle he had a great cavalry sabre, and he was wearing trousers and all the rest of the Scythian costume, and from his shoulder there hung a small black cape of thin material, as is usual with the people of Borysthenes. In fact, the rest of their apparel in general is regularly black, through the influence of a certain tribe of Scythians, the Blackcloaks, so named by the Greeks doubtless for that very reason.[35]

This scene should have been unthinkable, but Callistratus was not a lone individual isolated from Greek life. He was a prominent and clearly well-regarded member of his community – one that often interacted with the Scythians. No doubt wearing trousers made perfectly good sense. Herodotus describes the region as enduring frosts for eight months in the year, allowing the Scythians to drive wagons over large frozen bodies of water.[36] Also regular horse riding would have encouraged the Greeks to cover their legs.

For Dio, the people of Olbia had lost key elements of their Greek identity. He comments on their spoken Greek, in many ways echoing Ovid's complaints in Tomis: 'in general they no longer speak Greek distinctly.'[37] We know through their public inscriptions that the official Greek of Olbia looks exactly the same as it does elsewhere in the ancient world, so perhaps Dio is commenting on a local dialect that does not match the one he spoke; or perhaps he is simply exaggerating for effect. It is not uncommon for social groups moving into new areas of the world to exhibit two opposing transformations simultaneously: to adopt new customs and assimilate their new surroundings, while also cementing their old ethnic identities by clinging to age-old traditions. In Callistratus, we see the contrast between his Scythian dress and his obsessive love of the Greek poet Homer.[38]

Of course, this cultural assimilation was not one-way. We know that local Scythian groups began to adopt parts of Greek culture as well, not just from the cautionary tales of Herodotus, but in many other aspects of Scythian life. A familiar cliché about the Scythians promoted by Greek authors is their love of heavy drinking. In particular, they are said to drink undiluted wine. Now, by modern standards ancient wine was not particularly strong. On average, wine produced during this period would have been approximately 6–10 per cent proof, like a proper cider. But the Greek way of drinking this was to dilute it with water; how much water depended on how drunk one intended to get. As such, the use of water was as much a mark of refinement as an actual necessity, a matter of taste and preference. In not watering down their wine, Scythians were considered uncivilised, no matter how much alcohol they were actually consuming. One Greek drinking song from the turn of the fifth century BCE expresses this very clearly:

Come here, and so that peacefully,
I may honour Dionysus.
Come, let us not
Shout and crash
With our wine, as the Scythians drink,

But let us drink
Listening to lovely hymns.[39]

The Greeks told stories of men going mad after drinking Scythian wine. Cleomenes I, a king of Sparta no less, was said to have gone mad in exile. On his return, he began to assault anyone he met on the streets of Sparta, hitting them in the face. The authorities had him locked up. In jail, he took his own life in the most gruesome of ways: lacerating his flesh in long strips from his ankle up to his belly. The Spartan explanation for this onset of insanity was that he had grown accustomed to drinking wine in the Scythian way. In fact, it became customary for any Spartan who desired a strong drink to ask for a 'Scythian cup'.[40] To drink wine without inhibition, and to suffer the physical and psychological consequences of that drinking, was to be drinking like a barbaric, unrestrained Scythian. The irony of this is that the Scythians did not make their own wine. The Greeks and Persians introduced them to it.

* * *

While the city of Olbia was poorly understood in the wider Greek world, its influence was wide-ranging and so it always attracted outside attention. Its isolated position in the north forced the city to rely on powerful Scythians in the region to facilitate trade, and possibly for protection. Equally, the city's position on the Black Sea allowed it to prosper as a key trading hub throughout the Mediterranean. It was not long before Olbia attracted the interest of more dominant political powers.

In the late sixth century BCE, the most powerful empire in the Mediterranean was that of Achaemenid Persia. Their king, Darius I, was planning an expedition across the Danube; his goal was to subdue the innumerable Scythian tribes, or perhaps punish them for historic incursions into Persian lands.

With an enormous army at his disposal, Darius knew – as did the Scythians – that he could defeat a Scythian confederation in battle. Therefore, the various Scythian communities decided to work together to maximise their greatest strength: their mobility and nomadic lifestyle. Entire communities – man, woman and child – stayed on the move for sixty days and managed to keep Darius' army chasing shadows throughout the northern Pontic region. With no enemy to attack, the Persian king's plans were toothless, and the Scythians' own scorched-earth policy made life very hard for the Persian army. Darius' army ended up retreating in shame, returning over the Danube with his men. No Persian force would ever again attempt such an adventure.[41]

This at least is the story told to us by our Greek sources, but rather perplexingly the fate of the Greek cities in the Black Sea is never mentioned. We are left to wonder what the Greek citizens in places like Olbia were up to during these frantic few months: did they side with the Scythians or with the Persians? Were their cities safe from Darius' men, or were they besieged? It is not possible that the citizens of Olbia were able to join the Scythians in their hypermobile tactics, but there is no record, either in the literature or the archaeology, of any sustained damage during this period. Perhaps they were able to remain neutral in some way? All we do know is that the Persians did leave a mark on the Olbian landscape.

While the Persian invasion of Scythia might have failed, they were able to assert dominance over the Black Sea itself, aided by their control over Greek cities on the southern and eastern coasts. So, although Olbia may have maintained its independence, it was still reliant on Persian trade routes in the region. This may explain the discovery of a Persian clay weight at the site, made from local clay.[42] On it is an impression of a Persian archer examining his arrow. This artefact would have been used for weighing out produce or materials, offering a universally accepted weight standard, allowing for fairer trading. We find similar seals throughout the Black Sea region. To complicate matters, Olbia had more to navigate than simply *Persian* control of certain markets; from 479 BCE there was another major player in maritime trade: Athens.

The year 479 BCE saw the Persian invasion of Greece, initially led by Xerxes I, repelled from the Greek mainland. In their determination to defend Greece from future attacks, the Athenians joined a Hellenic alliance known as the Delian League. Athens took an early leading role in the league and began to use it to expand its own influence over the Aegean Sea. Our evidence is scarce but direct contact between Athens and the northern Black Sea seems to have been limited, at least initially. However, it is interesting that on the coinage of Skyles, the Scythian king mentioned earlier, we often find an image of an owl that imitates the Athenians' own coinage. This must surely suggest a growing influence of Athenian markets in the region.

Politically, Olbia was ruled by tyrants during the fifth century BCE. A tyrant was a non-hereditary sole ruler and, to the Greeks at least, the word did not hold negative connotations as a default as it does in modern usage; there were both good and bad ones. Tyrants often relied on powerful outside support to maintain their position, so the influences of Scythian rulers or the Persians would have played an important role in maintaining the status quo. This changed rather dramatically in 436 BCE, when the Athenians decided that their influence in the Black Sea was too weak and in need of enhancement.

The political mastermind behind this new Athenian policy was none other than Pericles, the man considered by many to be responsible for creating the classical Athens we think of today. His influence was remarkable in a democratic system which officially had no head of state. As the historian Thucydides, who was himself a contemporary of Pericles, states: Athens was 'a democracy in name but, in fact, governed by its first citizen'.[43] Pericles oversaw the rebuilding of the Acropolis complex, including the famous Parthenon. He spearheaded many of Athens' expansionist policies and led them from being simply leaders of the Delian League to becoming rulers of an empire in their own right. His arrival in the Black Sea with an indomitable Athenian fleet was therefore a sign of drastic change for the region. Pericles' purpose was clear:

> [In the Black Sea] he achieved whatever the Greek cities wanted and treated them kindly, while to the neighbouring barbarian peoples with their kings and rulers, he displayed the magnitude of his forces and the fearless courage with which they sailed wherever they pleased, having brought the whole sea under their control.[44]

The people of Olbia understood that the tide had turned in the Black Sea. Athens was now the regional superpower, and the city joined the Delian League as a tribute-paying member not long after Pericles' show of strength.

The time frame is hard to ascertain from the evidence we have, but we know that at some point after it joined the Delian League Olbia transformed itself politically from a tyrant-run state to a democratic one. Most notably, the city adopted a new cult of Zeus Eleutherios (the liberator). Inscriptions from the fourth century BCE attest to democratic constructs such as a *boule* (a council) and make reference to the *demos* (the people) as a source of authority and power. It is also noticeable how personal names disappear from the coinage, suggesting there is no longer a single ruler in Olbia.[45]

With democracy came a sense of political autonomy and cultural sovereignty. The people of Olbia could make decisions that were best for them, decisions that could help them most. This included making some radical changes to their social infrastructure in times of peril. In 330 BCE, during the early Hellenistic period, the Macedonian commander Zopyrion was appointed commander of the region of Thrace, on the western shores of the Black Sea. Alongside many other Macedonian commanders, his job was to help secure the imperial gains of his King Alexander III (the Great), while the king himself continued his expansion east into the Persian Empire and beyond. Zopyrion was not, it seems, much of a team player. News of Alexander's victories and the glory bestowed upon him encouraged Zopyrion to attempt similar feats. He quickly amassed an army of 30,000 men and declared war on the Scythian lands to his north-east. His first major target was the wealthy city of Olbia.

Olbia's defences had been well established by this point, including a large city wall; but an army 30,000-strong, led by a commander from the most successful military tradition the Mediterranean had seen to date, was no trifling matter. Zopyrion besieged the city and set about its destruction. The Olbians knew they were outmanned, and they would have known that one of the most common causes of defeat in Greek siege warfare was betrayal from within their own ranks. As a result, either before or during the siege, the people of Olbia did something rather extraordinary:

> When Zopyrion was besieging Olbia, the people freed their slaves and gave citizenship to foreign residents: with the citizen-rolls thus redrawn, they were able to hold off the enemy.[46]

By offering freedom and citizenship to these traditionally alien groups, the people of Olbia maximised the number of soldiers they could call upon and also minimised the likelihood of internal dissent and treachery. Their plan most definitely worked.

Zopyrion settled in for a long siege, one that relied on starving the Olbians into submission. Unfortunately for him, a great storm wiped out his supporting fleet, leaving his army stranded in hostile territory without any logistical support. His only option was to lift the siege and head back to Thrace, but he had many enemies between Olbia and home. We are told that the Getae tribes wiped out his entire army, inflicting one of the most devastating defeats on a Macedonian army and as a result destabilising Macedonian control in Thrace.

For Olbia, the decision to offer citizenship to non-Olbians and non-Greeks left an indelible mark on their cultural and political landscape. From the lifting of the siege onwards, it was now possible for Scythians to hold office in the city, and we do see a steady increase in foreign names on official decrees, denoting people in leading political and religious roles. The period also witnessed a booming of Olbian affluence, as witnessed by the extensive building projects undertaken and the ornate mosaics that were commissioned, no doubt attracting more Scythians into the city as a result. But this was not to last. By the middle of the third century BCE, Olbia went into swift decline, possibly as a result of regular raids on their agricultural land from external nomadic groups. The city began to rely on wealthy philanthropists to help plug the financial gap in the treasury; this included the sponsorship of a newly established grain-dole for the poorer citizens. It was not long before the inevitable occurred: Olbia relinquished its democracy in the second century BCE and accepted the rule of Scilurus, a Scythian king whose lands stretched across Crimea. He was himself quickly replaced by the growing power of the kingdom of Pontus, under the reign of Mithridates VI – a man who would become a considerable thorn in the side of the Roman Republic and one Pompey the Great.

Olbia was in a state of political flux, relying on strong external powers to protect it from migrating nomadic groups appearing in its lands. But the ephemeral nature of such empires in the region left Olbia exposed and at risk. By the mid-first century BCE, while Julius Caesar was rampaging through Gaul, a warlord of the Dacians (modern Romania) by the name of Burebistas crossed the Danube and ravaged the northern Black Sea coast. Olbia was destroyed and its people fled to the nearby Greek and Scythian communities further inland.

The city visited by Dio Chrysostom in the first century CE was not the Olbia of old. It was re-founded years later to re-establish a Greek trading presence in the area, so as to attract the Greeks back to the region with their wares. This was not done with the support of Greeks from around the Mediterranean, but, rather, requested by the Scythians themselves. For that, ultimately, is the story of Olbia. It was a city and a people that understood who they could rely on at the farthest reaches of the world. It was not their Greek brethren from far afield. It was, rather, the Scythian people they lived with every day.

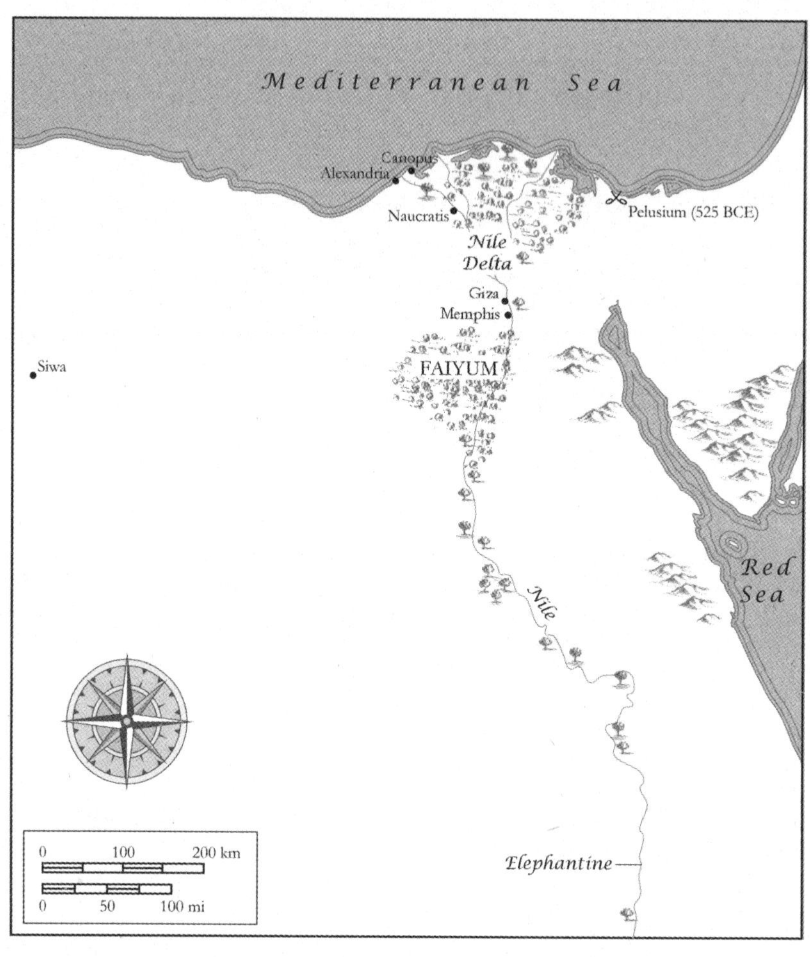
Mediterranean Sea
Canopus
Alexandria
Naucratis
Pelusium (525 BCE)
Nile
Delta
Giza
Memphis
Siwa
FAIYUM
Red
Sea
Nile
Elephantine
0
100
200 km
0
50
100 mi

# 5

# Naucratis, Egypt

In contrast to Olbia, life for the Greeks in Egypt began from an entirely different perspective. In the Black Sea, the Greeks could revel in a narrative of being a beacon of light in a barbarian wild – something that we saw did not live up to reality – but in Egypt this belief was not possible. For the Egyptians were already an ancient culture when the Greeks arrived. It often shocks people to learn that the death of the Egyptian ruler Cleopatra VII in 30 BCE occurred closer to the building of the world's tallest skyscraper, the Burj Khalifa, in 2009 (2,039 years apart) than to the building of the Great Pyramid of Giza (approximately 2,500 years apart). The Great Pyramid was more ancient to Cleopatra than she is to us.

The Greeks dated their own mythical, heroic past to around the thirteenth–twelfth centuries BCE; this is certainly true for the legendary Trojan War. Perhaps the most well-known date for the war comes from the Greek mathematician Eratosthenes, writing in the third century BCE, who calculated that Paris, prince of Troy, kidnapped Helen of Sparta and that this was the catalyst for the war in the year 1184–1183 BCE. Yet if we remove ourselves from the Greek world we know from Chapter 2 that, by the 1180s, the fortress of Buhen had been founded, extended and had already fallen into disuse. In terms of political rule, Egypt had already entered its 20th Pharaonic dynasty. Indeed, 1186 BCE saw Rameses III take the double crown of Egypt and begin his war against the elusive Sea People. By the time that Homer's *Iliad* had taken its final form in the seventh century BCE, the Egyptian kingdom had existed pretty much continuously for almost 2,500 years. What for the Greeks was a time of demi-gods and heroes like Achilles and Odysseus was for the Egyptians one of firmly historical events. It is for this reason that ancient Greek writers of the fifth and fourth centuries BCE were in awe of the cultural and historical memory of learned Egyptians.[1]

It is of little surprise, then, that the Greeks considered Egypt one of the oldest cultures in the world. Egypt's longevity was in itself a source of admiration: as Aristotle wrote, they were not only the 'oldest of nations, but have always had laws and a political system'.[2] Herodotus went further: he assumed that because the Egyptians were an older culture and therefore did certain things before the Greeks, the Greeks must have borrowed much of their culture from the Egyptians:

> The Egyptians were the first people to establish solemn assemblies, and processions, and services; the Greeks learned all that from them. I consider this proved, because the Egyptian ceremonies are manifestly ancient, and the Greek are of recent origin.[3]

Even the intellectual fields of philosophy and mathematics, as well as the art of writing, were all first ascribed by ancient Greek writers to the Egyptians. The Greeks felt this lack of comparable heritage quite keenly. Plato tells a fictional story of the Athenian lawgiver, Solon, travelling to Egypt and speaking with some old priests about ancient history. At one point, the oldest of the priests turns to him and says, in a rather patronising tone: 'Oh, Solon, Solon, you Greeks are always children: there is no such thing as an old Greek.'[4]

To the Greeks, the Egyptians were barbarians, as in not Greek, but there were more reasons to admire rather than to deride them. The Egyptians must have had some modicum of respect for the Greeks as well, if only for their trading abilities. In fact, some Egyptian sources refer to the Mediterranean as the Greek Sea, acknowledging their influence over maritime trade in the region.[5] There were long-standing exchanges between Egypt and Greece going back possibly as far as the Minoan period, but Egypt would never allow the Greeks to establish a permanent presence in the Nile Delta such as a trading post or settlement.

All this changed in the seventh century BCE as the Saite dynasty in Egypt began to employ more and more Greek mercenaries to fill out their armies. Psamtik I (r. 664–610 BCE) used a considerable number of Greeks to help secure his rule in Egypt and, in return, allowed them to settle in the Nile Delta. It was during his reign that the site of Naucratis appears to have been established, possibly as one of these settlements for veterans, along the marshy Canopic branch of the Nile.[6] Unlike other Greek settlements in foreign lands, such as Olbia and Massalia, Naucratis had no single mother city. The evidence suggests that at least twelve separate Greek cities were involved in the early history of the site, all from Ionia and Caria (the west coast of modern Turkey).

Thanks to a series of surveys of the site since 2012, we know that Naucratis was larger than originally thought. At its peak the town covered almost sixty hectares, with the river flowing to the west of the town in a south–north direction. The waterway was three metres deep, as an average, and around 250 metres wide, so it was perfectly suited to seafaring ships. As for the town itself, much of the remains exist under the modern villages in the area, and early surveys focused on buildings of religious significance. To the north of the site were temples dedicated to Greek gods such as Apollo and Hera, as well as a temple to

Aphrodite further south, and heroes like Castor and Pollux. To the far south of Naucratis is an enormous area designated the Great Temenos (religious precinct) measuring 298 metres x 259 metres, or eight hectares. Its design was most definitely Egyptian, but it is not easy to date accurately. We know that it underwent major renovations during the fourth and third centuries BCE, under the first Greek rulers of the Ptolemaic dynasty. Importantly, this Egyptian temple complex, which dominated the landscape of a Greek town and was heavily invested by Greek rulers, was dedicated to the Egyptian god Amun-Ra.

Away from the more glamorous finds, the most recent fieldwork has shown that the town was densely packed with houses and industrial areas, warehouses and workshops. These were not always neatly separated into distinct areas of the town, regularly alternating throughout, but some zones of industry are discernible from the archaeology. The houses were a mixture of compact, Egyptian-style tower houses and terraces. Capable of maintaining a population of around 13,000 inhabitants, the organic street layout and densely packed housing would have given Naucratis the feel of a busy, bustling, maybe even overcrowded town.[7]

The history of Naucratis is testament to Greek perseverance. Since its foundation, the town bore witness to numerous seismic political shifts, both in Egypt and in the wider Mediterranean. In 525 BCE, the Egyptian army of Psamtik III was defeated at the Battle of Pelusium by the might of Persia. The Persian king, Cambyses II, took the throne of Egypt and absorbed the kingdom into his empire. The impact this had on Naucratis is hard to discern, but we do know that archaeological evidence of trade in the town appears to diminish during the early years of the fifth century BCE, which chimes with the Greek revolt against Persia in Ionia (494 BCE) and the two invasions of Greece by Darius I (490 BCE) and Xerxes I (480–479 BCE). Yet, it did not take long for Naucratis to settle into its new arrangements and become a thriving market town. During the fifth century BCE, the town transformed itself into a city-state, with the construction of a *prytaneum* which served almost like a town hall, acting as a seat of government where magistrates and officials would meet to discuss matters of state.

Persian-ruled Egypt was consumed by regular revolts and uprisings. The Persian rulers had the power to control the area, but many of them failed to understand the Egyptian people and so their rule was a very uneasy one. At the end of the fourth century BCE, Persian rule was brought to an end by Alexander III of Macedon, or, as he would be remembered in history, Alexander the Great. Following his early death, the lands of Egypt were given to his trusted commander Ptolemy, the founder of the so-called Ptolemaic dynasty. The Ptolemies had a better understanding of Egyptian culture and what was expected of a legitimate Egyptian ruler. They regularly portrayed themselves as divine rulers, ultimately as pharaohs. Their fall in 30 BCE and the subsequent Roman rule of Egypt brought yet further change, including the spread of Christianity into the region during the first century CE. Through all these political and cultural changes, the small Greek outpost of Naucratis not only survived but flourished.

* * *

The settlement at Naucratis may have started life as a veterans' colony, but it soon transformed into one of the key trading ports of the Nile Delta. A Greek presence in the delta offered a unique opportunity for traders throughout the Eastern Mediterranean, and began to attract buyers, sellers and service providers – all of them looking to cash in on the untapped wealth of the Egyptian market. The dual presence of both military veterans and excess money also attracted sex workers to the town, the beauty of whom was legendary.[8]

Perhaps the best-known of them all was a *hetaira* (courtesan or mistress) named Rhodopis, 'the rosy-faced'. The word *hetaira* literally means 'female companion' and can equally refer to non-sexual relationships or to sexual ones; that said, Rhodopis was brought to Egypt enslaved, and the role assigned to her by her enslavers is clearly laid out in her life story. Originally, she was from Thrace, either born into enslavement or else taken as a young child. She was bought by a man called Iadmon from the island of Samos, the same enslaver who owned the famous storyteller Aesop. Iadmon sold her to another Samian named Xanthes, who took her to Egypt as a sex slave, possibly to Naucratis itself. It was there that her story takes on an almost legendary status. Having convinced a wealthy trader from Mytilene to buy her freedom, Rhodopis continued to ply her trade in Naucratis as a freewoman.

Her financial success as a freewoman is testament to her drive and ability to exploit the market. We are told by Herodotus that she used one-tenth of her wealth to buy a mass of sacrificial iron spits, the kind used for spit-roasting beef, and sent them to the sacred sanctuary at Delphi as an offering to Apollo. We do not know how much this cost, or even how many spits were bought – either would allow us to estimate her wealth. All Herodotus tells us is that she was clearly wealthy, but not quite as wealthy as people in his time were suggesting. Plutarch, a former priest at Delphi writing in the first–second centuries CE, also mentions numerous obelisks erected in her memory, which would have been remarkably expensive.[9] Over time, Rhodopis' story was mixed with that of other Egyptian women, and no doubt a lot of second-hand rumour, with many sources claiming it was she who paid for the smallest of the three great pyramids at Giza.[10] This is clearly false, but indicative of the reputation that followed her in death.

The mythos surrounding Rhodopis does not stop there. Our much later Roman sources tell another tale from her life which takes us from historical fiction into the realm of fairy tale. According to both Aelian and Strabo, Rhodopis (called Doriche in the texts) was favoured by the goddess Fortuna, the goddess of fortune and luck, while taking a bath.[11] The goddess sent an eagle that swooped down and plucked Rhodopis' sandal out of the hand of a startled slave. The eagle carried it south, to the royal residence of Psamtek (most likely Psamtek II) in Memphis, dropping it into his lap. The pharaoh marvelled at the shoe – its exquisite shape, appropriate size and neat design – but also at the actions of the bird; even in a culture where the supernatural existed all around you, and nature regularly offered signs and omens in need of interpretation, an eagle carrying a shoe was a bizarre event. He sent word throughout the land to find the woman to whom this sandal belonged. When he found Rhodopis he married her and made her his queen. If you think this story sounds familiar, you will understand why it is considered by some to be the earliest known version of the Cinderella story.

The fact that so much of Rhodopis' story, whether fact or fiction, survives in the ancient evidence is itself a cause for consideration. Herodotus claims that she was the most famous *hetaira* in all the Greek world, that her name was constantly on the lips of men in their gentlemen's clubs. His reason for this seems unsatisfactory: that she was sexually alluring, or as the third–fourth-centuries CE author Heliodoros puts it: 'There was no escaping or resisting the net of [her] sensuality.'[12] The same must have been true of many sex workers, both free and enslaved, so what was so different about Rhodopis? For this we must return to the earlier part of her story. The man from Mytilene, the one who bought her freedom, was a trader who had come to Naucratis by the name of Charaxus. Upon meeting her, he became not so much enamoured as obsessed with Rhodopis and is described as bankrupting himself during this time. Perhaps it was the ransom money he paid that ended up causing him such financial distress, as Ovid suggests in his fictional letter where he adopts the voice of Charaxus' sister, the famous 'tenth muse' of archaic Greece, the poet Sappho of Lesbos:

> My untaught brother was caught in the flame of harlot love,
> and suffered loss together with foul shame; reduced to need,
> he roams the dark blue seas with agile oar, and the wealth he
> cast away by evil means once more by evil means he seeks.[13]

Whether or not Charaxus actually did resort to piracy, as intimated by Ovid, is not easy to ascertain. But all the evidence we have about Sappho's relationship with her brother emphasises her disappointment in him for his 'past mistakes'.[14] These mistakes are not made clear in the scant remains of Sappho's poetry – not yet at least – but Herodotus suggests that there are poems out there waiting to be found, which may shed light on the matter. He tells us at the end of his account, in a rather matter-of-fact way, that Charaxus returned to Mytilene after buying Rhodopis' freedom and, perhaps as a result, he was 'bitterly attacked by Sappho in one of her poems'.[15] Which poem remains to be seen.

It would be a great injustice to leave Rhodopis hidden in the shadow of Sappho and her brother. The story of Rhodopis is one of enterprise and opportunity, of personal agency and emancipation. Naucratis was not the only Greek town that could play host to such a tale, but it comes as little surprise that it was that host, for it was a place of opportunity. The waterways on which it sat offered an unrivalled network of markets and facilitated the regular movement of people. Its primacy in the Greek enterprise for the region came courtesy of the Egyptians themselves. Sometime after 570 BCE, the pharaoh Amasis declared Naucratis as the only port where Greeks were allowed to trade in his lands. Any Greeks ships caught trading outside the town were forced to take an oath that they had done so by accident, after which they needed to transport their goods around the delta into Naucratis.[16] Presumably those which failed to do so were punished with fines or something similar.

Archaeological evidence of trade does survive. We have large Greek amphorae used to transport wine, and lots of it, as well as olive oil and maybe even foodstuffs such as figs. These finds corroborate the disparate written evidence: ancient tradition states that Charaxus was in Naucratis to sell wine.[17] We also know the Greeks traded gold and silver, as well as perishable items such as grain, and both timber and worked wood. In return, the Greeks bought raw materials such as natron, a salt mixture that was used for a plethora of different reasons including the curing of fish and the process of mumification. It was also the main ingredient in making faience and glass. The Greeks would buy grain during times of crisis or hardship; Egypt was, after all, one of the great bread baskets of the Mediterranean. They would also buy luxury items such as perfume, linen, local food products, papyrus and Egyptian-style amulets and scarabs.[18] The latter were so popular that Naucratis had its own scarab factory, which used moulds to mass-produce these beetle-shaped amulets for the Greek market. Many such scarabs have been found in Greek sanctuaries throughout the Hellenic world with rough hieroglyphs inscribed by either semi-illiterate Egyptian or simply non-specialist Greek hands. It seems that cheap counterfeits were all the rage in Naucratis for, within the sixth century BCE, we have evidence of Rhodian-style, small faience sculptures and vases that were mass-produced and of poorer quality being made for export from Egypt.[19] Seeing such industry in what was a trading settlement is quite unusual, but then, trade and opportunity so often create enterprise – although not, it seems in this instance, much in the way of fine art.

What is most interesting when considering trade in Egypt during these early years is not so much what the Greeks were trading in, but, rather, what they were not. We have very little evidence of iconic items of Greek culture, such as the painted crockery and vases for which Greece is so famous, being sold in Egypt. The items themselves are not what is important; rather, it is the lack of adoption of Greek culture which should interest us. We are often led by the histories to perceive Greek culture as somehow superior, and to think that the presence of this shining light of civilisation should have been enough to make any other society acknowledge this superiority and try to adopt some of its ways. But the people of Egypt did no such thing. Out here, at the edges of the Greek world, Egyptian culture reigned supreme.

It is notable how little evidence there is for Egyptian living quarters, or general signs of habitation at the site. They were most likely living there, but separately from the Greeks. Scholars disagree, however, about the Egyptian suburb on the site, whether it predates the Greeks' arrival or not. Either way, the Egyptians seem to rather successfully, and rather purposefully, separate the Greeks from themselves at Naucratis, stemming any real interchange of culture and social mores – a stark contrast with the cultural blending we have seen at similar sites such as Olbia and the Nubian–Egyptian frontier.

We have seen in earlier chapters how the Egyptians presented foreign groups, considering themselves to be surrounded by the 'wretched Kush' and the 'miserable Asiatics'. Like the Greeks, they projected an image of themselves as culturally superior to all others.[20] Perhaps this is why Amasis wanted to limit the interactions of Greek traders to a single town. Equally, perhaps this is why Naucratis was the only foreign trading centre that was allowed to have Greeks living there permanently, stemming a tide of Greek migration as best one could. We know that the few Greeks who had moved and lived further south, in Memphis, would intermarry with Egyptian women, adopting Egyptian names and even their burial customs, but there is no evidence that the Egyptians were doing the same in this period.[21] Herodotus may have been rather acute when he observed that 'the Egyptians shun using Greek customs'.[22] What he did not say, but is perhaps implied in his observation, is how bizarre an idea this was to the Greeks.

Much like the great Nile itself, cultural exchange flowed in only one direction – towards the Mediterranean. The permanent base at Naucratis gave the Greeks a prolonged exposure to Egyptian culture, not just in the town but within the wider Greek world. Many of the elements of Greek culture that we consider synonymously Greek do have some roots in Egyptian precedent. Early exposure to Egypt during this archaic period was also an exposure to a new form of monumental architecture – one that did not rely on small bricks, but, rather, on greatness and beauty cleaved from stone and painted in vibrant colours. The clearest example can be seen in the tall Egyptian columns, with 'elaborately carved capitals and bases'.[23]

Influence is a rather fickle historical concept to trace. That two things look a little alike does not prove that one influenced the other. In this instance, we have the appearance of Doric columns in seventh-century BCE Greece. These are perhaps the plainest of the classical Greek designs, with a fluted column, no carved base and a capital shaped like an inverted, shallow bowl. On top of this would be a frieze separated into panels by ornamental grooves called triglyphs. Most famously, these columns make up the awe-inspiring Parthenon atop the acropolis in Athens, with sixty-nine in total, each measuring over ten metres tall and nearly two metres in diameter.

The first appearance of Doric columns coincides with the prolonged exposure of Egyptian culture via places such as Naucratis. Equally, this chronologically chimes with the spread of Egyptomania throughout the Hellenic world. It has been argued that these columns share many similarities with the

Egyptians' own, and so an influence or source of inspiration makes sense. This also corresponds with a wider phenomenon observed by art historians known as 'the orientalising period', where the Greeks seem to draw much inspiration from cultures to the east.

There is no doubt that the Greeks took these ideas and influences and transformed them into something new and specifically Greek. Doric columns may look Egyptian in style, but the Parthenon in fifth-century BCE Athens looks decidedly Greek. Similarly, we can see a clear emulation of Egyptian sculpture in early Greek sculpture. The Egyptians had a long tradition of depicting large human bodies in hard stone, but the Greeks often made smaller figures in softer material. This changed during the archaic period, where we see life-sized or slightly larger statues called *kouroi*, which depict a young man or woman standing tall and proud. They emulate Egyptian statues in their square, head-on positioning, stiff arms to the sides, and clenched fists. But they also offer something a little different. Egyptian statues are always clothed, but the Greek preferred their young men to be completely naked; statues of young women, *kourai*, were, however, clothed. From these early statues would come the later, dynamic statues of warriors and athletes that we are used to seeing.

* * *

In his philosophical dialogue *Phaedrus*, the Athenian philosopher Plato has Socrates make up a myth to explain the invention of writing. The story goes that the ibis-headed god of Egypt, Theuth, invented letters as a means of improving communication and memory because, very simply, being able to write down a list enables a person to remember a longer list. Ecstatic with his new invention, Theuth went to tell the king of Egypt, the god Thamus – a made-up name, who Socrates says the Egyptians called Ammon.

The two gods have a heated debate about the value of writing and what it could mean for humanity. Theuth argues vehemently for its ingenuity, claiming the discovery as an 'elixir of memory and wisdom'. But Thamus urges justifiable caution against such boasts. He observes that it was for one person to invent something, but for another to judge its value and possible danger to others. His counter-argument for writing has a note of timeless concern for any new communication methods:

> For this invention will produce forgetfulness in the minds of those who learn to use it, because they will not practise their memory. Their trust in writing, produced by external characters which are no part of themselves, will discourage the use of their own memory within them. You have invented an elixir not of memory, but of reminding; and you offer your pupils the appearance of wisdom, not true wisdom, for they will read many things without instruction and will therefore seem to know many things, when they are for the most part ignorant and hard to get along with, since they are not wise, but only appear wise.[24]

More important for our interests is how Socrates begins the story: 'I heard, then, that at Naucratis, in Egypt, was one of the ancient gods of that country . . . the name of the god himself was Theuth.'[25]

This is clearly a story invented by Plato, or perhaps one he heard from Socrates himself. Its fictional basis is not really debatable; the same work makes this clear by having the eponymous Phaedrus accuse Socrates of always making up stories about Egypt (a claim that Socrates does not deny). But there are some echoes of truth in the story; like all good lies, it requires a veneer of plausibility. The Egyptian god of wisdom Thoth (Theuth) *was* associated with the invention of hieroglyphs by the Egyptians, for instance. Also, the name-dropping of Naucratis, giving a concrete location at the beginning that the Greek audience would know and associate with, adds a level of credibility. Yet it seems a strange choice: a trading town in the delta, as famous for its sex workers as it was for its produce. Why would he choose to name Naucratis as the town that Theuth came from?

According to a lost work of Hermodorus, one of Plato's own students, the philosopher actually travelled to Egypt at the age of twenty-eight.[26] This most likely followed the death of Socrates, a traumatically formative moment that was witnessed by both Hermodorus and Plato. We receive a little more information from Plutarch's biography of Solon, which tells us that Plato not only went to Egypt but that he sold oil there to fund his trip.[27] It is not much to go on, but some reasonable deductions can still be made. The chances of his trip beginning at Naucratis would have been high in any case, as a Greek outpost of a region under Persian control was always a safer option for any Greek traveller. Equally, for Plato the town was only ten miles from the Egyptian town of Sais, where he was said to have spoken with the priests. This makes Naucratis a likely destination, but still a little speculative based on the words of Hermodorus; however, if we are to believe Plutarch's story about Plato selling oil, we can more firmly place his position at Naucratis, as it was the only port where Greeks were allowed to trade.

Plato was not the first, nor indeed the most illustrious, Greek intellectual to visit Naucratis. Solon travelled there to see the country and for trade – trading in what we are not told, but trade means that Naucratis would have been his port of call.[28] It seems that Naucratis became a place that noted intellectuals were supposed to have visited, even if they hadn't actually done so. Our later sources write of sixth- and fifth-century BCE philosophers such as Democritus and Pythagoras visiting and learning mathematics and astrology. At its most bizarre, there is one tradition which suggests that the Athenian comedy playwright Aristophanes was actually born in Naucratis.[29] This is clearly not true, but it is indicative of the intellectual allure that Naucratis held; situated in the lands of ancient wisdom, it became an explanation for individual genius – they must have learned it in Naucratis.

Perhaps the most fascinating possibility is the visit to Naucratis of the father of history himself, Herodotus. It has long been debated how much Herodotus travelled around the Mediterranean and beyond while writing his *Histories*. His eyewitness accounts of sites and inscriptions lend credence to the idea that he travelled extensively, but equally he makes basic factual errors that we would not expect from someone who had actually been to these places. When it comes to Egypt, a country which makes up a large proportion of book two in his work, Herodotus is very clear about visiting the region:

> I learnt by the farthest inquiry that I could make, by my own travel and sight as far as the city of Elephantine, and beyond that by question and hearsay.[30]

Elephantine was to the far south, in Upper Egypt, so his claim suggests he travelled extensively down the Nile.

We must, as always, be a little sceptical about his descriptions of what he saw in Egypt. His assessment of Egyptian cultural norms is overly simplistic, if not always incorrect, but includes such important observations as 'Women urinate standing up, men sitting down'.[31] Equally, the less said of his description of the hippopotamus the better:

> They present the following appearance: four-footed, with cloven hooves like cattle; blunt-nosed; with a horse's mane,

> visible tusks, a horse's tail and voice; big as the biggest bull. Their hide is so thick that, when it is dried, spearshafts are made of it.[32]

Presuming that Herodotus is telling the truth about travelling to Egypt, it is worth noting that he never definitively claims that he went to Naucratis. This can only be inferred from the general situation for Greeks trying to visit Egypt, of course; but there is also a tantalising possibility that he left something behind. For, in 1903, the excavator of Naucratis, David Hogarth, presented two potsherds to the Ashmolean Museum in Oxford, each bearing the name of Herodotus.[33] One dates from the fourth century BCE, too late for our Herodotus to be the owner. But the other is dated, based on artistic clues, to the turn of the fifth century BCE, offering a provocative yet unverifiable possibility that this fragment of pottery was once held by the hands of Herodotus of Halicarnassus himself.[34]

Whether or not Herodotus actually left that cup behind, it would have been essential for him to visit Naucratis, for it had already established itself as a hotbed of intellectual writers, a tradition it maintained throughout the ancient period. Not only did it receive some of the biggest literary names as visitors and guests, but it gained a reputation for producing its own writers and thinkers alike. Their names are not well known today because very few of their works have survived the intervening years, but they come down to us as references made by other authors. Writers such as Staphylus, Phylarchus and Lyceas were renowned historians of local, regional and universal history. There was also Julius Pollux, an authoritative antiquarian and grammarian of the second century CE who, it is said, was handpicked by the Roman emperor Commodus to teach rhetoric at the Academy in Athens.[35]

Naucratis was also the home of a prolific author by the name of Athenaeus, a writer and grammarian who lived during the reigns of Marcus Aurelius and his son Commodus in the second and third centuries CE. Unlike his fellow Naucratites, some of Athenaeus' work does survive and provides historians with a crucial catalogue of quotations from dozens of lost works. It may not seem much by which to be remembered, but Athenaeus is singlehandedly responsible for some 10,000 lines of quoted verse, cites around 1,250 different authors and gives the titles of more than 1,000 plays.[36] He was a fastidious researcher, a thorough notetaker and an obsessive collector of information from all branches of knowledge; whether it was his intention or not, his work is vital to the study of ancient Mediterranean history.

His magnum opus is the *Deipnosophistae*, or *The Philosophers at Dinner*, a written discourse of intellectuals held at a fictional feast in Rome. Its subject matter is wide-ranging, but loosely tied together by the dining experience. It covers topics one might expect to have heard at such an occasion, what the Greeks called a *symposium*: food, drink, sex, history, poetry, linguistics, and so on. It must be said that the work is not a riveting read in and of itself, but its importance when trying to understand the ancient Greek and Roman worlds cannot be overstated.

Athenaeus was a proud Naucratite and he offers us insights into his hometown. He makes mention of the beautiful *hetaira* discussed earlier in this chapter, including the famous Rhodopis – although he does chastise Herodotus for getting her name wrong, suggesting that nearly a millennium later she held a somewhat legendary position in Naucratis.[37] We also see the town mentioned during a random discussion on the names of little fish, and a small tangent on the discussion of *kylixes*, a type of cup. He mentions that Naucratis makes exquisite versions of these cups, not on the lathe but by hand, which are dyed to look silver and therefore more expensive. The potters' workshops were all situated at one end of the town, next to the gate named the Ceramic Gate, for obvious reasons.[38]

So, it seems Naucratis was a logical place to set Plato's story. While the town was obviously not the place where writing was invented, it was a town synonymous with knowledge, a place of intellectual pilgrimage and discovery. A place where Egyptian wisdom and knowledge could be absorbed and adapted by classical Greek intellectuals. As time passed, Naucratis became a place where writers and scholars were born, producing yet another valuable trade item for Naucratis – knowledge.

* * *

In the late fourth century BCE, Egypt underwent a seismic shift of political leadership. Since 525 BCE, the Persians had ruled over Egypt, but it was a period of unrest and regular uprisings in the region. Regardless of the localised concerns, the Persian court had been able to maintain control by drawing upon the vast resources of their empire and quashing rebellions as they arose, at least in the earlier years of their rule. For the Greeks at Naucratis, this must have been a very unsettling time. Our sources suggest that often these Egyptian rebellions used Greek forces to assist them, but at other times Greeks would appear in the armies of the Persian king. With such fluctuating allegiances, one wonders how that would have affected the resident Greeks in the delta who wanted little more than to get on with their trades and lives. Unfortunately we have no evidence to answer this question.

In the fourth century BCE, Persian rulers regularly lost control of Egypt and mounted new invasions to restore their position. Following the crowning of Darius III in 336 BCE, Persia needed once again to reclaim its control over Egypt, something it achieved in a little under two years. But Darius had problems of his own in need of addressing, namely the imminent invasion of his empire by Alexander III of Macedon. Alexander's father, Philip II, had been murdered before he could put his own invasion plans into action, but Alexander was more than capable of taking on the mantle.

By 334 BCE, the same year in which Persia re-established control of Egypt, the Macedonians defeated a Persian army in battle at the River Granicus in Anatolia. Darius frantically called upon his satraps to provide more troops, amassing his army at Babylon before marching out to face Alexander at Issus in 333 BCE. The Egyptian satrap Sabaces took most of the military forces in Egypt with him to Babylon and on to fight at Issus, where he was killed in the thick of the melee.[39] Following his victory at Issus, Alexander had a choice to make: he could either chase the fleeing Darius and cement his victory by destroying his rival's remaining forces, or he could secure his position in the western part of the Persian Empire first. He chose the latter and, instead of heading east towards Babylon, he headed south towards Egypt.

Poorly garrisoned, poorly led and poorly motivated, Persian resistance in Egypt was minimal. The gamble Alexander was taking was not whether he could conquer Egypt, but whether the Egyptian people would welcome him as a liberator from Persian oppression. Fortunately for him, he made the right decision:

> The Egyptians, hostile of old to the power of the Persians … had taken courage at the prospect of Alexander's coming … Therefore a vast multitude of them had assembled at Pelusium, where they thought that Alexander would enter the country.[40]

Unopposed, Alexander was able to swiftly cement his position as ruler of Egypt, with the help of the priests at the Oracle of Zeus-Ammon at Siwa, who proclaimed him the son of Zeus himself. Before he left the region in 331 BCE, never to return, Alexander set about creating a new Hellenistic city, one that would replace Naucratis as the beating heart of Greco-Egyptian culture and enterprise. The site for Alexandria was chosen on the Mediterranean coast of the Nile Delta, making it the primary port for all trade in and out of Egypt. Interestingly, the person he left behind to oversee the project was not a trusted Macedonian, as one might have expected, but a local man from Naucratis by the name of Cleomenes.

Cleomenes is not a man whom history remembers fondly. The building of Alexandria not only usurped the primacy of Naucratis, but also that of the smaller harbour towns on the coast. Cleomenes planned for this by telling the inhabitants of Canopus, the largest harbour in the region, that they needed to move into Alexandria. The people refused and offered Cleomenes a large bribe to stop this from happening. They were successful in the short term, but once building in Alexandria was progressing, he returned to Canopus and demanded yet more money – more than the residents had available. Unable to pay him the extra funds, they were forced to move to Alexandria.[41]

Cleomenes' position in Naucratis did little, it seems, to enlighten him about the people of Egypt. When Alexander left, he not only left Cleomenes in charge of his pet project, but also named him governor of the east of Egypt. In addition to his position at Alexandria, this gave him a lot of authoritative power: power he used to line his pockets, or perhaps a more generous assessment would say to fill the wealth reserves of Egypt. During a famine, he banned the export of grain from Egypt. When people complained that such a ban would prevent them from paying their taxes, he allowed a small amount to be exported but raised the duty on grain exponentially. One Greek orator claims he went one step further and actually bought up excess grain and sold it at an inflated price.[42]

It was not just the laypeople he was exploiting and extorting, but also the Egyptian priests. One scam involved notifying all the temples in Egypt that the distribution of funding was uneven, so it was necessary to shut down some of them and get rid of their priests as well. Whether he intended to follow through on the threat is unknown, but the priests believed him wholeheartedly and sent him money not only from the temples' reserves, but also from their own personal wealth.[43] Perhaps his most egregious act as governor was when he threatened to commit sacrilege. While travelling through a region where the cult of the crocodile was particularly strong (presumably Faiyum, see Chapter 9), a servant of Cleomenes was taken and killed by one of the reptiles. In a rage, Cleomenes summoned the local priests and informed them he would take revenge on all the crocodiles in the region by arranging a mass cull. The priests frantically collected all the gold they could lay their hands on in an effort to stop him. They succeeded, but one can't help wondering if that was Cleomenes' intention all along.[44]

Cleomenes did not survive long after the death of Alexander in 323 BCE. The Macedonian Empire was divided up between Alexander's generals, with Egypt going to Ptolemy. Cleomenes was accused of being in cahoots with Perdiccas, another of Alexander's generals and a great rival to Ptolemy. Within his first year in charge of Egypt, Ptolemy had Cleomenes killed. No doubt this was equally motivated by the fact that Cleomenes had accrued personal wealth of over 8,000 talents, a damning legacy of his extortion of the Egyptian people. This was money that, on Cleomenes' death, could be assumed by Ptolemy himself.

Cleomenes' greatest impact on the story of Naucratis was his construction of Alexandria. No longer the primary Greek city in Egypt, Naucratis becomes less prominent in the written evidence. But we do know that during the reign of the Ptolemies, Naucratis remained one of the three major Greek centres in

Egypt. The town reached its zenith at this time in terms of population and prosperity, as shown by the final investments in the religious precinct, the Great Temenos. However, following the victory of the Roman politician Octavian over his rival Mark Antony in 30 BCE and the subsequent death of Cleopatra VII, the last Ptolemaic ruler of Egypt, Naucratis underwent a period of decline under Roman rule. This is especially apparent during the second and third centuries CE, when Egypt was hit particularly hard by the Antonine Plague, with researchers estimating that while the Roman Empire saw a population reduction of around 10 per cent, Egypt's was nearer 20 per cent and some towns' population loss closer to 33 per cent.[45] Combine this with regular unrest in Rome, which resulted in poor leadership, inconsistent policies and economic decline leading to a gross inflation, and then, to top it off, regular crop failure, it is perhaps unsurprising that there is a decline in archaeological material during the third century CE in particular.[46]

The town may have seen a slight resurgence with the introduction of Christianity into the region. The earliest attestation comes from the martyrdom of Epimachus of Pelusium, whose death in 303 CE occurred during the Great Persecutions of Diocletian. A fragmentary papyrus dating from the fifth or sixth century CE describes him as a twenty-seven-year-old man, a weaver by trade, who confessed to being a Christian at the court of the governor Polemius, at a dry riverbed near Naucratis. Christian iconography becomes prevalent in the town between the fifth and seventh centuries, including crucifixes, chi-rho symbols and even prayers written on pots, lamps and other items.[47] Furthermore, we know that a Bishop Harpocration of Naucratis is traditionally said to have been present at the First Council of Nicaea during the reign of Constantine.[48] More concrete evidence shows the Christian community was served by a bishop named Isaiah, in the fifth century, and there is also a passing reference to a monk name Taurus living near the town during the sixth century.[49] All this creates an impression of a thriving Christian community in Naucratis. This corroborates the archaeological evidence, which shows that the town was economically active up until the Muslim conquest of Egypt in the seventh century.

Our understanding of the town's history during the Roman period in particular is rather scant. A combination of factors have come together to underplay this vibrant story. The earliest excavations were primarily interested in classical Greek remains and big-ticket items like the Great Temenos. Very little attention was given to Roman and Byzantine artefacts. Equally, our written sources lose interest in Naucratis, especially after the construction of Alexandria. This blind spot continued into the Christian age and through to the modern, but there is hope that the site of Naucratis has yet more secrets it can reveal to us – secrets that will shed light on this most unique of Greek outposts, where the Greeks were welcomed but their influence stifled, and where knowledge was transferred between cultures, with the Greeks willing to learn. Out on the periphery, Naucratis was initially a place of experimentation without prejudice, but once the Macedonians brought Egypt more directly into the Greek sphere of influence, we see it shift to a more conservative place, a town dedicated to the conservation of knowledge rather than driving innovation. As it was brought back from the edges of the map it lost a small part of what made it special.

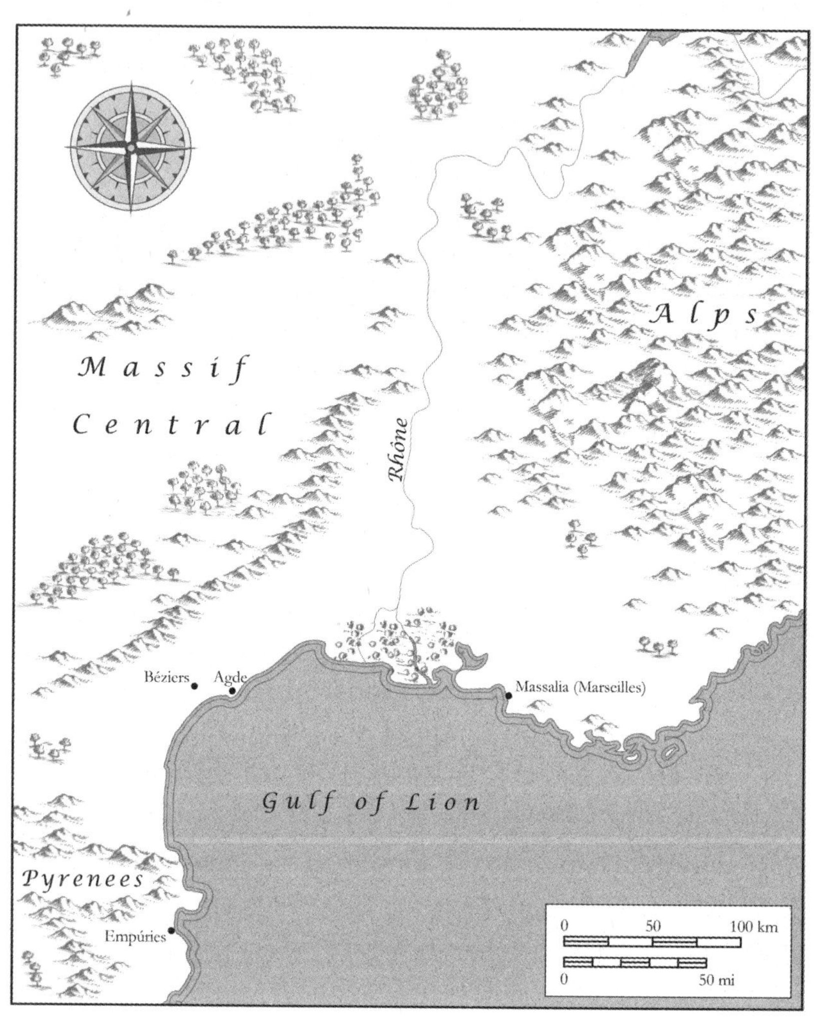

Massif Central
Alps
Rhône
Béziers
Agde
Massalia (Marseilles)
Gulf of Lion
Pyrenees
Empúries
0
50
100 km
0
50 mi

# 6

# Massalia, France

'[A town] placed in the extremity of the world and surrounded by tribes of Gauls, and washed with the waves of barbarism.'[1]

These words, written by the Roman politician Cicero in the first century BCE, describe the enduring perception of life at the edge of the Greek or, from his own perspective, the Roman world. The place he is describing is the Greek town of Massalia in southern Gaul, better known today by its modern name, Marseille. Set on the Mediterranean coast, but with easy access to the mouth of the River Rhône, Massalia was only sixteen days' travel from Athens by sea, and yet it might as well have been on the other side of the world.

Considering the continual importance of the town, from its founding right through to the modern-day city, it is amazing just how little we really know about its earliest years. It was founded at the end of the seventh century BCE as an *apoikia*, a term which is usually translated as 'colony' but quite literally means 'away from home'. The metropolis, the home from which the people of Massalia were away, was the Greek city of Phocaea in western Anatolia (modern Turkey) but Massalia was only one of dozens of colonies that Phocaeans established. Scholars have long debated why Phocaea, and many Greek city-states like it, began to establish colonies around the

Mediterranean, but, ultimately, we are not sure. Our sources do not tell us why Massalia was founded; it did not start life as simply a market town like Olbia and Naucratis, and it already existed when Phocaea was evacuated in 545 BCE as a result of Persian aggression.

The sources that describe its founding are often conflicting and create narratives worthy of the epics of Homer.[2] Perhaps our most complete version comes from the Gallo-Roman author Pompeius Trogus (first century BCE), whose account survives in an abridged form in the work of the later writer Justin (second century CE). He says that the Phocaeans arrived in the area and sought the friendship of the local Gallic tribe, the Segobrigii, in order to ask their ruler, Nannus, for permission to establish a town in his territory. On their arrival, Nannus was preparing a large feast for his daughter's coming of age where, according to their customs, her husband would be chosen at the banquet. The Greeks were invited to attend, and, with somewhat of an impending sense of narratological inevitability, the Greeks' leader Protis was chosen when the chief's daughter ignored all the other men and offered him a cup of water. In that instant, Protis was transformed from visitor into family member and was gifted the land on which to build Massalia.[3]

The story seems rather fanciful, but it is supported by an earlier account from Aristotle who tells a very similar version of events, but in less detail.[4] It is also important to note that Pompeius Trogus himself belonged to the Gallic people known as the Vocontii. His grandfather served under Pompey the Great and earned the family their Roman citizenship. His father later served as Julius Caesar's interpreter, meaning that Pompeius Trogus was raised as a member of the Roman elite, but he maintained the cultural roots of a Gaul. He lived in the town of Vasio in south-eastern France (modern day

Vaison-la-Romaine), so he would have known Massalia well, and his story may reflect the Massaliotes' own founding myth.

These early years of interaction brought the so-called Celtic world (*Keltika*) into the minds of the Greeks. 'Celt' is a rather vague designation for a variety of Iron Age societies in central and western Europe, who seem to have shared languages and important cultural links.[5] Our ancient authors are not very consistent in their use of ethnic terms, so sometimes we have cultures named as tribes such as the Vocontii, then more generically as Gauls, based on their geographical location, or indeed simply as Celts. Scholars have long debated the suitability of each term and the inherent issues surrounding them, but for our purposes it is best to recognise that this confusion is nothing unique: a man from Manchester, in the United Kingdom, can be equally described as a Mancunian, a Northerner, an Englishman and a Brit. These may have slightly different meanings in the grand scheme of things, but each is not without some validity.

As we may expect, the drip-feed of knowledge back to Greece about these hitherto unknown people began rather slowly. There is a vague allusion to them in the work of Hecataeus, a historian and geographer writing at the turn of the fifth century BCE; while Herodotus' *Histories* only mentions the Celts twice, but he offers no explanation about who they were or what their culture was like. By the fourth century BCE, however, Celtic warriors were becoming better known, appearing as mercenaries in an army sent from Syracuse, Sicily, to aid their Spartan allies.[6] It was also at this time, in 390 BCE, that the Gallic leader Brennus took an army across the Alps and finally sacked the city of Rome in 387 BCE, a pivotal event in the destiny of Rome, but not one that makes a great mark on the contemporary Greek evidence. One of the few such sources to mention the sacking is Plutarch's *Life of Camillus* which, rather notably, gets the identity of the sackers very wrong:

> For Heracleides Ponticus, who lived not long after that time, in his treatise *On the Soul*, says that out of the West a story prevailed, how an army of Hyperboreans had come from afar and captured a Greek city called Rome, situated somewhere on the shores of the Great Sea.[7]

The Hyperboreans, it may be remembered from Chapter 4, were a mythical people living at the far edges of the world who neither aged nor suffered any illness. Plutarch, it must be said, was not impressed with Heracleides Ponticus' error here.

By the mid- to late fourth century BCE, the Celts were firmly planted into Greek discourse. Aristotle correctly named the Celts as being responsible for the sacking of Rome, but got the name of the Roman dictator wrong, to the frustration of Plutarch once again.[8] However, his interest in the Celts, and that of his teacher Plato, was more to do with the natural temperament of the Celtic people and their supposed lack of moderation. The Celts are portrayed as heavy drinkers, lovers of war and combat, and recklessly courageous.[9] The accuracy of these generalisations can obviously be called into doubt, not least because these are common tropes assigned to many 'barbarian' societies by Greek writers, as we saw with the Scythians at Olbia. However, it may also reflect the regular conflict between Greeks and Celts, so these temperaments are not those of all Celts, but, rather, the warriors on campaign.

* * *

Surrounded by Cicero's 'waves of barbarism', Massalia becomes something of a beacon of light in the Greek and Roman world. The town grew from strength to strength. Originally situated over two hills, it had spread to a nearby third by the end of the sixth century BCE. It also cornered a trade market in the Western Mediterranean, establishing settlements and trading posts of its own along the southern coast of Gaul and down the Mediterranean coast of Iberia to the Pillars of Hercules in the south. These markets would then funnel their materials through Massalia and back to the larger markets further east; for example, the silver found in Iberia was said to have brought Massalia 'considerable revenue'.[10]

Our sources' admiration for Massalia did not rely simply on its financial successes. Its political system and continuity were marvelled at by many writers. While today we look back at the radical democracy of Athens as a model worthy of admiration, many of our sources – often written by wealthy elites – did not like the power democracy offered the poor at their expense. However, they were equally wary of monarchy and poorly run tyranny as well, which would equally limit the power and influence of the rich. Within this context, Massalia offered something a little different.

The constitution of Massalia was the subject of a work by Aristotle that has since been lost, but puts the city in illustrious company alongside Athens, Sparta and Carthage, whose constitutions were likewise studied and written about by the philosopher. Early details are elusive, but Aristotle does suggest that power in Massalia was originally held by a very small minority. Through some sort of public pressure, most likely from wealthy citizens who felt excluded from power, the city established the aristocratic oligarchy for which it was famous. This consisted of a council of 600 men, the *timouchoi*, or 'the honourable ones'. To qualify for the council you needed to be a free male, a father and able to prove that you came from a line of citizens going back three generations. Once in the council it was a position for life, so it is fair to assume that these were highly coveted roles. The council was led by fifteen of their number, chosen to manage the daily running of the city. Above these in the political hierarchy were three men chosen from the fifteen who held executive power, and from these three a single man was chosen to guide them.[11]

Alongside the town's reputation for good rule, Massaliotes were considered to embody this principle in the way they conducted themselves individually. The city had a reputation for temperance and self-restraint. They restricted the size and grandeur of private funerals, banned mimes from performing due to their common presentation of infidelity, and did not allow anyone to enter the city carrying a weapon. The women were said to be particularly restricted, being made to dress conservatively and allegedly banned from drinking alcohol.[12] We are even told, with an air of admiration from one source, that the *timouchoi* kept a supply of poison that citizens could request for the purpose of taking their own life. This state-controlled euthanasia required the person to put forward their claim and the council tried to ensure, on the one hand, that a person was not being unfair on themselves in ending their own life prematurely, but on the other hand that they were helping someone to die as quickly and as easily as possible if this was the best course of action.[13] The process is portrayed as very even-handed, very logical and even caring in its execution.

As a result of its glowing reputation, by the Roman period Massalia had become a place to send young, elite men for their education – it was more popular as a location of learning even than Athens.[14] The Roman historian Tacitus tells us that his father-in-law Gnaeus Julius Agricola, the man who would later make his name as the governor of Britain, was sent by his mother to Massalia, a place where 'refinement and provincial frugality were mixed and well combined'.[15] Agricola himself used to admit that he was an excitable youth with a passionate spirit, one who would have followed his interests in philosophy rather than politics if it had not been for his mother's decision. He would say that in his youth he was made to learn the most difficult of lessons – moderation. To the Romans, there was no better place to learn this than Massalia.[16]

We do not want to get the wrong idea about Massalia; it was not an inward-looking, navel-gazing society that stuck to its traditions and looked no further than its own city walls. Far from it. Massalia was not only at the forefront of the Greek cultural world, but it was also in some way responsible for its expansion. The city lays claim to two great explorers of the ancient world, Euthymenes in the sixth century BCE, and more famously Pytheas in the fourth. Quite rightly, these two men are featured prominently in the modern city as well, with their statues adorning the Palais de la Bourse in Marseille.

Euthymenes has no surviving works, and he is only briefly mentioned in a few later texts – and not often in a positive light. What we do know is that he sailed out of the Mediterranean and around part of the West African coast. He even claimed to have discovered the origin of the Nile, a hotly debated topic during the sixth and fifth centuries BCE:

> Euthymenes of Massalia tells an eyewitness account: 'I have ... been on a voyage in the Atlantic. The Nile flows from there, and in greater volume as long as the Etesian winds are blowing in season ... Moreover, the taste of the sea is fresh and its creatures are like the ones in the Nile.'[17]

Euthymenes made quite a considerable leap in logic here. On discovering a large river filled with crocodiles and other animals similar to those found in the Nile, and knowing as he did that the Nile emptied through the delta in Egypt, he concluded that this must be the place where Oceanus – the ocean which the Greeks once believed encircled the landmass on the map – fed into the Nile. What Euthymenes had not considered was that he had simply found another large river that was home to crocodiles and the like. The exact location of this river is impossible to ascertain from the available evidence, but scholars have suggested he may have found the Senegal River, or maybe even the Gambia.[18]

It is a shame that his work was ridiculed by later writers – Herodotus does not name Euthymenes, but he most vehemently attacks the idea that the Nile was fed by Oceanus and it is not a theory that is given much credence in the subsequent discourse. Yet perhaps he has been unfairly treated. His expedition and the information he gathered must have made its way to other navigators and explorers in the Mediterranean. In the fifth century BCE a Carthaginian by the name of Hanno undertook a similar voyage, possibly going as far south as modern Cameroon. Along the way, Hanno described meeting indigenous peoples, wild animals, and one particular oddity for which he is most well known:

> [T]here was another island, full of savage men. But there were a lot more women, with their bodies covered in hair: our interpreters called these people *Gorillai*. When we pursued them in the chase, we were unable to capture any of the men; for they all fled to the high ground and kept us at bay by throwing stones. However, we took three of the women, who bit and clawed at their captors and did not want to follow. So we killed and flayed them, and brought their skins back to Carthage.[19]

This story of a wild tribe of hairy people, with strong, powerful men who were outnumbered by women, living in West Africa stuck in the European imagination. In 1847 CE, when Thomas S. Savage sent a partial skeleton of a large, powerful, hairy ape from West Africa to Jeffries Wyman at Harvard, the story of Hanno immediately came to mind as he wrote up the first scientific assessment of a new great ape. We do not know whether Hanno was actually describing a troop of gorillas, but one thing is certain – it is because of his account that gorillas have acquired their name.

While the travels of Euthymenes leave no equitable mark in the historical record, the same cannot be said of his heir apparent, the Massaliote navigator Pytheas. Pytheas set out on his greatest voyage towards the end of the fourth century BCE. Having entered the Atlantic, he did not head south but instead explored northern Europe. He was the first Greek ever to reach Britain, and what's more he circumnavigated it. His exploration was so important to the Greek and Roman world that his account, the thus far undiscovered *Periplus*, is the origin of many place names still in use today – most notably he called the island *Bretannika* (Britain) and its most northern point was called *Orcas* (the Orkneys), both names most likely coming from indigenous languages he encountered on the way.[20]

If his account had ended with this simple yet impressive encircling of Britain then Pytheas could well have expected the respect and adulation of future generations. However, what he achieved was considered by many to be exponentially more improbable, so much so that Strabo describes him as a habitual liar.[21] Strabo's cynicism is understandable, if misguided. Pytheas described a land six days' sailing north of Britain called Thule – considered by many subsequent geographers to be the most northerly inhabited land on the map – where the summer nights lasted for only a couple of hours, and which was near to the frozen sea. It is likely that Pytheas was the first Greek to reach the Arctic Circle, with its short summer nights and proximity to ice floes. Scholars cannot unanimously agree about the location of Thule, but from the evidence we have the best candidates are either Iceland or more likely western Norway. His journey was not complete before he ventured further east into the Baltic Sea and then sailed back around the western coast of Europe and into the Mediterranean.

Pytheas' tales of frozen waters and unending days, plus some rather inconsistent estimations of distance in his account, were enough to split the intellectual communities of both Greece and later Rome. Strabo did not believe him, nor did the historian Polybius, and Pliny was sceptical. But Eratosthenes, the Greek mathematician remembered in history for calculating the circumference of the world to a fair degree of accuracy, accepted Pytheas' account entirely, as did the Roman historian Tacitus and the geographer Ptolemy. Pytheas' voyage was on an unprecedented scale compared to that of any Greek mariner who went before him. It also had direct benefits for his hometown; his knowledge of Britain no doubt enabled Massalia to establish their lucrative trade in British tin.[22] He had truly pushed back the boundaries of the known world and in effect expanded the edges of the map. Naysayers be damned.

* * *

The story of Massalia is inextricably linked to the Gallic tribes that surrounded them, and the wider Celtic world. From the very beginning, as laid out in the foundation story, Massaliotes and Gauls were interacting almost as equals: the tribes were given names, as were their rulers. Gauls were not dismissed as simply barbaric inhabitants in need of removal. Instead there is a suggestion of an almost symbiotic relationship between Greek and Gaul similar to the one we saw in Olbia, one that grew into prolonged trade and cultural exchange.

Our lack of extensive physical evidence makes this topic hard to explore – hard, but not impossible. Our written sources emphasise the impact of Greek culture on the Gauls, something that neatly contrasts with the resistance to Greek culture in Egypt. Strabo described Massalia as a 'school for the barbarians', instilling in them a love of Greek literature.[23] This is confirmed by Julius Caesar's account of his wars with the Helvetii, on the Swiss side of the Alps, where he describes them using the Greek alphabet in their record keeping.[24] Pompeius Trogus goes a step further and identifies key elements of Greek culture brought by the Massaliotes:

> They learned to prune the vine and plant the olive; and such a radiance was shed over both men and things, that it was not Greece which seemed to have immigrated into Gaul, but Gaul that seemed to have been transplanted into Greece.[25]

In the modern day it is hard to imagine the lands of France without wine, but their reputation for viniculture owes everything to this introduction of the grape vine by the Massaliotes. Wine itself had already been introduced into the region by the Etruscans in central Italy, by way of trade. When the Greeks arrived, they simply grew the demand, in part due to their own large consumption of the drink (ancient wine was actually quite a bit weaker than modern versions and was regularly drunk by ancient Greeks).

The Massaliotes were not content simply to buy in wine. They soon began to grow their own vines, but to do this they first needed to import them. How this was achieved can be deduced from the remains of a remarkable discovery off the coast of Mallorca. A Carthaginian shipwreck was found containing numerous amphorae, drinking cups and also cauldrons, which we know were used for making alcoholic drinks. More importantly, also found were grapevines which had been embedded in soil, primed for transplantation. Of equal importance is the fact that grape seeds have also been discovered in large quantities within Massalia itself, suggesting local cultivation using plants that had been originally transplanted from elsewhere.[26]

Wine became very popular within elite Gallic culture so the Massaliotes, much like the Etruscans before them, found a strong market for not only the drink but also all of the accoutrements associated with it. These included ornately designed cups, vases and mixing bowls, many of which survive in burial contexts. The most striking example was found in Vix, in northern Burgundy, where a large bronze krater (a bowl for mixing wine with water) was discovered in a rather grand burial mound. The so-called 'Vix Krater' is the largest metal vessel discovered from the Greek archaic period. It is decorated with intricately cast images of Greek warriors, chariots and gorgons; as a piece of Greek metalwork it is unparalleled in its size and artistry. The vase weighs over 200 kilograms, and the suggestion is that the krater was dismantled for transportation, coming from either the Greek mainland or from one of the Greek cities in southern Italy.[27]

The Gallic elite used Greek culture and Greek imports as high-status items to assert their own authority and power. This was not just about buying expensive drinks, but also emulating things associated with the Greeks. We have examples of Celtic attempts to recreate Greek vases, for instance. Most notably, we have early Gallic coins which clearly attempt to copy Greek originals, even to the point of using the Greek alphabet, and copying the image of identifiable Greek kings such as Philip II of Macedon, or gods such as Apollo.[28] This fashion spread quickly; we have coins from the second-century BCE Britain which are clear copies of Macedonian coins, nearly 150 years before Britain was successfully invaded by the Romans. The Celtic world was originally a moneyless trade network, so the decision by a ruler to try and mint their own coinage was not only an attempt to control wealth, but to align the ruler's projection of authority and power with that of the Greeks and later the Romans. This suggests that the Gauls were influenced by the people at Massalia, but they were not specifically emulating

Greek culture. This was not a Hellenisation of local people, but, rather, an adoption of Greek items – a cultural appropriation, of sorts – to cement the status quo within their own society.

In contrast to this Gallic cultural flexibility, Massalia is presented as abnormally conservative for a city so far from the mainland of Greece, especially when it comes to their own Greek culture and identity. They seem to have clung tightly to an old identity through fear of somehow losing or diluting it by allowing Gallic and wider Celtic culture inside. This seems at odds with most other Greek colonies, especially in the Western Mediterranean.

We know that the relationship between Gauls and Massaliotes went deeper than simply trade. The foundation story specifically describes intermarriage with local families, a common occurrence in the Greek colonies as a way of cementing their place in foreign lands. We also know that Massalia would hire Gallic mercenaries, to the point where in the first century BCE we are told that they had a permanent auxiliary force of neighbouring tribesmen prepared to be fully incorporated into their forces at a moment's notice.[29] In fact, if we can remove ourselves from the conventional descriptions of our elite writers, whose interest was ultimately in describing the elites of Massalia, we can see a rather different side to the city.

On a deeper cultural level, the city was at one point notably trilingual – speaking or at least writing in Greek, Latin and a Gallic language.[30] We have no direct archaeological evidence to support this as yet, only literary. We do know that local languages appear in inscriptions in the surrounding area, but they are written in the Greek alphabet.[31] We also have evidence of a Massaliote living in Ptolemaic Egypt during the second century BCE. His name was Cintos, a decidedly Celtic rather than Greek name.[32] There is a suggestion that this trilingualism influenced the pronunciation of even the most educated of men.

In a scathing poem attacking the Massaliote orator T. Annius Cimber, Virgil mocked his Gallic pronunciation of the letter *tau*, perhaps indicating an accent influenced by locals in the region.[33]

The use of multiple languages indicates an inclusive society, one where it was necessary to go beyond a simple lingua franca (Greek being the obvious choice) and learn to communicate with one another on an almost equal footing. I say almost because there was still a power dynamic in Massalia, where the Greek and later Roman citizen was dominant. Gauls would come to Massalia for trade, business, or simply as part of a broader process of immigration. One area where close interactions would take place on a daily basis would have been employment, with local people offering a good supply of manual labour. The opportunity or resources available to the Gallic people must have been enticing, if the story told by Poseidonius is anything to go by:

> Poseidonius tells us that in Liguria, his host Charmoleon, a man who came from Massalia, related to him, that having hired some men and women to dig his land, one of the women was seized with the pains of labour, and going a little distance away from where they were working, she gave birth and then returned immediately to her work, for fear she might lose her pay. He saw that she was evidently working in considerable pain, but was not aware of the cause till towards evening, when he became aware of it and sent her away with her wages. She then carried her infant to a small spring and, having washed it, wrapped it up in as good swaddling clothes as she could get, and made the best of her way home.[34]

These cultural interactions and influences stretched further afield than southern Gaul, aided in no small part by the settlements Massalia established in Iberia. Athenaeus describes the Iberian locals wearing richly ornate tunics, yet he notes them to be courageous warriors, which contrasted directly with their luxurious clothing. Immediately following this description, he mentions the Massaliotes wearing the exact same kind of dress as the Iberians, but says they lacked the overt masculinity of their Celtic counterparts. He describes the men of Massalia as shameless and effeminate, and informs us of a Greek expression 'May you sail to Massalia' in reference to this supposedly soft lifestyle.[35] What Athenaeus is ultimately judging here is Greek men acting like barbarians, something that our other sources suggest would not be possible in the Massalia they describe. The fact that this becomes proverbial suggests that Athenaeus is not making this up, nor was he the first to say it.

So, we are torn between our sources. Massalia is presented as a conservatively Greek city by some but not by others. This dichotomy can even be apparent in a single source. The Roman writer and historian Livy mentions the nature of the Massaliote relationship with the Gauls on two separate occasions, once during a speech by a Roman consul preparing his army for battle against the Galatian Gauls in 189 BCE, and once during the speech of a Rhodian embassy to Rome. The consul claims that the Massaliotes had 'assimilated something of the spirit of their neighbours', whereas the Rhodian describes the complete opposite, saying that they remained culturally intact and 'free from contamination by their neighbours'.[36] Logically, we should conclude that the city exhibited both tendencies, that they were in some ways similar to what we saw in Olbia: both fiercely protective of their Greek identity and willing to integrate foreign people into the mix. But this still raises a problem because these are two very different and conflicting ways of running a city. Perhaps we should accept that these dual identities cannot be easily reconciled, and acknowledge that Massalia's place so far removed from the beating heart of Greek culture allowed it to be whatever people wanted it to be.

* * *

A solution may be found in another relationship that Massalia navigated from its very foundation: its ties with Rome. According to Trogus, the Phocaeans who first set out to found Massalia stopped en route in Rome, then under the kingship of Tarquin. Here they established a treaty and a long-standing friendship between the two cities.[37] Considering that Trogus was writing this account during the height of the Roman Empire, it is perhaps best if we treat this story with a degree of scepticism; however, all the evidence we have from the sixth to the first centuries BCE suggests he may well be correct.

At the turn of the fourth century BCE, a fledgling Rome was engaged in conflict with the Etruscans. Following a long siege at Veii in c.396 BCE, the forces of the Roman dictator Marcus Furius Camillus were able to take the city and in turn destroy one of their local rivals. Before the battle, Camillus made an oath to Pythian Apollo, the god of prophecy whose home was at Delphi in Greece. After the victory, we are told that he fulfilled his promise and that the city of Rome dedicated a golden bowl to the god, which would cost the equivalent of one-tenth of the spoils taken from Veii.

In Delphi, offerings such as these would be dedicated and stored in a state-owned treasury. Most of the big city-states had one, but Rome did not. Instead, Rome placed this bowl in the treasury of their greatest Greek allies, the Massaliotes.[38] Within a few years of this triumph, Rome was sacked and held to ransom by the Gallic army of Brennus. When news of this reached Massalia, the people were distraught and publicly mourned the tragedy. So deep was their affection for Rome that the

Massaliotes used both private and public money to help pay the ransom needed to make the Gauls agree to a peace.[39]

By the third century BCE, Rome had recovered from its trauma and begun to establish itself as a great political and military power in the Mediterranean. Its main rival was the north African city of Carthage, and the two powers engaged in a series of conflicts known as the Punic Wars. Massalia held firm as an ally to Rome, a position that was truly challenged during the Second Punic War, which saw a large Carthaginian army under the command of Hannibal Barca march up from Spain, pass by Massalia and cross the Alps into Italy itself.

The town was used as a staging ground for Roman military activity and reconnaissance. It also supplied ships and marines to help fight the war at sea, in particular around the coast of Spain – the one area where Massaliote interests were directly undermined by Carthaginian expansion.

Our Roman sources are rather coy about the role of Massalia, but oddly enough a surviving source from a Greek writer who fought on the side of the Carthaginians highlights their importance in the battle:

> They all fought outstandingly, but most of all the ships of the Massaliotes, who were the first to join battle and were wholly responsible for the success of the Romans. In sum, their leaders encouraged the others and made them bolder, while they themselves attacked the enemy with exceptional bravery.[40]

Again, our penchant for scepticism would serve us well here: should we be surprised to find a Greek source speaking very positively about the Greek contribution to a victory? However, as the tide of power shifted and Rome became the dominant force, the Roman state never forgot the help and support given by Massalia over the years. When Massalia's colonies came under attack from the local Gauls, the Ligurians, Rome secured the victory but ensured that the peace settlement was entirely in favour of Massalia. In 125 BCE, Rome went to war once again at the behest of the Massaliotes who were having trouble with another local group, the Saluvii.[41] In 102 BCE, Rome and Massalia had yet another common enemy, the allied Ambrones and Teutones tribes. After securing victory, the Roman commander Gaius Marius later dug a canal to free up passage along the Rhône. Because of their assistance in this war, he gifted control of the riverway to Massalia, allowing the city to collect tolls from boats passing through.[42]

The mutual dependence between both cities and their long-standing friendship allowed the Massaliotes special privileges rarely offered by the Romans. They were, as Cicero once said, Rome's 'most faithful allies'.[43] But this position was particularly difficult to maintain when Rome itself was split into factions, something that occurred most dramatically during the civil war of the first century BCE between Julius Caesar and Pompey the Great. Caesar had already subjugated all of Gaul, but he left Massalia independent from the empire. When Caesar crossed the Rubicon (both literally and metaphorically), the Massaliotes needed to choose between Pompey and the city of Rome, and the rising star and conqueror of Gaul himself.

It was inevitably a gamble for Massalia; whichever side it supported could backfire if it was defeated. Massalia chose to remain as neutral as possible, but it was not a simple decision because most of the towns and peoples of Gaul had already sided with Caesar. Their reasoning was clear and logical, but unfortunately somewhat naive:

> They said that they were allies of the Roman people and felt friendly towards both sides, and that they were neither intermeddling at all nor in a position to decide which of the two was

> in the wrong; consequently, in case they were approached in a friendly manner, they would receive them both, they said, without their arms, but if it were a question of making war, neither of them.[44]

Caesar was not a man to be shut out. To him, this neutrality was as good as siding with Pompey, so he laid siege to the city in 49 BCE for four long months. The odds were always stacked against the people of Massalia, but this did not stop them from putting up a fierce resistance. The siege was bloody and the forces of Caesar were ultimately victorious, but the memory of this Massaliote stand was never forgotten by the Roman people. Facing one of the greatest military leaders ever seen in the ancient world, Massalia chose to honour its alliance with Rome over siding with this usurper. The poet Lucan immortalised their actions in his poem about the civil war:

> Then did the Grecian city win renown
> Eternal, deathless, for that uncompelled
> Nor fearing for herself, but free to act
> She made the conqueror pause.[45]

Caesar did not punish the city for resisting, but he did take away its primary role as the gateway to southern Gaul; Massalia even lost control of the canal gifted to it by Marius. Yet Massalia was always permitted a degree of autonomy in the Roman Empire. That was the depth of affection, the depth of bond shared between the two cities.

It was either during or after these events that our main sources for the history and culture of Massalia were written. So the city that was being lauded by Roman authors such as Tacitus and Strabo was Rome's greatest ally: a city that had stuck by them during the darkest periods of their Republican history and remained steadfast against some of the most formidable powers in the ancient world. It was a place whose long history was entwined with the story of Rome itself. Massalia accepted its role in the new Roman world order and as good as disappears from the records that we have.

The story of Massalia does not end there, though it is notably absent from much of the literary record and the limited archaeological evidence does little to fill any gaps. During much of the Roman Imperial period we hear very little from or of Massalia, but this changes rather dramatically from the fourth century CE onwards, when the city becomes something of a hub for the new religion spreading through the empire: Christianity. The city reappears in the record as a vibrant, lively place filled with intellectuals, writers and religious thinkers, attracting people from all around the Mediterranean.

Its re-emergence as a city of knowledge appears to chime with, or perhaps assist in, its restitution as an important trading port, especially after the fall of the Western Roman Empire in the fifth century CE. Ceramic remains found at the ancient site of the city show evidence of a thriving trade network throughout the Mediterranean. They also show an almost exclusive trade in African fine ware, specifically expensive, high-quality pottery coming from the region of what is now modern Tunisia.[46] The city was also minting gold coins, struck in the name of the Eastern Roman Emperor, which highlights just how plugged in Massalia was to the world outside the post-Roman lands of Francia. These were connections that enabled its continued success as it transformed from Massalia into the modern Marseille. It was no longer a Greek city out on the periphery, but an influential cultural centre in its own right.

Massalia benefited in many ways from its serendipitous location. Being situated in a land that would become one of the cultural and political cornerstones of European history, and a foundational influence on the concept of western civilisation, meant that it could never be forgotten. Olbia and Naucratis are examples of what can happen when the edges of the known world are transformed into the edges of known history. But these sites were no more remarkable or unique than any other. They are each proof of the flexibility of ancient Greek culture and thought. Away from the conservative eyes at the centres of Greece, they broke social norms, defied cultural truisms and pushed the Greek perceptions of the world, and themselves within it, to the very edge and beyond. While to our modern eyes they lived on the edges of the map, from their perspective they were simply at the beginning of a new map in need of drawing.

Section III

# THE ROMAN WORLD

Chapter 7
[SCOTLAND]
Hadrian's Wall
North Sea
Elbe
Oder
BRITANNIA
London
Rhine
GAUL
Rhône
Rome
HISPANIA
Tagus
Chapter 8
Carthage
Tingis
Thapsus (46 BCE)
Volubilis
MAURETANIA
Atlas Mts.
Lixos (Drâa)
NUMIDIA
LIBYA

The Roman World
0 200 400 600 800 1,000 km
0 100 200 300 400 500 mi
Vistula
Southern Bug
Dnieper
Don
Danube
Black Sea
Troy
ASIA
Athens
Euphrates
Tigris
LEVANT
Mediterranean Sea
Chapter 9
Ptolemaios
CYRENAICA
Alexandria
Cairo
Karanis
EGYPT
Nile

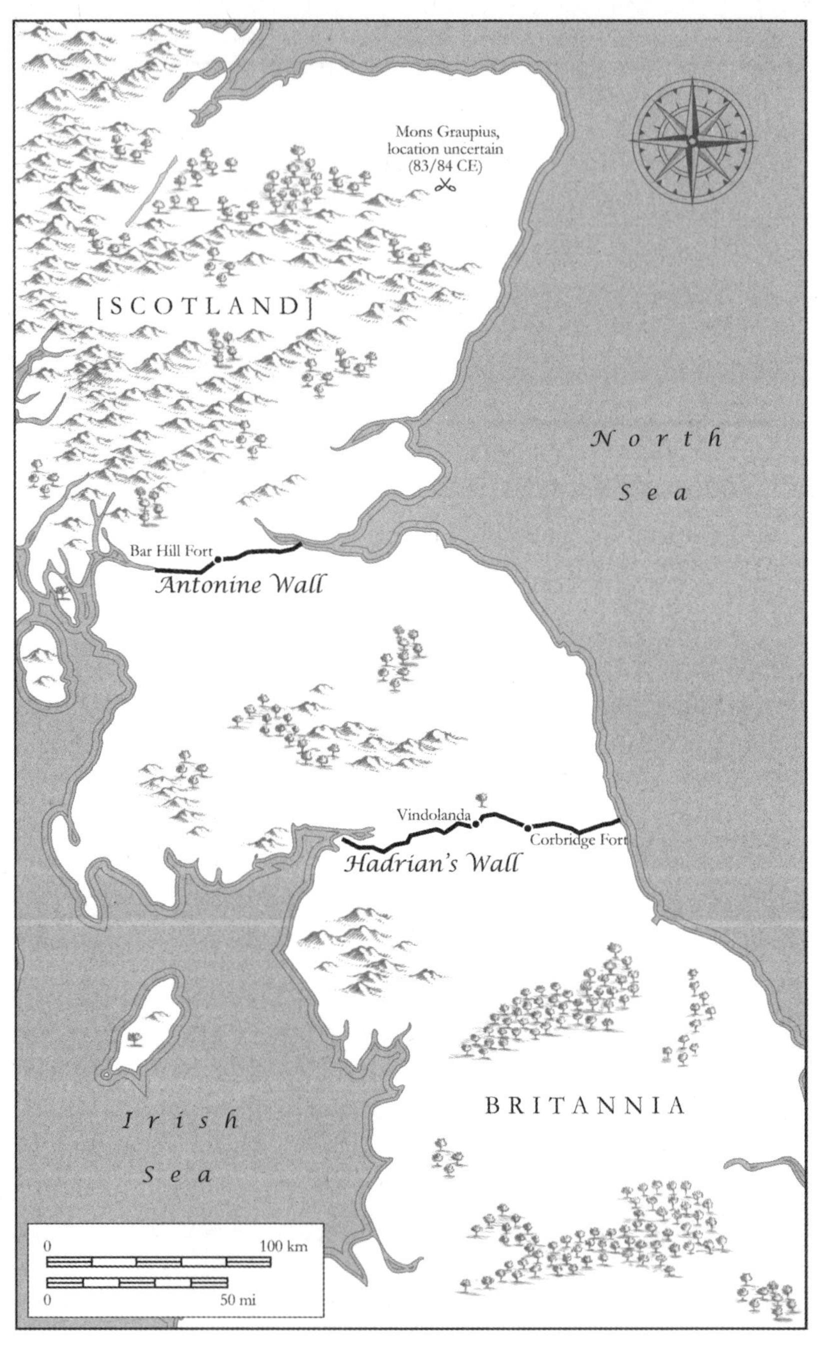
Mons Graupius,
location uncertain
(83/84 CE)
[SCOTLAND]
North
Sea
Bar Hill Fort
Antonine Wall
Vindolanda
Corbridge Fort
Hadrian's Wall
BRITANNIA
Irish
Sea
0
100 km
0
50 mi

# 7

# Hadrian's Wall, England

The Roman Empire gave the history of Europe and the wider Mediterranean something it had never really had before, or at least not on such a scale: firm borders. This gave clear boundaries between the Romans and their colonies inside the empire, and everyone else outside it. In essence this is when the Greek concept of the 'barbarian' as a foreign speaker was transformed into the more modern usage of the term meaning a savage and uncivilised person or culture. This is a Roman paradigm, one built on the fear of foreign invaders or migrations infiltrating the empire. Unlike the Greeks', Roman ideology feels more similar to that of the Egyptians that we saw in Chapters 1 and 2: this was not simply one of cultural superiority, but a polarity of civilisation and order with barbarism and chaos.

This ideology is one that modern historians often, and unwittingly, emulate when they write the history of the Roman Empire. When we write about barbarian hordes, large migrations, the 'fall' of Rome and onset of the Dark Ages, we are telling a very specific story, one told from the perspective of Rome itself and, if truth be told, our own cultural perspectives and fears today. It comes as little surprise that when news stories break of refugees entering the country or of continental migrations of people displaced by war or natural disaster, commentators express unfounded concerns that we are witnessing the modern-day 'Fall of Rome'. For Rome has become a symbol of something much greater than itself. It is the framework around which Western civilisation has been arranged, and so the story of Rome is one with a strict narrative. It is one of progress, of learning and education, of domination and cultural development. It is also a story filled with moral lessons, in particular of hubris and the dangers of hedonism or debauchery.

However, to embrace this narrative fully you need to narrow your focus onto only those stories that fit it. This means that even the most enthusiastic of Roman history readers will be exposed to a very Rome-centric perspective: one that is interested more in the emperors, their families and the cultural elite, or else the military as an efficient fighting machine as opposed to a force made up of an eclectic mix of individuals. This narrative does not ignore the periphery, in fact it often embraces it wholeheartedly, focusing on foreign groups crossing the borders, battles being fought and chaos ensuing. But it sometimes ignores the normal, everyday lives out there. These next three chapters do not rewrite the history of the Roman Empire, but flesh out the rather abridged story that is commonly told. They also reveal that behind the veneer of 'Rome' lies a complex, multicultural world that had more to divide it than it had to unite it, and yet it held together for hundreds of years.

Our first Roman location epitomises life at the edge of the empire, but is also perhaps the most well-known example in this book. Situated over 2,000 kilometres away from the heart of the Roman Empire, Hadrian's Wall formed its permanent northern boundary. It was not the end of the empire, so to speak. Roman influence stretched well into Scotland, as did their legendary road system, but their frontier was demarcated by this curtain of wood and stone. An attempt to push the boundary further north was made during the reign of Hadrian's successor Antoninus Pius, but this new wall was short-lived.

Hadrian's Wall, or what remains of it today, runs along the dramatic undulations of the Cumbrian and Northumberland countryside. The beauty of its surroundings is hard to ignore as you scramble up the uneven paths to reach the wall, often with only the local grazing sheep to keep you company. The serenity of the landscape, mixed with the beautiful shifting colour palettes of the seasons, is regularly punctuated with blasting cold winds and driving rain which will soak you right through. It is one of the most dramatic ancient sites in the world, but the experience is not to everyone's liking. In the first century CE, the Roman historian Tacitus noted that the sky in Britain is 'deformed by clouds and frequent rains', while at the turn of the second century an auxiliary commander at the fort of Vindolanda, which sits just a few miles south of the wall, had this letter drafted:

> Flavius Cerialis to his September, greetings. Tomorrow, which is 5 October, as you wish my lord, I will provide some goods [...] by means of which we may endure the storms even if they are troublesome.[1]

As is so often the issue with our evidence from Hadrian's Wall, which includes the amazing Vindolanda Tablets that have survived with the inked letters intact, we are left with gaping holes in the text. Here, the commander Cerialis is arranging some form of transaction with Caecilius September to take place on 5 October, when Cerialis will receive some supplies to help his men weather the local storms. This letter, and hundreds like it, show the lived experience of many men, women and children on the frontier. It gives the strong impression of an organised and logistically efficient setup.

You would be excused for thinking that the Romans had established themselves in Britain for a long time before this letter was drafted, but they had not. Claudius' initial invasion of Britain was only staged sixty years earlier, and only Julius Caesar had dared to attempt a military excursion on the British mainland up until that point, in 55 and 54 BCE. In fact, until Caesar first landed on the Kent coast, these northern reaches of Britain and Ireland were the subject of much debate for Greek and Roman writers:

> [T]he island itself was said to have been so large that no one could believe it existed at all. Writer after writer had entered the bitter controversy. Britain was just a name and a legend they said; the island did not exist and never had existed. Now Caesar attempted to conquer it, and advanced the Roman Empire beyond the bounds of the human world.[2]

To writers during the Roman Republic, Britain, if it existed at all, was without doubt the furthest northern point in which humans lived. Strabo describes Ireland, which he places above Britain geographically, as a cold and miserable place inhabited by a savage race of men. He even decides, based on no real evidence, that northern Britain must be the absolute upper reaches of habitable earth.[3] This idea is echoed in later Roman poetry, where Britain is often described in such terms; as the writer Horace so eloquently describes it, Britain was at the *ultimos orbis*, the world's edge.[4]

Perhaps this perception of Britain in the minds of the Romans goes some way to explain their rather slow attempt to take control of the island, beginning with Julius Caesar's two rather half-hearted invasions in which he spent less than three months in Britain in total.[5] (Not that this prevented him from receiving twenty days of thanksgiving pronounced in his honour by the Senate – being the first Roman to take an army beyond the edges of the world did come with its own perks.) His adopted heir, Augustus, also planned numerous invasions of Britain but he was always too distracted by other events ever to put those plans into action.[6] The emperor Gaius, remembered in history as Caligula, took an army as far as the north Gallic coast in 40 CE but decided against crossing the Channel, allegedly ordering his men to collect seashells instead to take back to Rome.[7] Even the famous invasion of Claudius in 43 CE, the first Roman to follow in the footsteps of Caesar, only secured control of south-east Britain. In 83–84 CE, during the reign of Domitian, the Roman commander Agricola won the Battle of Mons Graupius in Scotland. Only then had the Romans finally managed to complete a task that had begun over 140 years before.

The history of this period was written by Tacitus, who also happened to be Agricola's own son-in-law, and he was clearly not impressed with the way Rome had handled its conquest of the island. He put a scathing assessment of Roman imperial actions in the mouth of the Caledonian commander Galgacus, who describes the Romans as creating 'a desert and calling it peace'.[8] But Tacitus' most cutting comments about the whole process are kept for his own voice when he summed up the impact of Agricola's success: 'Britain was thoroughly subdued and immediately abandoned.'[9]

He is not being literal, of course: the Romans did not abandon Britain in any shape or form. But Mons Graupius was most probably fought in the very north of Scotland, whereas Hadrian's Wall would be built over 200 miles to the south.

* * *

Following the death of Domitian in 96 CE, imperial power in Rome entered a new phase of non-familial succession: one where each emperor would adopt a chosen heir who was arguably best suited for the role. Much later, Niccolò Machiavelli (1469–1527), the political philosopher, identified this series of rulers, from Nerva to Marcus Aurelius, as the best, giving rise to their later moniker the five 'Good Emperors'. How good they really were is up for debate, but what we see in the actions of the first three (Nerva, Trajan and Hadrian) is a keen understanding of the true state of the empire. Nerva only ruled for a short time, knowing that he did not command the respect and loyalty of Rome's mighty legions. Trajan understood that Rome had stagnated as an imperial force. He also knew that his greatest strength was as a military leader, and so he stretched the borders of the empire to its greatest outer limits. When Hadrian became emperor, we see yet another reassessment of what was needed:

> On taking possession of the imperial power Hadrian at once returned to ancestral custom, and devoted his attention to maintaining peace throughout the world. For the nations which Trajan had conquered began to revolt; the Moors began to make attacks, the Sarmatians were waging war, the Britons could not be kept under Roman control, Egypt was thrown into disorder by riots, and finally Libya and Palestine showed the rebellious spirits.[10]

Hadrian's policy, one that he actually inherited from Augustus, would have a dramatic impact on the shape of the Roman Empire. Many of the lands annexed by Trajan were swiftly abandoned and the borders of the empire were purposely shrunk, but more clearly defined and supported. He invested in the so-called *limes*, garrisoned borders which existed in varying forms of construction. In North Africa this saw the development of the *Fossatum Africae*, a long ditch and embankment with sporadic stretches of stone walling supported by a large network of watchtowers and small forts. In the volatile region of Germania the fortified frontier was extended with wooden palisades filling the gaps between natural boundaries such as the Rhine and Danube rivers. For Britain, however, Hadrian chose something a little bit special:

> [Hadrian] set out for Britain, and corrected many abuses there; he was the first to construct a wall, eighty miles in length, to separate the barbarians from the Romans.[11]

This wasn't some mere project to shore up the northern border: Hadrian wanted to make a statement. The wall stretched for seventy-three miles (117 kilometres), bisecting Britain and, according to Cassius Dio, also its people – the Maeatae to the south and the Caledonians to the north.[12] Once completed, Hadrian's Wall must have been a formidable sight, standing over four metres tall and three metres deep. The wall was also broken up at regular intervals: milecastles stood at every Roman mile (1.5 kilometres) with a gateway through the wall, and two towers between each milecastle, giving the boundary a suitably military feel. The Romans also, rather uniquely, built twelve large forts on the wall line, as well as relying on other forts both north and south of the boundary. But this was not all: a defensive ditch was dug on both the northern and southern sides as well, creating a clearly marked frontier zone; there is even evidence that native settlements were cleared from the immediate areas either side of the wall.[13]

We are not sure why Hadrian took such dramatic measures. Forts such as Vindolanda were already established in the region where the wall was built, so the likelihood is that there was trouble brewing with the Caledonians. When Hadrian succeeded to the imperial throne in 117 CE, following his adoption by Trajan on his deathbed, there is a suggestion that there was unrest in Britain. Our written sources do not give any useful details or specifics, but a damaged tombstone discovered at Vindolanda dedicated to a centurion called Titus Annius offers us some insight. The style of the epitaph dates it to the start of the second century CE and Titus Annius is said to have 'died in war'.[14] There is no known war in the region during this period, except for this unrest at the ascension of Hadrian. We also know that Hadrian sent 3,000 men drawn from three separate legions to Britain, possibly suggesting that the two British legions may have suffered some heavy losses at this time, maybe including the infamous Ninth Legion, although scholars are not in complete agreement about this.[15] There is even evidence that London was purposely burned during this time. Was this all part of a coordinated uprising by the Britons? Were the Romans struggling to keep the Britons under their control? If so, this goes some way towards explaining why Hadrian felt the need to build such an imposing monument: to affirm Roman imperial power in the region.[16]

Yet this boundary was much more than simply bricks and mortar. To be able to protect such a long frontier, it needed to be garrisoned by many soldiers. It was as much a human boundary as anything else. And whenever I stand on Hadrian's Wall, it is these men who come to mind alongside an old American military maxim: 'hurry up and wait'. The expression encapsulates the lived experience of many soldiers who are constantly pushed to be ready, to move quickly and be prepared to act, and then they must wait. Wait for the impending attack, wait for the next set of orders, wait for direction, wait for other troops to do their jobs first. This wait can last hours, days, weeks, years even, so let us consider one part of the military experience we are not often encouraged to think about: boredom.

Evidence of boredom can be difficult to identify in ancient texts, but we do know that it was a problem even in armies. For instance, the Greco-Roman biographer Plutarch (first–second centuries CE) describes one commander's attempts to alleviate the boredom of his men during a siege by giving them a designated space in the city to walk and run.[17] The contemporary histories do not discuss boredom and inaction on the frontier: why would that be of interest to their audience? So our literary evidence offers a very sketchy image of a soldier's life along a frontier like Hadrian's Wall. However, while we have no Roman accounts of bored young soldiers getting into mischief while on campaign, as we do from classical Greece, for instance, we do have archaeological evidence that Roman soldiers would while away their time with board games and dice.

One particularly popular game on the British frontier was *Ludus Latrunculi* ('Game of Little Brigands'), a strategy-based board game similar to chess. The tactical aim was to try and trap a piece from your opponent with two pieces of your own; once trapped, this captured piece was removed from the board. The strategic goal was to take all your opponent's pieces while losing as few of your own as possible. It was a game of guile, cunning and tactical finesse, one which no doubt attracted both players and punters gambling on the outcome. Its appeal was also aided by the ease with which soldiers could fashion a board by scratching lines on a flat rock, or by drawing them on the ground. For the coloured pieces you simply needed shards of pottery or even just light and dark stones. Some of these items have been found inside the milecastles, so this is not just soldiers playing while off duty, but when they were supposed to be guarding the wall.

Another easy set of games to play involved dice, an object that is regularly found along the frontier. Dice offer the same ideal attributes as the ad hoc board games: they are light, portable, easy to use and even easier to gamble with. One game, *tesserae*, was played with three dice and the winner was the one with the highest cumulative score after a roll. What could be simpler? We know of other dice games with different objectives such as trying to get odd or even scores from the roll. Needless to say, when money and competition are involved, there is also cheating. At the Corbridge fort, for instance, researchers have discovered a trick die, where the number 6 is missing and was replaced with a second number 1. These types of fake dice have been found throughout the empire, including loaded dice weighted to land on certain numbers, so it was not just the British garrisons that had a penchant for dishonest play.[18]

Soldiers who endured long periods of inactivity were considered something of a problem. In an extraordinary piece of evidence, an imperial tutor named Marcus Cornelius Fronto wrote a letter to the emperor Lucius Verus during the second century CE, which lays out a somewhat caricatured portrayal of troops in Syria, somewhere that was often considered a very relaxed military assignment compared to the western frontiers:

> The army you took over was demoralized with luxury and immorality and prolonged idleness ... Gambling was rife in camp: sleep night-long, or, if a watch was kept, it was over the wine-cups.[19]

While the garrisons at Hadrian's Wall can hardly be accused of living in luxury, there is ample evidence of the ready supply of beer and wine for the men. The concern about 'prolonged idleness' is equally appropriate; indeed, our evidence for military life at the frontier paints no more exciting a picture. Of the hundreds of tablets surviving at Vindolanda, there is no mention of combat or enemy raids; in fact the Britons as a collective group only appear once throughout the existing corpus, where they are given the derogatory name of *Brittunculi* (little Britons).[20] The majority of these letters concern the boring humdrum of day-to-day life:

> I have sent (?) you ... pairs of socks from Sattua, two pairs of sandals and two pairs of underpants, two pairs of sandals ...[21]

But this is not to say that life on the frontier was without its dangers. Although raids and combat are notably absent from so much of our evidence, we do know of one particular incursion which saw the Britons cross the wall. In 180 CE, the year in which Commodus inherited the throne from his father Marcus Aurelius, the new emperor faced what one ancient author described as his 'greatest struggle'. The Caledonian tribes managed to cross Hadrian's Wall and wreak havoc to the south. We cannot be sure how many, or in how coordinated an action, but it must have been a sizeable force because it managed to defeat a Roman army:

> When the tribes in that island, crossing the wall that separated them from the Roman legions, proceeded to do much mischief and cut down a general together with his troops, Commodus became alarmed but sent Ulpius Marcellus against them.[22]

It is difficult to visualise what actually happened; the idea of a full Roman legion being defeated by a large raiding party is hard to reconcile. Perhaps it was a small garrison, or maybe a Roman commander had been caught out with a personal retinue; we can never truly know. What we do know is that Commodus reacted very quickly to the news and sent a former governor of Britannia, Ulpius Marcellus, to quell the potential uprising. We do not hear much about Marcellus' life, but Cassius Dio paints a very eccentric picture of the man. He is described as being temperate and frugal, almost perfectly built for military life, and was 'openly incorruptible', but he was also an arrogant and unkind man who was generally unpleasant to be around. Marcellus had a strange way of doing things; for instance, he would only eat stale bread to prevent him eating more than was necessary. He would also create the impression to his men that he never slept; for instance, he would have orders written on a number of tablets that, during the night, his aides would deliver to his officers at set times to create the impression that he was still awake and working even in the dead of night. It is not even clear if Commodus actually liked or respected him as a man. At some point in his career Marcellus was almost put to death by the emperor before a very late reprieve and the issue of a pardon. But no matter his personal foibles, Marcellus took ruthless action against the British tribes.[23]

Danger did not just lurk in the British countryside, however. We know that life inside the Roman forts and the accompanying *vici*, civilian settlements that grew alongside the forts themselves, was dangerous in its own right. On the northern frontier, we know of at least three possible murders occurring on-site. In one civilian settlement, archaeologists discovered two bodies buried beneath the floorboards of an as yet unidentified building. The disposal of the bodies is suspicious enough – the Romans buried their dead outside their settlements as a rule – but one of the victims still had a knife among his remains from when he was stabbed either in the back or through the ribs.[24]

More disconcerting is the recent discovery of a suspicious body disposal found in the fort of Vindolanda itself. In a shallow pit uncovered in the corner of a barrack room, researchers found a young child, no older than ten, who seems to have been buried with their hands tied behind their back. It is hard to say for certain but cause of death may have been blunt-force trauma to the skull. What seems certain, whether this death was accidental or deliberate, is that the eight men who shared that room must have been able to smell the body decomposing and chose to do nothing about it, which suggests a cover-up. The child is of indeterminate gender, and researchers have named them Georgie. While Georgie's story reminds us of the volatility and violence of the Roman world, it also raises some interesting questions.

Studies of Georgie's tooth enamel shows that they were of North African origin. There are two plausible explanations for Georgie's presence: either they were enslaved, or they were a child of one of the soldiers.[25]

* * *

The Roman invasion of Britain and their subsequent abandonment of the country are foundational moments in the history of the British Isles. The invasion is often cited as the moment that Britain really joined the history of Europe, while the withdrawal of the Romans is likewise considered a watershed moment when civilisation left and the Dark Ages began. Many recent histories have dispelled this myth of the post-Roman Dark Ages, but what is not perhaps as well known is that the Romans in question were not as Roman as you might think.

The term 'Roman' is often used as a simple way of explaining who held power, but it can create the false impression that when we talk about the Roman army, or a Roman commander, we are automatically talking about Romans (i.e. someone from Italy). This is not an error that can be blamed on our ancient evidence; they knew that the army was not just full of Italians. But it is a more modern problem, where we project Roman identity through a very narrow lens that often omits the murkiness of who exactly was considered Roman. The Roman army was made up of a wide variety of auxiliary cohorts from around the empire, the ranks of which were filled with *peregrine* soldiers (free subjects, who were not citizens). In the second century CE, Hadrian's Wall was manned by maybe as many as 9,000 men drawn from across the empire. While these men were sometimes commanded by Roman citizens, the bulk of their numbers were not. This means that the Roman occupation did not simply bring Roman culture over to the British Isles it brought a lot more besides.

One inscription found near Hadrian's Wall, dating from the second or early third century CE, epitomises the multicultural make-up of the army:

> Virgo, in her heavenly realm, is close to Leo:
> holding ears of grain, the inventor of justice,
> foundress of cities:
> gifts that allowed us to recognise the gods.
> Thus she is also the Mother of the Gods,
> Peace, Virtue, Ceres, the Syrian Goddess,
> administering shares of life and justice with her scales.
> Syria gave rise to this constellation, to be seen in the sky,
> to be worshipped in Libya;
> that is how we all have acquired our knowledge.[26]

The dedicant is given as one Marcus Donatianus who was most likely a Roman officer from North Africa. His name is strongly associated with the region, and this specific reference to the goddess being worshipped in Libya cements that connection. Equally interesting, he is clearly at pains to acknowledge that the divine virgin, Virgo, was worshipped by different cultures under different names: Cybele (Mother of the Gods), Pax (Peace), Virtus (Virtue), Demeter (Ceres) and Dea Syria (Syrian Goddess). This list suggests that Donatianus was sensitive to the beliefs and cultural influences of other people, but which people? The most logical answer would be his own men. Syrian troops were a mainstay at Hadrian's Wall, and the reference to the Syrian goddess is amplified by his claim that Syria and Libya are linked through this shared deity.[27]

In fact, ancient Syrian culture left a clear, if fleeting, imprint on Britain long before the Saxons and Normans of later years. We know of various Syrian cults being practised along the wall. Two dedications dating from the third century CE have been discovered, one to the semitic goddess Astarte and the other to Hercules of Tyre, the Romanised name for the semitic god Melquart.[28] Both inscriptions are in Greek and in hexameter verse, and the commonalities between them have led some researchers to suggest they may come from the same shrine. The formality of a place of worship is supported by the dedicant for Hercules of Tyre, who was an archpriestess:

> For Hercules
> of Tyre:
> Diodora,
> Archpriestess [set this up].[29]

More famously, the length of Hadrian's Wall has numerous shrines (Mithraea) dedicated to the cult of Mithras. Originally from Syria and Persia, Mithras was adopted by the Romans, who transformed his following into a mystery cult with initiates and secret rituals.[30] His was a popular cult among the Roman army during the second and fourth centuries CE, but we actually know very little about it. Most of our information comes from the Mithraea themselves, which often depict important scenes related to Mithras: his birth from a rock and his killing of a bull. Due to the secretive nature of the cult, many false claims have been made about Mithras over the years, such as being born of a virgin in a stable, where he was visited by wise men; and that he later died on a cross before being resurrected days later. All our evidence for the cult of Mithras, of which there is little, actually disproves many of these claims to begin with.

Our evidence shows that people from across the empire made their way to the north of Britain. While far-flung locations like Syria and North Africa often catch the eye, we also see Gauls from modern France and Belgium, Greeks, Sardinians and more besides, each culture leaving a small piece of themselves in the

British Isles. But alongside this intricate tapestry of cultures, we also see an interesting attempt to maintain a sense of Roman identity along the frontier. While we have evidence of brewers and much beer drinking at Vindolanda (beer being associated with barbarousness and a lack of taste), we also have ample evidence of wine, olive oil and garum fish sauce being imported for those with more Roman tastes.[31] But Roman identity was not just one of preferences: it enabled personal progression and status if it was emulated effectively. Evidence from the forts suggests that some soldiers, or perhaps their children, were trying to learn Latin. Some of their writing exercises survive in the archaeological record, including copied-out lines of important cultural writers, with Virgil being an obvious favourite.[32]

Perhaps the clearest attempt to maintain a semblance of 'normal' Roman life can be seen in the lives of elite women. One famous example is a letter written on behalf of Claudia Severa, the wife of Aelius Brocchus, at an otherwise unknown fort of Briga. The recipient was Sulpicia Lepidina, the wife of Flavius Cerialis, who was the prefect of the 9th cohort of Batavians stationed at Vindolanda. Most of the letter was written by a scribe, but a few words at the end are in a second hand, the only real explanation being that it is her own hand, making this among the earliest known examples of Latin written by a woman. The letter's content speaks for itself:

> Claudia Severa to her Lepidina, greetings. On 11 September, sister, for the day of the celebration of my birthday, I give you a warm invitation to make sure that you come to us, to make the day more enjoyable for me by your arrival, if you are present. Give my greetings to your Cerialis. My Aelius and my little son send him their greetings.
> [Second set of handwriting]

> I shall expect you, sister. Farewell, sister, my dearest soul, as I hope to prosper, and hail.[33]

There is something quite endearing here. This woman, living at the edge of the world in what was characterised as a brutal, austere and male environment, is trying to arrange the most normal of events for a member of an elite Roman family. Roman birthdays were not celebrated in quite the same way as we celebrate today, so think less jelly and cake and more rituals and prayer – nevertheless, it was an important social occasion and her affection for Lepidina is obvious.

What letters such as these also highlight is the importance of family and extended family relationships. Lepidina and Severa were not actually sisters, but the use of the word 'sister' as a greeting, alongside the male counterpart 'brother', is very common in the personal correspondence. So, too, is the concern for family members; Severa asks after Lepidina's husband and also extends the greetings of her own husband and son. We also have letters from soldiers writing to family members, asking for news and showing the usual concerns of men who are far from home.

The role of family along Hadrian's Wall was, for a long time, an unstudied area of frontier life. The reasoning was simple: family should not have been there. This has been a long-standing misconception about Roman military life, one born from a law governing the lives of the soldiers. Most likely dating from the time of Augustus, a decree banned Roman soldiers from marrying.[34] This meant that a rank-and-file soldier could not have a legally recognised wife or legitimate children. It has often been the case that historians have read about a law in the literary evidence and immediately assumed that it was followed. In this case, the ban on legal marriage was presumed to mean that these soldiers did not have families of their own, not until they were discharged anyway. However, these two things are not mutually exclusive: official law is not always reflected in social reality.

The Roman law did prohibit soldiers from marrying *and* many Roman soldiers had wives and families – but those wives and families were not legally recognised. Livy gives us clear evidence of this dissonance when he describes an embassy from Spain who were descended from Roman soldiers:

> Another embassy, also from Spain, of a novel class of people, arrived. Stating that they were the children of Roman soldiers and of Spanish women, between whom legal marriage could not exist, and that they numbered over four thousand souls, they asked that a town be given them in which to live.[35]

Ignoring evidence such as this, however, scholarly assumptions went a step further: researchers assumed that because families were apparently banned and because our Roman sources are very dismissive of women being in the military environment, then women themselves were not permitted in forts. This idea persisted for over a century, but it was never going to last because, as archaeologists excavated many of the forts along and behind Hadrian's Wall, the evidence was overwhelming: women and children *were* present.

Thanks to the anaerobic conditions in the archaeological layers at Vindolanda, we have a veritable treasure trove of surviving organic material. Items of everyday use made from things like wood or animal hair have survived in good condition. Leather is particularly abundant in the archaeology, including excitingly mundane items such as drawstring leather bags. But among it all is an overwhelming quantity of shoes and socks which survive and, thanks to their size, allow researchers to identify them as being for children or women. Many have been found in the barrack lodgings, others in the officers' quarters, showing that women and children were living with soldiers at all levels within the hierarchy. While Vindolanda may hold the most extensive collections, it is certainly not unique here; researchers have found children's shoes in large quantities as far north as Bar Hill Fort in Dunbartonshire, Scotland, when it formed part of the Antonine Wall.[36]

It was, after all, worthwhile having a family while serving in the Roman auxilia. First, if a soldier enlisted at, say, twenty years old, he would not be allowed to marry until he was at least forty-five. Second, and more importantly, when a member of the auxilia was discharged, usually after twenty-five years of service, he was awarded a military diploma bestowing Roman citizenship upon him and, rather paradoxically considering the Roman laws in place, citizenship was also given to his unofficial wife, or future wife if he did not already have one, and any children they might have.

The story of one soldier, a man by the name of Longinus Sestius, encapsulates the multicultural nature of life at Hadrian's Wall. We only know of him because his military diploma was recently published from a private collection. He was an archer within a specialised auxilia cohort, the *cohors I Hamiorum sagittariorum* (First Cohort of Hamian Archers) who we already know from other inscriptions along the wall. The Hamii came from central Syria, just over 100 miles north of Damascus, but the diploma was not found in either Syria or Britain – rather, it is believed to have come from Bulgaria. It was issued in 132 CE, meaning that Longinus joined the army in 107 CE, the year following the end of the Second Dacian War (105–106 CE) that Trajan had been waging in the region. One researcher has argued convincingly that the First Cohort of Hamian Archers most probably fought in Trajan's war in Dacia and, having taken losses, decided to recruit archers from within the area.[37]

As a member of the cohort, one of maybe 480 archers, Longinus would then travel over 2,000 miles to northern Britain, where he would stay. We cannot be certain when this took place, but inscriptions in Britain that name the unit do not appear until the time of Hadrian, so perhaps they were part of his mission to reinforce troops on the island shortly after becoming emperor. If we assume that Longinus was redeployed in 118 CE, then he would not return to his homeland for fourteen years – fourteen years stuck as a Dacian surrounded by Syrian comrades, serving in the Roman army, all while stationed at the edge of the world map. He was a foreigner among foreigners, which could have been a very lonely existence, but his diploma does mention two children, a son and a daughter. Perhaps he took a young wife with him from Dacia, but her absence from the diploma does hint at the possibility that she died before he was discharged. She would have been entitled to citizenship alongside her husband, but the real incentive was that their children received it as well – ensuring that the family would for evermore be considered citizens of Rome.

The history of Hadrian's Wall does not end in the second century. Antoninus Pius' attempt to push the Roman frontier further north into Scotland was something of a disaster. Construction on the new wall began in 142 CE, taking about twelve years to build, only to be abandoned in 162 CE and the garrisons withdrawn back to Hadrian's Wall. This failure to extend Roman control north seems in no small part to be a result of Caledonian unity and resistance, something neither Antoninus, nor his successor Marcus Aurelius, could properly subdue. We have seen how Commodus dealt with the growing situation in Britain, sending Ulpius Marcellus to try and quell any revolts in the region. But even this had minimal success.

From the third century CE the northern frontier was becoming increasingly uncontrollable. Equally, its remoteness from

Rome along with its comparatively poor revenue benefits for the empire meant that it became less and less of a priority for successive emperors. The situation was made worse by the fact that the Roman Empire was itself undergoing a long political crisis, a problem that is epitomised by the year 238 CE – the so-called 'Year of the Six Emperors'. As a result, Britain became a hotbed of mutiny and rebellion. More than once Britain was absorbed into breakaway empires, such as the Gallic Empire under the command of Postumus in the mid-third century. Another attempt was made by Carausius. Originally from Belgic Gaul, he had been given the job of ridding the English Channel of the growing number of Frankish and Saxon pirates in 286. Unfortunately for him, his best efforts were deemed inadequate and he was quickly accused of purposely allowing the raids to occur before attacking the pirates so that he could take the loot for himself. He was tried and sentenced to death by the emperor Maximian, so perhaps in an act of desperation or amazing self-belief he proclaimed himself emperor and took control of Britain.[38]

His reign was short-lived, and Britain would be invaded by several more emperors, each trying to reassert their control over the edge of the map, before the eventual withdrawal of troops at the turn of the fifth century. But the reign of Carausius is revealing for the messages he left behind. During his rule, he minted coins that seemed to purposely target local dissatisfaction at Roman rule, referring to himself as *Restitutor Britanniae*: the restorer of Britain. His attempt to annex the land from Roman rule may be seen as somewhat inevitable as Rome grew less capable of managing Britain as a territory, but that would be misleading. As we shall see in the next chapter, some towns at the edges of the empire were capable of devout loyalty to Rome, even when that loyalty does not seem to have been well earned by the Romans.

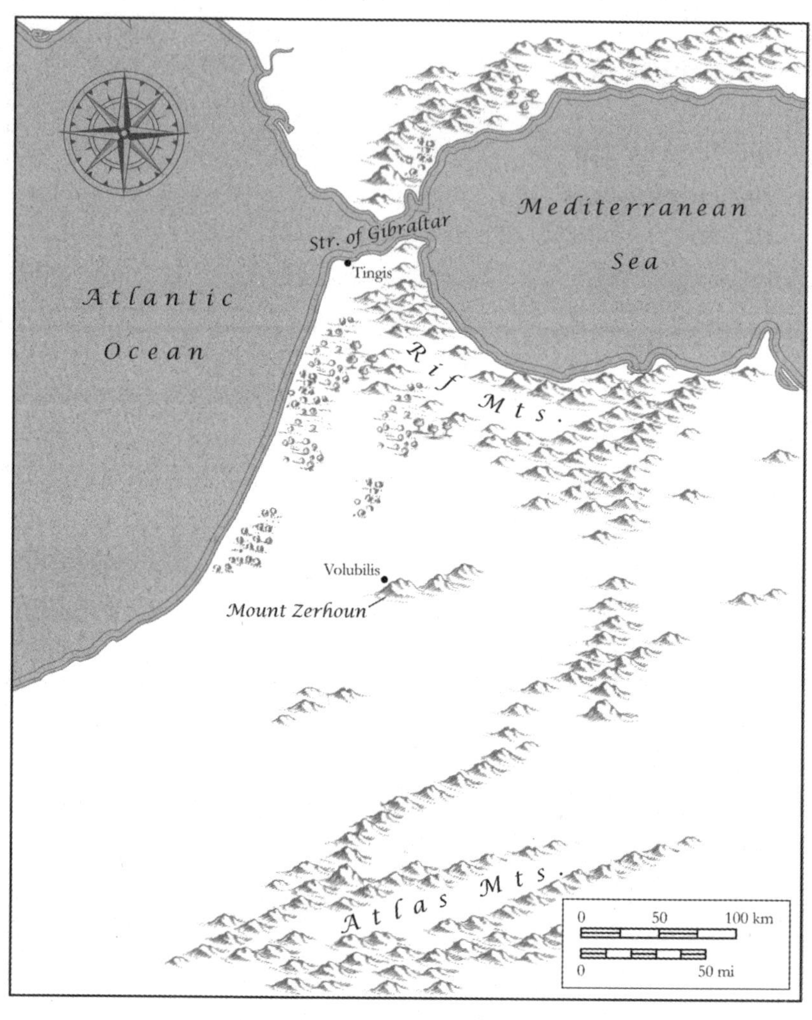
Atlantic
Ocean
Mediterranean
Sea
Str. of Gibraltar
Tingis
Rif Mts.
Volubilis
Mount Zerhoun
Atlas Mts.
0
50
100 km
0
50 mi

# 8

# Volubilis, Morocco

It is easy to look at an ancient object and attribute it to a single culture. Our decision to label it will be based in part on what culture we associate the object with, and in part on which culture we consider most dominant in the region at any given time. However, to do so can often disguise the cultural complexity of what is actually on display. One such object sits in the ruins of an enormous house with more than forty rooms, in the ancient town of Volubilis, which lies about thirty-two kilometres north of Meknes in modern Morocco (ancient Mauretania). The object, from which the house derives its unofficial name, is a mosaic depicting the twelve labours of Hercules.

The mosaic is clearly Roman in style, and the choice of the Greco-Roman hero par excellence was quite a common choice of decoration. The mosaic is very large and covered in geometric patterns, with a number of distinct oval frames inside which sit depictions of the celebrated labours. In vibrant colours that have survived the winds of time, we can clearly make out Hercules wrestling the Cretan bull, hunting the Stymphalian birds, and even his capture of Cerberus, the three-headed hound of hell. The artistic quality, it has to be said, is rather poor even if we take into account that it has been heavily reconstructed. The images lack both depth and definition and do not have the usual dynamism associated with Hercules' legend, but, considering its placement in such a grand house, it must have been expensive. There are certainly more impressive mosaics in other houses at Volubilis, but this one stands out for its depiction, not of one of Hercules' labours, but of a battle he fought along the way. One image shows the hero standing behind another man with his arms around his waist, trying to lift him up. Hercules' opponent here is the half-giant Antaeus, who was said to have ruled in the region in which Volubilis was located.

The story goes that Antaeus was the son of Poseidon, god of the sea, and Gaia, mother earth. While the king of Libya (an ancient name for a land that encompasses all of North Africa to the west of Egypt), Antaeus would take the opportunity whenever he could to challenge travellers to a wrestling match. Being part giant, he was a powerful opponent in his own right, but his close connection with the earth via his mother meant that he was invincible as long as his feet stayed on the ground. Antaeus' matches would always end in the death of his opponent and he would then use the skulls of the fallen to build a temple in honour of his father. One day he made the mistake of challenging the hero Hercules, who was passing through his lands on his way to the Garden of the Hesperides to collect their golden apples. Hercules was the more talented wrestler, but he noticed that each time he almost threw Antaeus to the ground, the giant would be aided by Gaia and thrust upright ready to continue the fight. Hercules changed tactics and began to lift his opponent up, taking his feet off the ground and sapping him of his divinely inspired strength. During one such exercise, Hercules used his own legendary strength and squeezed Antaeus, expelling the breath from his lungs and crushing him to death.[1]

This myth was popular in Greece but, according to our sources, it was also popular in Mauretania. During the early first century BCE, a Roman commander called Quintus Sertorius was taken to the supposed tomb of Artaeus, near the city of Tingis:

> In this city the Libyans say that Antaeus is buried; and Sertorius had his tomb dug open, the great size of which made him disbelieve the Barbarians. But when he came upon the body and found it to be sixty cubits [almost thirty metres] long, as they tell us, he was dumbfounded, and after performing a sacrifice filled up the tomb again, and joined in magnifying its traditions and honours.[2]

As counter-intuitive as it may seem, the mosaic reflects the local myths, beliefs and culture of the 'Libyans' (by which the author, Plutarch, means locals of western Africa) almost as much as those of the Romans. Hercules was a hero of Greece and Italy, and Antaeus was as much of a legend in Mauretania. But the reason it is counter-intuitive is because of how we have been encouraged to see the history of Africa as a passive participant in European or Mediterranean history rather than part of a dynamic exchange of cultures and stories.

The position of Africa in the classical world is often misrepresented. Egypt, with its obvious and impressive cultural achievements, is usually accepted by historians into the ancient Mediterranean story but much of the African continent – what the Greeks and Romans called Libya and its southern region of Aethiopia – is ignored or even discarded unless it plays a part in the story of either Rome or Greece. It has been assumed that the Greeks and Romans looked to the rest of Africa as a barbaric and wild place; an idea influenced, no doubt, by eighteenth- and nineteenth-century ideas more than ancient ones. But our ancient sources do not portray so simple a picture.

In some classical traditions, ancient Libya was the land of the gorgons, of the Amazon warriors, of giants like Antaeus, and the beleaguered Titan Atlas who was punished for his part in the Titanomachy (the Titan War) by being made to hold up the sky. But Libya was also the land of the hero Memnon, king of the Aethiopians, who led an army to Troy to help defend the city and drew blood from the mighty Achilles before the Greek hero was finally able to kill him. Memnon's mother Eos, goddess of the dawn, begged Zeus to give him immortality and this wish was granted.

In many ways, the story of Memnon mirrors that of Achilles: a warrior-leader, with a divine mother who approached the smith-god Hephaestus for special armour, who dies heroically on the battlefield before being granted immortality at the behest of his mother. His story was well known and formed part of the Epic Cycle which tells the broader story of the Trojan War. We do not have a full copy of the epic, the *Aethiopis*, but its synopsis survives in the work of other writers, and scenes from the epic were a popular motif on Greek vases.

The concept of 'Libya' is imbued with a nuance that reflects the Greek and Roman relationships with the African continent. What the Romans called Mauretania, which roughly equates to modern Morocco and parts of Algeria, was considered to be the south-western edge of the world's landmass. It was thought to be buffered up to Oceanus, the waterway that encircled the world's land. Mauretania was a land where myth and wonderment were written into the very landscape with the mountains of Atlas to the east, the Pillars of Hercules to the north and the grave of Antaeus that served as a tourist attraction near the coastal town of Tingis.

For all its mythological status, this area of the world was well known by the sixth century BCE. The Carthaginian navigator Hanno wrote an account of his journey to circumnavigate the continent of Africa, as discussed in Chapter 6, and it begins with his trip around the north-west coast of Mauretania, with mention of a River Lixos, which is most likely a reference to the modern Drâa, the largest river in Morocco. While on his

Selection of bead pendants and earrings discovered in graves at Lake Turkana

CAVRVS·CHORVS·VEL·IAPIX·SIVE·ARGESTES
CIRCTVS VEL TRESIAS
FAVONIVS·ZEPHIRVS
mare glaciale
EVROPA
DATIA
Pontus euxinus
Getulia
Sinus hesperius
LIBIA INTERIOR
AFFRICA
ARABIA
Circulus equinoctialis
Ethiopia
ETHIOPIA·INTERIOR·
Terra incognita sed'm ptholomeum
Sinus Ba
AFRICVS·VEL·LIBS·
LIBONOTVS·EVROAVSTER·

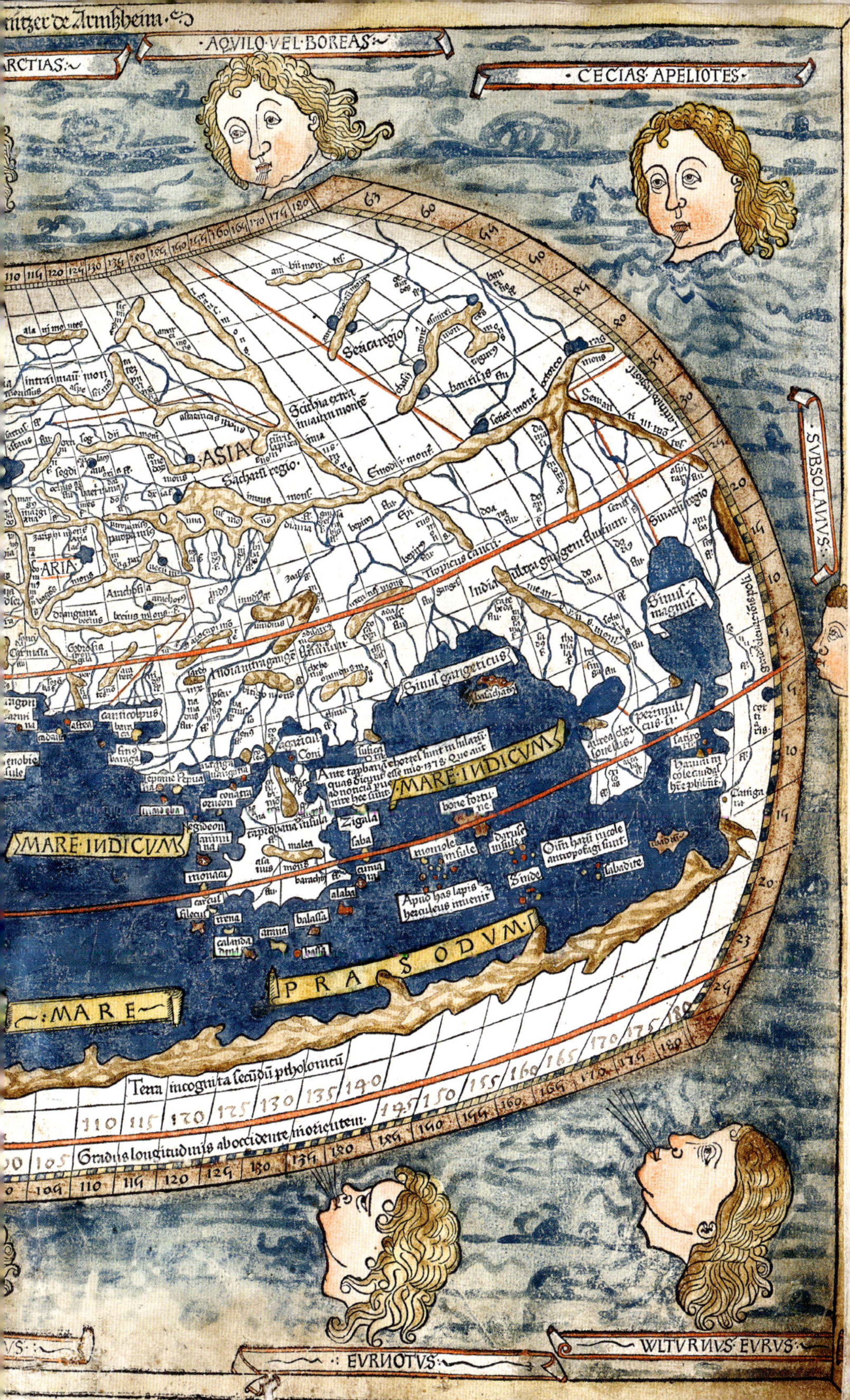

AQVILO VEL BOREAS
CECIAS APELIOTES
SVBSOLANVS
ASIA
ARIA
Sacharū regio
Sithia extra imaum montē
Serica regio
Tropicus cancri
India ultra gangem fluuium
India intra gangem fluuium
Sinus gangeticus
Sinus magnus
MARE INDICVM
MARE INDICVM
Taprobana insula
PRASODVM
MARE
Terra incognita secūdū ptholomeū
Gradus longitudinis ab occidente in orientem
EVRNOTVS
VVLTVRNVS EVRVS

Remaining defences of Buhen Fort

Pillars being transported before the site was flooded

*Previous pages:* A reconstruction of Ptolemy's world map (90–168 CE), by Nicolaus Germanus in 1482 CE

Relief at the Karnak Temple complex of Thutmose III killing Canaanites after the Battle of Megiddo

A selection of the Megiddo ivories dating between 1300–1000 BCE: two female figures either side, and a winged sphinx in the centre

Site of Olbia

Artefacts discovered on the site, including an iconic dolphin-shaped coin or token, beautiful examples of jewellery, and a small vase most likely used for holding perfume or maybe massage oils

GENERAL VIEW OF RUINS OF THE TOWN OF NAUKRATIS.

THE OLD NAUKRATIS-MEMPHIS CANAL, AS DESCRIBED BY HERODOTUS.

MARBLE RAM FROM GATEWAY OF THE GREAT TEMENOS.

Contemporary news report of Petrie's excavations at Naukratis, *The Illustrated London News*, 21 November 1885

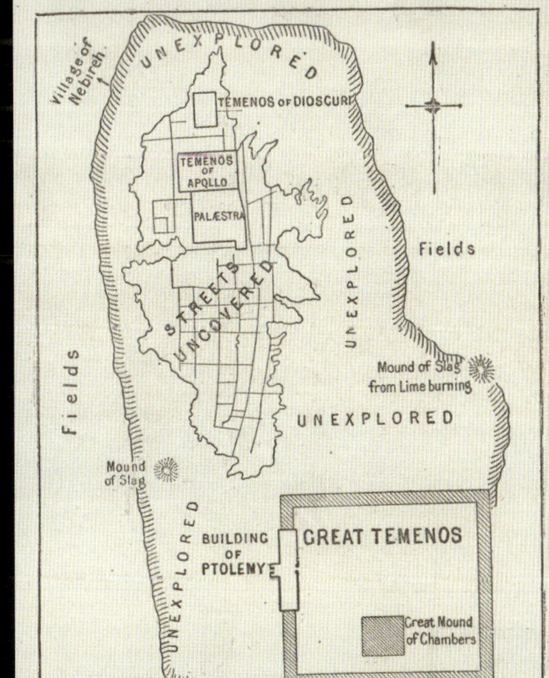


GROUND PLAN OF THE TOWN OF NAUKRATIS, AS EXPLORED BY MR. PETRIE.

Ground plan of the town of Naukratis, *The Illustrated London News*, 21 November 1885

Hadrian's Wall as it stands now, with the appropriate weather

Reconstruction of Roman town at Hadrian's Wall

*Top left:* Staffordshire Moorlands Pan which names some of the forts on Hadrian's Wall. It may have served as a memento or even a souvenir from the frontier.
*Bottom left:* A Gallic imitation of a Massalian coin
*Right:* One of the two Basse-Yutz Flagons, around 400 BCE. The shape is Etruscan in design, the decoration is an early La Tène style, but the swirls in the dog's ears may suggest Scythian influence as well.

Vindolanda tablet from Hadrian's Wall; the handwritten piece is a party invitation written in ink, from Claudia Severa to Lepidina

Hercules mosaic from Volubilis. The top right-hand oval depicts Hercules wrestling with Antaeus.

Volubilis, Morocco, now

Karanis, Egypt, now

Alexander fighting Porus, taken from an early seventeenth-century work from Mughal India

The temple of An Duong Vuong in Co Loa (Hanoi) now

The Trung sisters on war elephants pursuing fleeing Chinese warriors during their failed rebellion. Traditional folk painting from Dong Ho village, twentieth century.

Obelisks at Aksum

Pages from the Garima Gospels between circa 330 CE and circa 600 CE

journey, he describes founding colonies, seeing wildlife such as elephants, and also meeting with local people:

> Continuing our voyage from there, we reached the Lixos, a large river flowing from Libya. The Lixites, a nomadic tribe, were pasturing their cattle beside it. We remained with them for some time and became friends.[3]

The name given to these local inhabitants has changed time and again. The Greeks referred to them as an ethnic group called the Mauri. This name transformed into the word Moor, which took over as the collective term for people in the region. But before long the word Moor became a pejorative, meaning simply North African 'savages'. The Arabic term Berber, first attested in the medieval period, is the more common one used today to describe the indigenous people living in Mauretania but to use it in the ancient world creates the illusion of unity, suggesting that the people of Mauretania had a shared culture and language family. The evidence suggests that this was not entirely true.

The nomadic lifestyle mentioned by Hanno becomes a common trope when describing the Berbers living in Mauretania, but Mauretania was a land of varying landscapes. It has high mountain ranges, arid steppes and coastal plains, and is also cut up by deep river valleys. Each ecosystem offered new opportunities for its inhabitants and encouraged different ways of life. As a result, we hear of nomadic cultures, semi-nomadic pastoralists and more sedentary lifestyles, too.[4]

Hanno came from Carthage, a city situated on the coast of modern Tunisia near what is today Tunis. Carthage was itself a colony of the Phoenicians, who lived in the Levant region and were famed mariners, but the Carthaginians had by the time of Hanno established themselves as an independent city-state with a strong economic and cultural influence in north-western Africa. The Carthaginians originally focused on the Western Mediterranean and the West African coastlines, but their desire for more trading goods drove them inland. One such town was founded in southern Mauretania around the third century BCE, on the foothills of Mount Zerhoun, which was twenty days' travel from Carthage itself. Set on a triangular plateau, it overlooked a fertile valley that has evidence of human habitation stretching back 5,000 years. The Punic town was most likely built on, or an extension of, a local settlement, one that was named after a local shrub that grows in abundance in the region: the oleander. In Amazigh, the Berber language family, the name of this plant is *Walilt* which, it is believed, was Latinised into the name Volubilis.

Volubilis was not a large town, but pre-Roman remains reveal the foundations of Punic temples, a mausoleum dedicated to a member of the local elite, sanctuaries and funeral stelae inscribed in both Punic and Libyan languages. It was run in the Carthaginian tradition, with magistrates using the title of *suffet*, but the presence of inscriptions in local languages does suggest that there was not simply an imposition of Punic culture but that local Mauri or other Berber people were incorporated into the town.

Its founding in the third century BCE is interesting, considering what was happening in the Mediterranean at this time. Unfortunately, we do not have any written accounts from the Carthaginians explaining why Volubilis was established, but it is perhaps no coincidence that the third century saw Carthage engage in two brutal wars with the growing power of Rome. In 264 BCE, the two powerful city-states went to war and dragged with them their extended network of client states and allies. The First Punic War would continue until 241 BCE when an uneasy peace treaty was signed, but a second war would break out in 218 BCE – the famous campaign of Hannibal Barca.

Carthage relied heavily on its North African territories for both produce and manpower. During the latter years of the First Punic War, the historian Polybius tells us that they doubled their demands on towns like Volubilis, requiring 50 per cent of their agricultural produce rather than the usual 25 per cent. It is unlikely that Volubilis was established to increase this revenue stream during the war, but it would not have been long before the strains of war started to take their toll on the small town. By the time of Hannibal, we have one of the first historical mentions of the Mauri people:

> With his brother Hasdrubal in Iberia he left ... cavalry consisting of eighteen hundred Numidians of the Massolian, Massarsylian, Maccoeian and Maurian tribes, who dwell by the ocean.[5]

As we saw with the Celts previously, Roman authors can seem inconsistent in their labelling of foreign people. Numidia was an African kingdom which incorporated much of Mauretania, and of the tribal groups mentioned it is only the Mauri who are regularly referenced in the surviving source material.

Following Rome's successful defeat of the Carthaginians in 201 BCE, any immediate interest they had in the region focused on the lands around Carthage itself. In fact, they held very little interest in the lands of Mauretania and, for the next 400 years, this attitude never really changed.

* * *

Writing in the first century BCE, the Roman historian Sallust gives an account of the Jugurthine War (112 106 BCE) between Rome and the king of the north-west African kingdom of

Numidia, Jugurtha. During this war, Mauretania and by extension Volubilis was ruled by Jugurtha's father-in-law, Bocchus I, who initially allied himself with the Numidians before betraying him to the Romans in exchange for a cut of his kingdom. Bocchus had the moment immortalised in a ring he gifted to the Roman officer to whom he handed over Jugurtha. This officer's name was Lucius Cornelius Sulla Felix, and he would later become one of the most notorious dictators of Rome.

The role of Bocchus is pivotal for the narrative of Sallust's history, so his introduction to the king is important:

> The whole of the Mauri were governed by Bocchus, a king who knew nothing of the Romans but their name, and who, before this period, was little known to us, either in war or peace.[6]

Bocchus' support for the Romans brought the region into the Roman psyche, but not enough to directly take control. Roman intervention in Mauretania was usually limited to being supportive of a local regime. The Roman commander we met earlier, Sertorius, who visited the tomb of Antaeus, was in the region around 80 BCE to help Bocchus' successor, his son Mastanesosus, secure his rule in the north. It was not until 33 BCE that it came under direct Roman rule, and even then it was not for very long.

During the civil wars in Rome – firstly between Julius Caesar and Pompey the Great, and then during the Liberators Civil War between Caesar's heir Octavian and his ally Mark Antony on one side and the enemies of Caesar on the other, before finally the war between Octavian and Antony themselves – the co-rulers of Mauretania were the grandsons of Bocchus I: Bocchus II, who ruled in the east, and Bogudes, who ruled in the west, possibly using Volubilis as his seat of power.[7] Caesar had acknowledged their co-rule and gained their support as a result, but during the war between Octavian and Antony the brothers chose opposing sides. Bogudes chose incorrectly and supported the doomed Antony, allowing Bocchus II to take control of his half with the support of Octavian. On Bocchus II's death in 33 BCE, with the civil war still raging, the king gifted the crown not to his brother or any other family member, but to Octavian himself. Octavian in turn gifted the kingdom to a Numidian prince, Juba II. This decision seems to have been an astutely political one.

Juba's father, Juba I of Numidia, had sided against Caesar in his war with Pompey and was part of the defeated loyalist forces at the Battle of Thapsus in 46 BCE. The elder Juba took his own life before his capture, but his young son was taken to Rome and was part of the victory triumph for Caesar:

> Then Juba, his son who was a mere infant, was carried along in the triumphal procession, the most fortunate captive ever taken, since from being a barbarian and a Numidian, he came to be enrolled among the most learned historians of Greece.[8]

Juba II would grow up to become a real polymath and scholar, writing books on a variety of topics from history and geography to painting and theatre. His works do not survive today in full, but they are regularly quoted by surviving authors such as Pliny, Plutarch and Galen, and he is referenced by writers as a well-respected expert in a diverse range of subjects. But his education was not solely academic. He was raised in the household of Caesar and then Octavian, joining the latter on military expeditions.

Around the year 25 BCE, Octavian, who had by now been given the title of Augustus by the Roman senate, chose Juba to rule Mauretania and run it as a client kingdom. In addition, Augustus decided to cement the political potency of this decision by offering him the opportunity to marry a woman of royal pedigree from another North African kingdom – Cleopatra Selene, the daughter of Cleopatra VII and Mark Antony. In effect, Augustus had solved numerous problems at the same time by uniting the children of his past enemies and rewarding them handsomely for their loyalty to him and to Rome. For it was a reward. Mauretania may have been palmed off by the Romans time and again, but the lands of Mauretania were very wealthy, and Juba and Cleopatra wasted little time in making the kingdom their own.

Much of the pre-Roman remains of Volubilis are dated to this period. We cannot be certain how much directly coincides with the reign of Juba II, but many temple foundations and shrines have been dated by archaeologists to the first century. Unfortunately, the Mauretanian shape of the city is hard to deduce. As we have seen in previous chapters, the history of cities on the peripheries is at the whim of the interests of the earliest researchers and Volubilis is no exception. The first wave of archaeologists were more interested in the Roman remains and so the earliest layers of the city are still in need of the systematic research that is now happening. We do know that in the Roman Imperial period, Volubilis was producing large quantities of olive oil; this is a tradition that may have preceded the Romans, if the discovery of a pre-Roman olive mill in the south-eastern corner of the city is anything to go by.[9]

Juba and Cleopatra merged their respective cultural influences, blending Greek, Roman, Punic, Egyptian and Mauri cultures as they invested in their kingdom. It was something they could easily achieve over 2,000 kilometres away from the judging eyes of Rome. While their direct investment in Volubilis is, thus far, difficult to date accurately, we know that the pre-Roman city had a structured urban centre to match any Greek or Roman town. It was predominantly populated by local Mauri people, but it tapped into the wider Mediterranean trade networks, as proven by the discoveries of vases from Italy and coins from Spain, as well as bronze statues and busts most likely imported from Greece or Italy. One bronze bust depicting Juba II is a particularly striking example.

It is also probable that Volubilis was an important part of a growing trade route for a very special form of timber between Mauretania and the Roman world. Pliny the Elder writes in the first century CE about a citronwood, the forests of which populated the Atlas Mountains, that was used to make fine tables that were the envy of all who did not have one. He mentions two antique tables owned by Juba II being sold at auction for the equivalent of millions of pounds sterling in modern money, similar in many ways to how mahogany has been coveted in modern times. One highly desired attribute was to have knots in the wood, which apparently added to the esteem and value of the table. The irony of this defect, in addition to the desirability, was not lost on Pliny who notes 'that which we buy at so high a price is in reality a defect in the tree'.[10]

Following Cleopatra's death at the turn of the Common Era, Juba chose a new co-ruler to help him command his large kingdom, his son Ptolemy. Named after the paternal line on his mother's side, Ptolemy epitomised the cultural complexity of his parentage, their histories and the manner in which they ruled Mauretania. Ptolemy was raised in the same vein as his father, possibly even being sent to Rome from a young age. He was proud of his Egyptian and Mauretanian cultural heritages, but while co-ruler he fashioned his image most often in the vein of the Julio-Claudian emperors in Rome, stressing his youthful face and with a characteristic hairstyle that models those of the imperial family.[11] He maintained an interest in Greek culture, which held a strong influence over him throughout his education. As he grew older, he would even portray himself with a beard in the Greek style – showing his ability to transform his image according to his intended audience.[12] We also know that he invested money in the city of Athens: the Greek travel writer Pausanias describes a *gymnasium* in the city that was funded by Ptolemy and included statues of him and his father.[13]

When Juba II died in 23 CE, Ptolemy became the final king of Mauretania and also the last Ptolemy to rule an ancient kingdom. He was able to rule amicably alongside the Roman emperor Tiberius, even helping him to subdue a Numidian uprising led by Tacfarinas in 24 CE, for which he was awarded an ancient honour of an ivory sceptre and magnificent robe; the Romans also bestowed upon him the titles of 'king, ally and friend'.[14] But his esteemed position would not survive a regime change in Rome itself. In 37 CE, Tiberius died and was succeeded by the notorious Gaius (Caligula). Within three years of his succession, Gaius had Ptolemy murdered and Mauretania had become an official province of the empire. The motivations behind his assassination are not clear-cut. Some sources claim it was related to how wealthy Ptolemy was and how that wealth was displayed during a fatal trip to Rome, but some modern scholars have argued that Ptolemy may have been involved in a failed conspiracy against Gaius.[15]

The death of Ptolemy threw all Mauretania into disarray. A popular ruler who had overseen an affluent reign, Ptolemy was a king who represented the glory of the region. His familial links to famous North African rulers included Hannibal Barca, and even stretched back, according to his father, as far as Tinga, the consort to the Libyan giant Antaeus who was killed by Hercules, which, when combined with his maternal links to Egypt, ensured a legitimacy and acceptance to his rule.[16] After his assassination, Mauretania witnessed a revolt led by an elusive figure called Aedemon. Aedemon was said to be a freedman, a former slave, of Mauri origin who owed his freedom to his enslaver, Ptolemy.[17] The revolt was widespread, but not everyone in Mauretania sided with their kinsmen. In the isolated town of Volubilis, the inhabitants stood firm in their loyalty to Rome. Part of the city was destroyed by fire at this time, suggesting that this was not simply an ideological stand but one that brought aggression and retribution upon the city.[18]

The impact of the revolt on Volubilis must have been extreme. The city did survive and Aedemon's revolt was put down but not on Caligula's orders. Caligula was killed in 41 CE and succeeded by his uncle Claudius, who sent experienced commanders to bring an end to the issues in North Africa. Claudius rewarded the commander of Volubilis' auxilia, whose name survives thanks to an inscription found in the city that was erected by his wife, Fabia Bira:

> In honour of Marcus Valerius Severus, son of Bostar, of the tribe Galeria, *aedile*, *sufes*, *duovir* and the first high priest in his city, leader of the auxilia against Aedemon, who was defeated in war; because of his services to the state and the success of his mission, when he gained for his fellow citizens from deified Claudius Roman citizenship ...[19]

Marcus Severus' embassy secured Roman citizenship for his fellow citizens and the right to marry non-citizen wives, allowing for the continued integration of Mauri into the city. But then Claudius offered more, which is suggestive of how much Volubilis needed to recover from the war: he exempted them from paying taxes for ten years and allowed more settlers and inhabitants to join the city. He also allowed the disposal of property and wealth left behind by those who died in the conflict without any living heirs.

Volubilis had now become a Roman city, a *municipium*. It has been fairly argued by historians that the city continued to 'Romanise', that is to adopt Roman cultural practices and systems of operation, a process it had been undertaking since the reign of Juba II. Yet we can still see in this inscription the full heritage of the city. Marcus Severus may have had a Roman name, and many Roman positions of office, but he had also served as a *sufes*, the Punic term for a magistrate. His father, Bostar, had a fairly common Punic name, while his wife's name Bira and that of his in-laws, Izelta, are Mauri in origin. Indeed, citizens of Volubilis would often adopt the Roman custom of using three names (*tria nomina*) to appear Roman, or to display their citizenship, but within these names, much like with Fabia Bira, we can see their Mauri and Punic heritage as well.[20]

* * *

Walking around the modern site of Volubilis, it is the Roman vision of the city that comes through most strongly. The city grew exponentially with the support and investment of Roman finance, growing from its pre-Roman footprint of around fifteen hectares to its largest size of over forty hectares. At its height, the town played host to maybe 12,000 people.[21] There was not a mass influx of migrants, but we do see the multicultural empire on display in surviving inscriptions such as a dedication to Mithras made by a Roman centurion called Aurelius Nectoreca, who was originally from Britain and was stationed in the area.[22] There was also a synagogue with funerary inscriptions in a variety of languages. One particularly poignant one was in honour of Matrona, the daughter of the Rabbi, which is thus far unique in the city for its use of Hebrew.[23]

Between the first and third centuries CE we can see many of the hallmarks of a Roman provincial town appearing: the city walls and gates, aqueducts, public fountains, baths. There is also a triumphal arch dedicated to the Berber emperor of Rome, Caracalla Severus, in 217 CE, which in a rather cruel twist of fate was the year he was murdered – we do not know if he was killed before or after the arch was completed. Towards the south you can still see the remnants of the forum, the beating administrative heart of the city, with the remains of the Capitoline temple – dedicated to a holy triad of Jupiter, Juno and Minerva – still standing nearby. The lasting Roman impression of the site has left its mark on many visitors over the years, none more so than General George S. Patton, who wrote in his diary following his own visit to the site in January 1943:

> Harmon and I could not but think that we, the modern equivalent of a Legate, were walking the very streets where our predecessors had walked in shining brass 2,000 years ago.[24]

The remaining temple ruins and columns are romantic and evocative to walk through, but it is the domestic spaces within the city that give Volubilis its fame. The concentration of impressive villas is indicative of the accumulated wealth for the local elite. Many of these families' names are lost to history, but the houses retain the names of their most striking features, their mosaics. We have already seen the House of the Labours of Hercules, with its less than perfect artistry. In contrast there is the House of Venus, a most luxurious home with its own private baths and impressive mosaics. The mosaic to which it owes its name is now housed in the Kasbah Museum, Tangier, but you can still see others in their original positions depicting famous scenes from mythology. Even with these grand houses there are firsts among equals, with the House of Orpheus in the south a particularly impressive example. Its large and varied mosaics, dedicated pool with its own marine-themed mosaics, and bath suites with underfloor heating, betray the opulence and comfort that this villa must have exuded in its heyday.

The regular discovery of olive presses in the town, including within many of these grand villas, is a constant reminder of where this money came from. They were ancient oil tycoons: agricultural barons offering employment and pay in exchange for hard labour and their own excessive personal profits. The growth in agricultural commerce alongside that of the population in and around Volubilis meant that the Roman settlement required more land in the surrounding area for food production. This brought them into conflict with local, nomadic Mauri groups; in particular we hear about one group called the Baquates people, who relied on much of the land in the valley for pasture during the autumn and winter months.[25] Rising tensions between the two peoples no doubt encouraged the Romans to increase their military presence in the region, as evidenced by the number of Roman camps that have been identified.

A collection of eleven inscriptions dating from 168 to 280 CE records regular peace treaties between rulers of the Baquates – usually given the title *princeps* or, on one occasion, *rex* – and the Roman governor of Mauretania Tingitana (the Roman province which incorporated the western part of Mauretania). In the absence of any historical narrative describing this period of discontent between the two cultures we are left to piece together these small snapshots of diplomatic concordance. The clustering of these inscriptions within a period of about a century suggests that each agreement was built on shaky ground. A sympathetic reading would note that each inscription contains the name of a different ruler of the Baquates people, so perhaps these are reassertions of the cordial détente with each succession of leadership. However, we know that during this period the city walls of Volubilis were reinforced. We also know that before 168 CE the Baquates were implicated in the raiding of towns in Mauretania alongside other Mauri groups. So the idea that some or maybe most of these recorded agreements may reflect sporadic outbursts of violence or raids is not unrealistic. By the third century, they suggest that the Baquates were making alliances with other Mauri communities – one such alliance with the neighbouring Bavares forced the local garrison to be reinforced by more troops, suggesting this was a little more sinister than a simple pastureland dispute.[26]

The Romans did try different methods of control over the Baquates. In a few inscriptions we see the adoption of Roman *nomen* by their leaders, suggesting that they were given citizenship. Although, rather ominously, these names are often followed chronologically by a ruler without a Roman *nomen*, suggesting that this policy did not guarantee any success.

For the people of Volubilis, these raids and the constant failure to control the Baquates were exacerbated by just how isolated the town was from the rest of the Roman world. The nomadic or pastoralist lifestyle of the Baquates was considered the antithesis of Roman identity, something lacking the civilised ideals held by members of the empire. Sallust described nomads in Africa as such:

> [They were] rude and uncivilized tribes, who subsisted on the flesh of wild animals, or, like cattle, on the herbage of the soil. They were controlled neither by customs, laws, nor the authority of any ruler; they wandered about, without fixed habitations, and slept in the abodes to which night drove them.[27]

Needless to say, this prevalent attitude towards nomadism shows no attempt to understand it on its own terms. Even more sympathetic observers, such as Diodorus of Sicily, who describes their culture as 'not entirely savage or different from that of civilized men', cannot help but contrast the way they lived with a sedentary lifestyle. So, too, we may assume, the people of Volubilis – with their blending of Mauri, Punic, Greek and Roman cultures and people – saw themselves compared to the nomadic Baquates.

But this is to look at Volubilis through purely Roman eyes. The people may have enjoyed Roman citizenship, and emulated Roman elite culture, but they were still descendants of a local elite with a strong sense of identity. Nowhere is this clearer than in 284 CE, when the Roman emperor Diocletian had brought the chaotic third century's political crises to an end. As part of his stabilising reforms for the empire he made the decision to shore up the boundaries; in Mauretania, this meant abandoning much of the land to the south including Volubilis. The administrative and military abandonment of a town could very easily lead to its demise, but this was not the case here. Volubilis continued as normal. In fact, we know that some of the grand mosaics commissioned in the large villas date to *after* this period of Roman withdrawal, which suggests two things: one, the local elite stayed; and, two, the city remained as connected to the Mediterranean trade networks as it ever was.

We can assume that relations with the Basquates and other local groups must have improved, as there is no evidence of either peace agreements or attacks on the town. Perhaps the Roman withdrawal freed up some agricultural land, allowing for a re-establishment of pasturage for the pastoralists. We do not know. What we do know is that Volubilis was not abandoned until the fifth century CE, following a devastating earthquake. But considering its fertile location, the site would not remain abandoned for long. A new, unknown group moved in and built on the western slope of the town, creating another stage of evolution for Volubilis. It had already seen dominant cultures come and go, but each one left a small part of itself behind. This created a unique microcosm of the ancient world, where Carthage and Rome became blended, and Egyptian culture merged with that of the nomadic Mauri. It highlights the lack of homogeneity at the edges of the world, where personal identities do not disappear just because political powers change hands. Even at this later date, following the fall of the Western Roman Empire, we see continuity. The discovery of Latin inscriptions dating to the sixth and seventh centuries and using the Roman dating system suggests that the Roman shadow still loomed over this isolated place.[28]

Mediterranean
Sea
Alexandria
Canopic
Rosetta
Nile
Delta
Damietta
Naucratis
Cairo
Giza
Memphis
Karanis
Philadelphia
Faiyum
Lake
Moeris
Oasis
Nile
Antinoopolis
0
50
100 km
0
50 mi

# 9

# Karanis, Egypt

Sometimes, living on the periphery and away from the cultural or political centres of the world can be as much a feeling as it is a physical reality. Unlike northern Britain or southern Mauretania, which were isolated locations far at the edge of the Roman Empire or any major cultural centres, our final Roman example is nothing of the sort. Located in the rich and fertile lands of the Faiyum Oasis to the south-west of Giza and modern Cairo, the small village of Karanis would appear to be well situated within the wider Roman world. Egypt was distant from Rome, but, as we have seen in previous chapters, it was a thriving cultural region that attracted Greeks, Persians and Romans. To describe Greco-Roman Egypt – the name given to the period spanning from the first Macedonian ruler Alexander the Great's invasion in 332 BCE to the Arabic annexation in 646 CE – as somehow peripheral or on the edge of the known world is not very accurate. But this does not mean that many people felt this way.

By the time of Roman rule, following Octavian's victory over Mark Antony and the final Ptolemaic ruler of Egypt, Cleopatra VII, in 30 BCE, Egypt was a complex and intricate blend of Egyptian, Greek and Roman culture. The city of Alexandria was a beacon of knowledge and learning, drawing scholars from around the empire to its famous library and museum. The city was Greek in design, on the orders of its namesake Alexander the Great, but it incorporated non-Greek ideas, such as Egyptian and Jewish knowledge, into the fold. As such, Egypt sat in a unique position within the Roman Empire, maintaining this cultural blend at both social and political levels. Superficially, however, we may think that it appears almost inclusive in its approach. Unfortunately, this was not the case.

One key issue was that many of these historically dominant cultural identities held different statuses in Roman Egypt. For the Romans created a legal hierarchy: Roman citizens, citizens of the three Greek cities – Naucratis, Alexandria, Ptolemaios, and later Antinoopolis – and then the Egyptians (i.e. everyone else). This hierarchy did not actually take into account whether a person was or was not Greek, Egyptian, Jewish or Nubian for instance; what mattered was citizenship. So, a Greek who was not a citizen of Rome, or one of the named cities, was by legal definition an 'Egyptian' and liable to pay poll tax. A further exception was made for the descendants of Greek settlers in the Faiyum region, but still, this did not account for every Greek in Egypt.

To add further tension, the administrative language of Egypt was by this time Greek and, thanks to Ptolemaic rule, Egyptian culture was very Hellenised with its local political structures, magistracies and even its elite social clubs (*gymnasia*) emulating Greek practices. Even before Roman rule, these cultural tensions were insurmountable for many, including one poor trader who wrote a letter to a Greek businessman called Zenon, complaining of his treatment at the hands of Zenon's clients on account of his non-Greek status:

> They have treated me with scorn because I am a 'barbarian'. I beg you therefore, if it seems good to you, to give them orders that I am to obtain what is owing and that in future they pay me in full, in order that I may not perish of hunger because I do not know how to act like a Greek.[1]

But it was not all one-way. A petition survives from a Greek recluse named Ptolemaeus who lived in the Serapaeum, a sanctuary dedicated to the goddess Serapis, in Memphis, dating from 161 BCE, who asked his local magistrate to intervene with the violent abuse he was receiving from the local Egyptians:

> [T]hey came to the temple of Astarte in the sanctuary . . . some of them holding stones in their hands, others sticks, and tried to force their way in, so that with this opportunity they might plunder the temple and kill me because I am a Greek, attacking me in concerted fashion.[2]

His letter goes on to remind the magistrate that Ptolemaeus had already sent a petition complaining about these same people attacking him in a similar way before, but nothing had been done about it.

It is very easy to get lost in the larger narratives at play in Egypt – not least the revolts and violence in Alexandria that pitted Greek and Jew against one another. But what letters such as these remind us is that these tensions occurred in the everyday lives of people up and down Egypt. For the people of Karanis, these were just part and parcel of life in the Faiyum.

* * *

The drive from Cairo to the modern site of Karanis, now called Kom Aushim, takes only forty minutes, but your approach brings you into what seems like an entirely different world from the hustle and bustle of the city and the barren landscape of the desert. For Karanis sits almost exactly at the point where the beige hues of the rocky, sand-littered tundra transform into a riot of green that is the tell-tale sign that you have reached the Faiyum Oasis.

The oasis is not, as is usually the case, formed from a natural source of local water but is fed by the Bahr Yussef, an ancient canal that connects the region to the Nile. This canal system empties into Lake Moeris, which sits just to the west of Karanis. This lake, now saline, was fresh-watered in the ancient period and served as a vital lifeline to the many villages that grew in the area. Herodotus described the lake as a magnificent wonder during his own travels in the region, and observed with candid respect how it was reliant on man-made canals and responsible for considerable income through the trade of fish.[3]

The village itself is, paradoxically, unremarkable and yet unique in the ancient world – not for what it once was, but for what it has become. Karanis was a small and relatively poor rural village that relied on its agricultural produce to make money. The village has no large villas to walk through or fancy housing, and while its three temples are still in good condition for the modern tourist to walk around, they are of an appropriately modest size for the location. However, it was never the architecture or the grandeur of the site that interested its earliest excavators:

> We have seen the letters these people [of Karanis] wrote to one another, the accounts they kept in business transactions, the kinds of food they ate, the grain they planted in their irrigated plots of land, the cloth they wove to make their garments, the wooden boxes in which they stored their treasures, the glass that must have been highly cherished, the pottery that served as common household ware, the toys that delighted the hearts of their children, the lamps that gave such feeble light . . . The people who wrote and read the papyri, which have become so valuable as source material for the history of this period, are revealed to us as a living people in a living town.[4]

As a result of the arid conditions, the material remains at Karanis are simply astonishing. As stated by Enoch Peterson, the director of excavations at the site during the 1920s and 1930s quoted above, we have organic material still in good condition such as wooden boxes, clothing, shoes, even wooden toys that were loved and cherished by local children. Equally important is the survival of papyri, a writing material made from the ubiquitous papyrus plant, which survive to record everything from private letters to accounts and tax returns.

These discoveries are made all the more pertinent because many of the written documents that have been found were hidden away by their ancient owners. That is to say, researchers have found what amounts almost to family archives, bundles of paperwork and important documents that an ancient Egyptian, Greek or Roman citizen deemed important enough to stash away for safe-keeping. This gives us access to useful documents we otherwise do not often see in ancient excavations, such as leases and land deeds; but it also means that we know any letters found were of some emotional or legal importance to the person or family who decided to keep them. These can usefully be supplemented by more papyri that have been unearthed around Karanis and some other sites in the Faiyum, no doubt discarded as rubbish at one time or another. All this material gives us an amazing insight into ordinary, everyday life in Karanis and other villages in the Faiyum that is unmatched anywhere else in the ancient world.

* * *

Karanis was one of many villages founded in the region by the second member of the Ptolemaic dynasty, Ptolemy II Philadelphus, following his reclamation project to secure more fertile land in the area. Ptolemy II was also in the process of reorganising the infrastructure of Egypt, breaking up the land into administrative lots called *nomes*. Karanis sat in the newly established Arsinoite *nome*, named after Ptolemy's sister-wife

Arsinoe II, and it greatly benefited from Ptolemy's other important decision to reinvest in the irrigation and canal systems throughout the Faiyum. This was not done out of the goodness of the king's heart but had two important payoffs: first, it secured and exploited an agriculturally rich area of Egypt; second, it gave him valuable land to donate to the military veterans who had helped him secure peace in the east with the Seleucid kingdom. These parcels of lands, called *kleroi*, established an important social hierarchy in Karanis from its very foundation. The owners of these estates, the local elite, were both veterans and usually Greeks or Macedonians, while the farming and labouring was performed by Egyptians who were moved into the village from elsewhere.

Unlike our earlier example of a town established in Egypt for Greek veterans, Naucratis (Chapter 5), the veteran identity of Karanis remained ever-present, even when the Romans took control of Egypt. Much like the Ptolemies before them, Rome incentivised military service with the offer of citizenship and sometimes land, placement in established veteran colonies, or a golden handshake to help them set themselves up in retirement. So, while we know that veterans were living there in the Ptolemaic period, all our evidence and family archives for them date from the Roman Imperial period (first–fifth centuries CE).

Our history books often focus on the domineering presence of the mighty Roman army and its role in forging an empire, but we often forget that those same men had then to leave the army and pick up life in a civilian world – a world in which they had not really existed for nigh on twenty-five years and were finally re-entering in their forties or even fifties. The transition was not always an easy one. Those lucky enough to have strong family connections in their homeland would have had support, but at Karanis we know of one veteran named Terentianus who was in need of help:

> Valerius Paulinus also called Ammonas, to his brother Valerius Apollinarius, warmest greeting. I want you to know that I am in military service next year only, and (then) I am released: if the god wishes, I will come to reverence your countenance along with the ancestral gods. Now then I ask you, receive with my recommendation the discharged soldier Terentianus who brings you this letter, and let him know what sort of villagers we have, lest he get into trouble.[5]

Paulinus' concern for his comrade is clear throughout the letter, but it also points to a rather lonely reality for Terentianus. He is not returning to his own family for support, but is, rather, relying on the extended social networks from his brothers-in-arms. We are told that Terentianus was a man of means, capable of renting a house by himself, but that it is his social relationships he needs support with.

Paulinus' letter of recommendation here does more than simply make his brother aware of a friend coming to town; it establishes a peer support for the veteran as he starts life in his new home, creating links that branch out like the 'threads of a spider's web' spreading through the community and out into neighbouring villages.[6] Accordingly, it is not a unique form of letter. We have another, written by a veteran from Karanis called Gaius Iulius Nepotianus who swore the 'oath customary for the Romans ... to be surety for the stay and appearance of Iulius Saturnilus, veteran, landholder in the same village'.[7]

This network was valuable, but exclusive to a limited elite. In the surviving tax lists between 171 and 174 CE, the village had no more than 14 per cent of its population using Roman names and therefore enjoying citizenship. We cannot know how many of these were veterans – this was not recorded on these lists – but it is presumably far fewer still considering that many of these would be legacy citizenships inherited from earlier generations who earned their status through military service.[8] What we do know is that their elite status was not particularly tied to personal wealth. While we do have examples of veterans leaving large tracts of land in their will, this is not the norm and many would not have been notably more affluent than their neighbours. Their social position was instead tied to their unique legal status in the Roman Empire.

Veterans of the Roman army were granted many things once they were honourably discharged. In particular, they were exempted from certain civic obligations. To be granted this was no simple feat, especially at a time when photographic ID did not exist and anyone could easily claim to be someone else. The solution was effective, if a little simple. We have the examination records for one Valerius Clemens which were conducted to clarify his veteran status; in it he is described as having an identifying mark: 'Valerius Clemens, aged 52, with a scar above the right ankle.'[9]

The underlying premise to this reward for veterans was that a man who had spent the majority of his adult life serving the empire had earned the right to no longer serve. This at least was the idea, but the experience of one poor veteran in Karanis suggests that it was not always the case:

> It has been laid down sir, that veterans after their discharge have a period of five years' respite. Contrary to this ruling, I was threatened after two years of my respite and was arbitrarily chosen for compulsory public service, and up until the present moment I have been continuously performing those services without a break.[10]

The writer of this petition is well known in the papyrological records. His name is Gaius Julius Apollinarius and he served in *legio III Cyrenaica*, which was one of three legions stationed in

Egypt during the second century CE. His career was aided by his father, Gaius Julius Sabinus, who had served in the same legion. Apollinarius' military career took him as far away as Arabia, but his family archive has preserved letters he sent as a soldier as well as those he wrote later as a veteran, following his discharge at the age of forty-eight. His letter here highlights a discontent, a sense of injustice no doubt felt by many veterans in Karanis. His claim ends with outright incredulity. Not only was he being asked to do something he had no obligation to do as a veteran, but the fact that he was also being made to continuously perform his duties without a break was forbidden for everyone, including the Egyptians. His concern was not that there was injustice for all, but, in his own words, that 'the rule ought to be more strictly observed in my case since I have served for such a long time in the army'.

Apollinarius, for all his experience and long-standing ties in Karanis alongside that of his father, was learning a difficult lesson for many at the far edges of the Roman provinces: legal protection is only as good as the officials who are executing it. But he was not alone: we hear in another petition by a group of veterans their concern for what they witnessed on a visit to the Temple of the Caesars in Philadelphia, a village just down the road from Karanis:

> We were in the village of Philadelphia in the Arsinoite nome ... at the temple of the Caesars, and that is how we happened to see Gaius Maevius Apelles, veteran of the Appian division, being flogged with rods and scourges by two guards on orders of the *strategos* [chief official] Hierax.[11]

Veterans were supposed to be exempt from being beaten as a form of punishment. They were also protected from being condemned to the beasts in the arena, from working in the mines and any public works. In the case of Gaius Maevius Apelles here, it seems the *strategos* – a chief official in the nome of Arsinoite – has chosen to ignore this.[12]

Of course, the lives of these veterans were not all focused on personal rights violations and legal petitions; this is just a survival bias in our source material. Veterans were no different from any other citizen in the empire: family was at the heart of their lives. From the private letters we see the omnipresence of important women in their lives, from mothers and wives to sisters and aunts: the love between family members is palpable on the papyri. One rather poignant example was written by Apollinarius to his mother Tasoucharion while he was still serving in the military in 108 CE. He was stationed in Arabia at the time, while his mother had moved to the big city of Alexandria with his father and siblings, so the fact that this letter was kept safe is therefore rather notable and indicative of its sentimental importance. Perhaps with good reason:

> My lady mother, many greetings. Before all else, I pray for your good health ... For each time I remind myself of you, I do not eat, nor do I drink, but I cry.
> [Before he ends the letter, he writes:]
> I ask you without delay to reply to me concerning your health, so that I also may have consolation.[13]

We do not know much about Tasoucharion other than the fact that she was the devoted matriarch of the family, with a husband and four children. She died at some unknown point after this letter and her husband remarried. With no details we can only speculate, but Apollinarius' concern for his mother's health may suggest something a little deeper than a passing illness.

Of course, with so many young boys growing up to follow their fathers, brothers and uncles into the army, our evidence also speaks of the inevitable reality of widows and single women left behind. Recent studies of the local census that occurred every fourteen years have revealed some rather surprising results. Contrary to the common presumption that single women would have been required to remarry or move back into their father's home, we see a considerable number of them living with their adult sons, brothers, brothers-in-law in the case of widows, or even continuing to live with their ex-husband.[14] We even have one example in Karanis, one of the thirteen examples that appear in the surviving census records for all of Egypt, which shows an all-female household with three generations living under one roof. It lists the declarant as a fifty-year-old woman, her twenty-one-year-old daughter and one-year-old infant granddaughter.[15]

These women's decisions would have been based on what was best for both them and their children. While they were not legally autonomous – women needed a theoretical male guardian for certain documentation – many women established financial autonomy for themselves. We know of one fifty-eight-year-old woman called Aurelia Libouke who was an expert weaver and was paid to take on apprentices.[16] The contract that survives describes Aurelia as acting 'without a guardian by right of her children'; this is a reference to the *ius trium liberorum*, a law which gave autonomy to freeborn women with three children of their own. This law may well have enabled another resident of Karanis who, according to the census, lived by herself with her three children, to do so without much fuss.[17] Outside Karanis, we know of a variety of women who sold their skills and wares, and others who ran their own businesses.[18] In an economic environment where women could inherit part of their family estate and also earn their own money, it is perhaps not surprising that some chose to remain single.

There are even instances where childhood was not a barrier for a girl to assert herself and claim what was rightfully hers.

One young orphaned girl called Aurelia Tapais was able to petition against the illegal sale of her inherited land by two men. The petition makes no mention of a guardian, which is doubly unusual on account of both her gender and her status as a minor. Whether or not she was the child of a veteran we do not know, but her case will not have been unique: orphaned children were at the whim of their guardians, some of whom tried to find ways to relinquish their responsibilities. Aurelia's letter ends with a suggestion that she was not alone, and that help was there for her when she needed it:

> Farewell. I, Aurelia Tapaeis, have submitted this. I, Aurelios Dioskoros, wrote for her as she is illiterate.[19]

There was, of course, a more sinister side to life at Karanis. The contract for Aurelia Libouke that we have does not concern a father signing over his child for an apprenticeship, but instead a slave owner signing over his young, nameless slave for a period of one year. We also have contracts of sale for enslaved people in the village such as Aphrodite, who was only ten years old, and her mother, whose name does not survive on the fragmentary papyri; both were bought by a woman called Ptollarous with the support of her husband-guardian.[20] At Karanis there were freedoms for some, not freedoms for all.

* * *

The story of Karanis is a story of perseverance above anything else. For 700 years, from the age of the Ptolemies through to the collapse of the Western Roman Empire, life in Karanis continued relatively unchanged. Even down to its pre-Roman footprint, Karanis maintained its own style, its own way of doing things which, as we have already seen with the mistreatment of veterans, was sometimes at odds with the Roman way.

As you walk around Karanis, you do not feel as if you are in a Roman town. The road layout is irregular and there is no intersection of two major roads. To cross the site between east and west is something of a nightmare, made easier by the fact that today very few of the old housing blocks remain at any height. Instead, you scurry along what must have once been short streets and alleys, trying hard not to step on the copious quantities of broken pottery shards that litter the ground.

Houses were small in their ground plans, even the more expensive ones, with the average house size measuring no more than forty-five square metres. They were multi-storey, whether it was with two above ground, or one above and one below.[21] These houses are in close proximity to one another, but they were built independently and free-standing, sometimes sharing outdoor spaces for communal activities such as milling grain and preparing bread; however, they usually retained their own entrances and exits onto the streets outside.[22] Of course, it is hard to deduce if these buildings held more than one household or family at a time. They presumably did: surviving documents show various houses and courtyards being split between family members as part of their inheritance.

Even the two temples blended Greek, Egyptian and then Roman ways of doing things. Both are built in an Egyptian style, using limestone blocks and employing a distinctive layout. The north temple has the subtle presence of Greco-Roman columns at its outer corners and internal doorways, but they do not dilute the clear, culturally Egyptian identity of the buildings. Both are likely to have been dedicated to a crocodile god, either Pnepheros or Petesouchos, who were different manifestations of the crocodile-headed god Sobek, himself a particularly important deity in the Faiyum.

According to a rather mysterious and enigmatic text known as the *Book of the Faiyum*, which dates to the Greco-Roman period but draws upon earlier Egyptian mythology, it was an enormous crocodile that first arose from Lake Moeris following the Great Flood. The embodiment of a primeval creator god, the crocodile is drawn wearing the red crown, a symbol of power that signified one's rule over Lower Egypt. The text that sits above it describes him as the one 'who has created for himself, who emerged from the Wadj-wer [the Great Green] … Ra-Harakhte is the one, he does not set, he does not tire. He is Sobek of Shedet, Horus of Shedet.'[23]

The crocodile had become a symbol of creation, of life, as well as one of destruction and death. The Faiyum was filled with cults of the crocodile, and the largest cultic centre in the region was at Arsinoe. The name of the town was originally Shedet, but the Greeks had already given it a different one: Crocodilopolis, the Crocodile City. The geographer Strabo visited during the first century BCE and described his experience of the cult:

> [W]e come to the city Arsinoe, formerly called Crocodilopolis; for the inhabitants of this *nome* worship the crocodile. The animal is considered sacred and kept apart by himself in a lake; it is tame and gentle with the priests … We found the animal lying on the edge of the lake. The priests went up to it; some of them opened its mouth, another put the cake into it, then the meat, and afterwards poured down the honey and milk.[24]

There is no evidence that the temples at Karanis hosted any live crocodiles, not yet at least, but the mummified remains of crocodiles have been discovered in the temples. There are also deep recesses in the walls that were used to store the mummified remains before their use in various rituals. We can only speculate about what these rituals looked like, but the discovery of the image of another crocodile-god called Socnopaeus, with its distinctive falcon's head on the body of the reptile, raises the possibility that the temple may have served as an oracle as well.[25]

These Egyptian cults remained a focal point in the lives of the people in Karanis: their temples were continuously invested in during the Roman Imperial period, and we know of extensions during the reigns of Nero and Vespasian for certain. But this did not preclude the presence of other religious groups, ones that could not easily be included in these sacred spaces. For instance, much like in Volubilis, we have evidence of people in the village who were Jewish. Some of the names that survive do suggest Jewish descent, but the most concrete evidence comes from their liability as Jews to pay certain taxes, which survive in the tax records.[26] We can also see the development of Christianity in the village, especially from the end of the third century onwards – approximately around the time the temples fall into decline and then disuse.

While no church has been satisfactorily identified in Karanis, the Christian influence is clear to see in the later material evidence. Items imprinted with Christian iconography include various forms of pottery, and lamps and also textiles have been found, with crosses, lambs and even images of saints on them. Various symbols of the old cults were reappropriated to become Christian in meaning, such as the image of the infant god Harpocrates being fed by his mother Isis, which has obvious commonalities with the Virgin Mary nursing the baby Jesus.[27] The growth of Christianity in the village coincides with its spread throughout Egypt and the founding of numerous monasteries and monastic communities. By the 320s CE, we hear of one Karanis resident who was in desperate need of some Christian charity:

> The cattle of Pamounis and Harpalos damaged the planting which I had done … I caught the cow and was leading

> it up to the village when they met me in the fields with a big club, threw me to the ground, rained blows upon me and took away the cow ... and if I had not by luck received help from the deacon Antoninus and the monk Isaac, who happened to walk by, they would probably have finished me off completely.[28]

It was not only the village or its culture that shows great perseverance: so do the people themselves. Life in Karanis was tough. If they were not having to deal with rogue officials ignoring laws or having their neighbours beat them up, residents were navigating poor harvests, balancing debts and dealing with illness. At the end of the second century (c.165–180 CE), the Antonine Plague caused an unknown disease to spread across the empire without prejudice. The doctor Galen lived through it and noted various symptoms in passing, including rashes, fever, vomiting, diarrhoea and coughing. What he does not make clear was how deadly it was.[29] Scholarly estimates suggest there was a population drop across the Roman Empire of around 10 per cent. But in Egypt this plague hit particularly hard, and the population drop may have been as much as 20 per cent. For Karanis, we know from the tax records that survive, covering 171–174 CE, that the village may have lost as much as 40 per cent of its population.[30] We cannot know if this loss of population was a result of deaths due to the plague, or people choosing to move away from the village in an attempt to escape its effects, but what is clear is that this was a period of flux for Karanis.

By the mid-third century, scholars have noted a sizable drop in written evidence from Karanis.[31] Between 220 and 270 CE Karanis almost goes missing: researchers have found very few confirmed documents at the site dating from this period, but equally the village is rarely named in evidence from other Egyptian sites either. For whatever reason, Karanis saw a notable decrease in activity within a generation of the Antonine Plague. It did recover, of course, as we know the settlement was in use through to the fifth century, but its character most definitely changed. Agricultural land being used to grow crops was reduced by 81 per cent, at a conservative estimate, and surviving letters by tax collectors show a local resistance to paying their dues resulting in a drop of 95 per cent in tax revenues compared to before the plague.[32]

In the fifth century, our very sporadic evidence suggests that the people of Karanis were moving further away from the village itself in search of better farmland. In 439 CE, a declaration was made by a group of landowners whose farms bordered a nearby reservoir that asserted their right to destroy any attempts made by villagers from Karanis to draw water or in any way use the land.[33] Clearly, local government had stopped investing in the irrigation systems of the northern Faiyum region. This is all but confirmed by a tax collector who wrote a letter to his superior complaining that he had been assaulted. He begins with a rather telling statement:

> Even before my writing, your worship will not be unaware that there the people from Karanis are not concerned to inhabit the village, nor indeed to pay their taxes to the emperor.[34]

While the more central towns like Arsinoe were still flourishing, those at the far edges were having to travel further and further afield to find good agricultural land. For these people to continue to survive, they needed to leave Karanis to the sands of time.

# Section IV

# BEYOND THE CLASSICAL WORLD

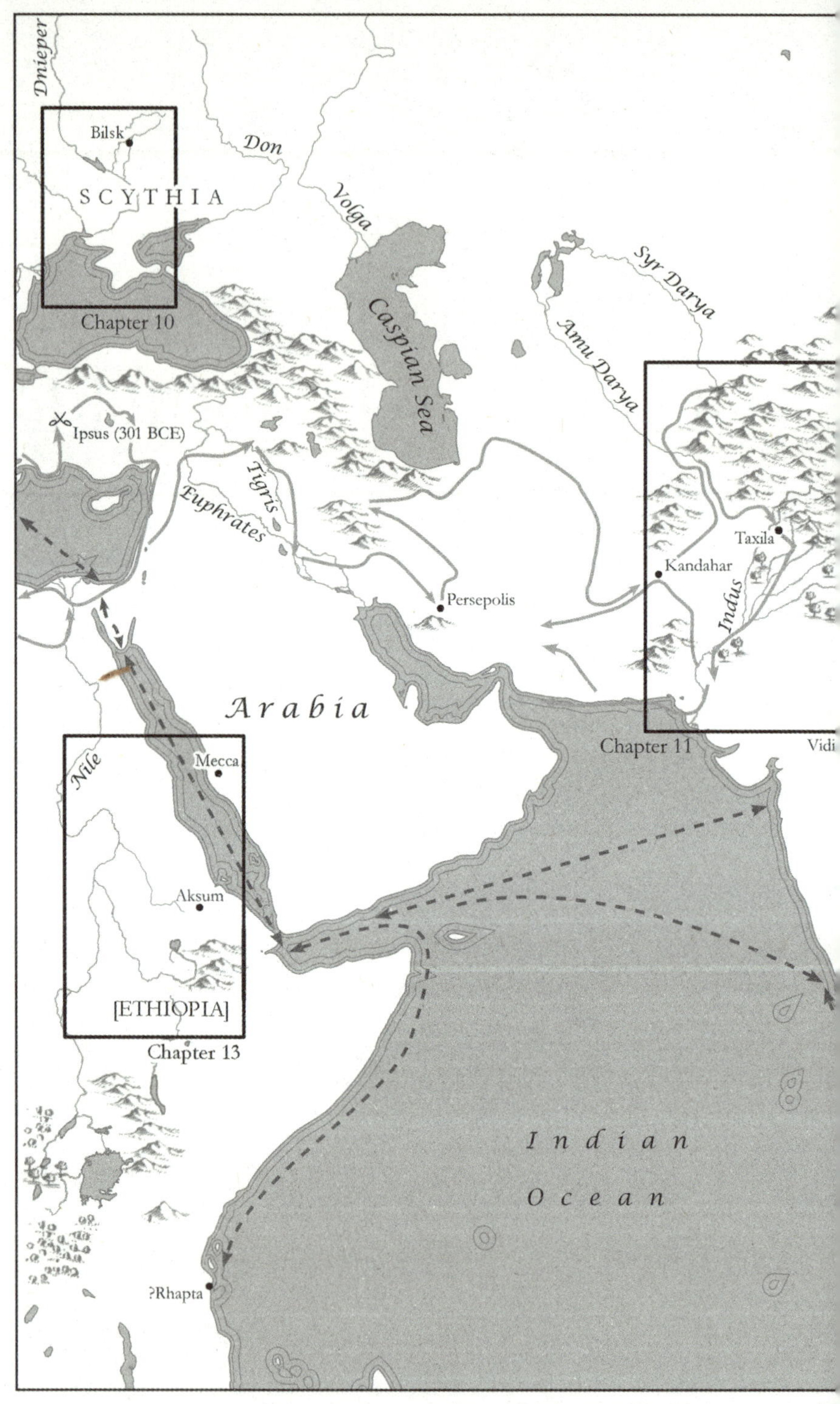

Dnieper
Bilsk
Don
SCYTHIA
Volga
Chapter 10
Caspian Sea
Syr Darya
Amu Darya
Ipsus (301 BCE)
Tigris
Euphrates
Taxila
Kandahar
Persepolis
Indus
Arabia
Chapter 11
Vidi
Nile
Mecca
Aksum
[ETHIOPIA]
Chapter 13
Indian
Ocean
?Rhapta

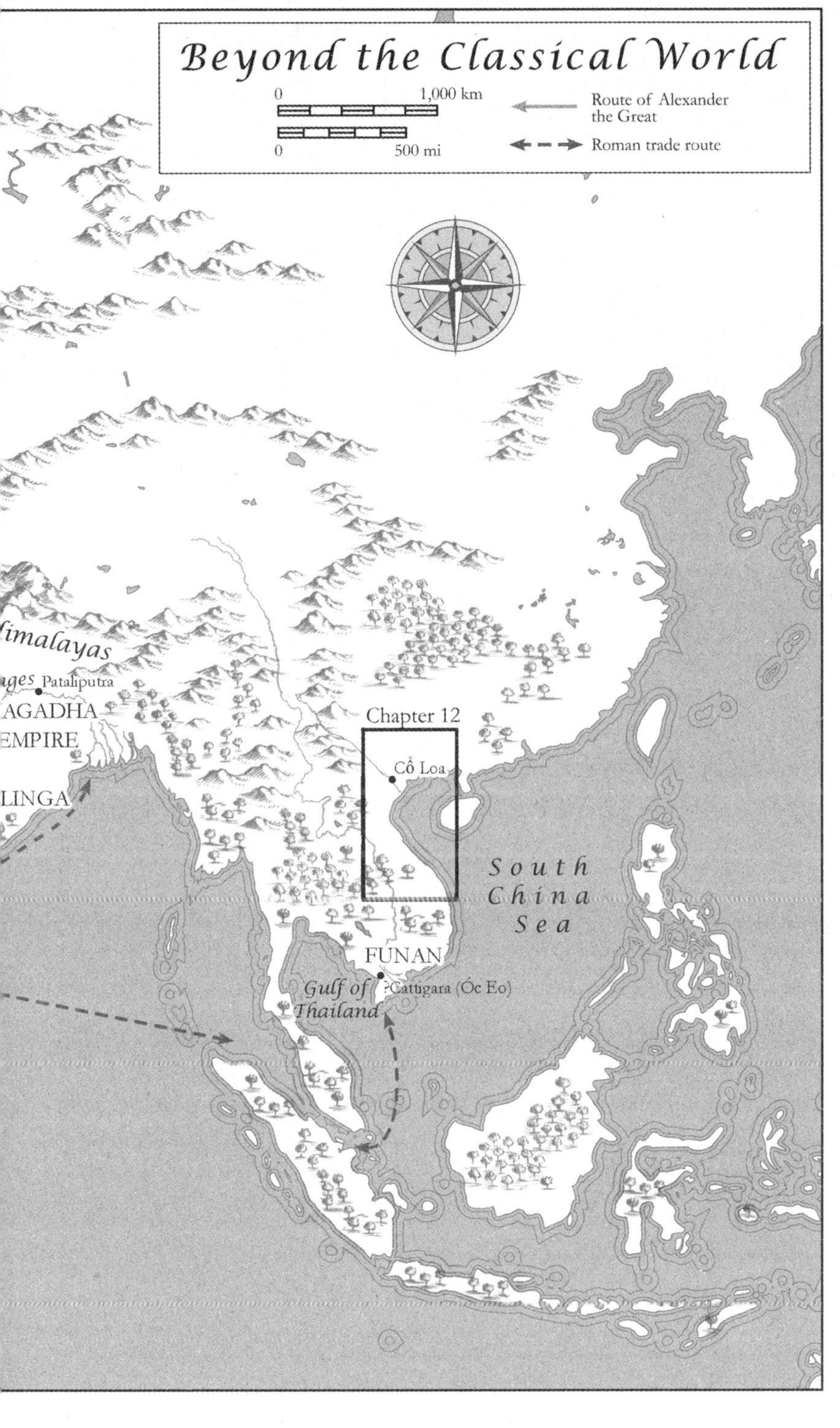

Beyond the Classical World
0
1,000 km
0
500 mi
Route of Alexander the Great
Roman trade route
imalayas
ges
Pataliputra
AGADHA
EMPIRE
LINGA
Chapter 12
Cổ Loa
South China Sea
FUNAN
?Cattigara (Óc Eo)
Gulf of Thailand

Vorskla
Sukhaya
Grun
Bilsk
Psel
Dnieper
SCYTHIA
Southern
Bug
Berezan
Olbia
Sea of
Azov
Crimea
Black Sea
0
50
100 km
0
50 mi

## 10

# Bilsk, Ukraine

The previous chapters have shown the need to look beyond the cultural centres of our histories not only to learn important nuances, but also to recapture narratives that are often ignored. We have looked to the far edges of the known world for a disruption of our assumptions and accepted truths. In this final section, we will actually leave the 'known world' behind. To those of us raised in the European traditions of history, this means leaving the Mediterranean Basin entirely, both geographically and also in terms of cultural influence. For while Greece and Rome were spreading their influence so, too, were other global cultures, such as the Scythians, India and, of course, China. These cultures do not play a big part in Mediterranean or European political history, but socially and economically the interconnected nature of Eurasia is undeniable.

What we find beyond the edges of the map are similar stories to our own. Ones that highlight human perseverance, ingenuity and resourcefulness. We see the same power imbalances at play and the need to adapt in order to survive. We also find cultures that do not live up to some of the stories told by our classical authors. These are not barbaric, uncivilised harbingers of chaos: they are complex societies, some of whom chose very different social infrastructures. So perhaps it is best to begin with the quintessential barbarian group, the one that the Greeks and Romans would identify as their antithesis – the Scythians.

Imagine for a moment that a fourth-century BCE Greek merchant decided to travel out of the Greek city of Olbia that we met in Chapter 4 and up the Dnieper River, in search of a large market to sell his wares. Carrying a cargo of fine tableware and probably wine in large amphorae, his journey could have taken him hundreds of miles north in his hunt for somewhere to trade. On his journey he would begin to hear of the ideal place, a giant market town that sat on the crossroads of Scythia and Europe. The merchant would branch off the Dnieper, onto one of its many eastern tributaries, finally making his way onto the Sukhaya Grun river. As his journey came to an end, he would have been greeted with a most unexpected sight: high up on the plateau was an enormous wooden fortification the size of a large city, seemingly in the middle of nowhere.

The fortification of Bilsk would have left a great impression on our merchant. Its wooden walls stood nine metres tall, with surrounding ditches five metres deep. The perimeter was over thirty-three kilometres long, forming an almost triangular shape which actually combined three smaller forts together, one to the west overlooking the Sukhaya Grun, one to the east overlooking the Vorskla and a third to the north-east as well. To give a sense of perspective and scale, the Aurelian walls that were built to encircle third-century BCE Rome only measured nineteen kilometres in length. In total, these wooden walls at Bilsk enclosed a space of roughly 4,800 hectares – an area almost double the size of Imperial Rome, five times the size of Babylon; or, for the modern-day reader, Bilsk would just about fit on Manhattan Island with wriggle room to spare.[1] The magnitude of this site cannot be overstated. To travel through the settlement north to south meant walking over just over eleven kilometres. Most intriguing of all for this monumental hillfort is that the evidence suggests it never served as the home for any substantial population. That is to say, the wooden walls enclosed an enormous space, but it was mostly empty space, nonetheless.[2]

On his return to Olbia most likely carrying a tidy profit in the form of precious metals, grain or even enslaved people, how would our merchant describe what he saw to his fellow Greeks? Where would he say he had been, and who would he describe as living in this enormous city made of wood? To our Greek protagonist, he was in the lands of Scythia which, as we have established, were considered to be shrouded in mystery. The inhabitants must therefore have been Scythians, a collective term given to a rather large array of tribal groups and identities. However, there was one small problem: the Scythians were thought to be nomads. Why would nomads build this enormous city, at the point where the wide-open plains of the steppes – ideal for their horse-based migratory lifestyle – meet the forest steppe?

Our ever-faithful guide to the Scythians, Herodotus, epitomises the confusion here. In his *Histories* an entire section is devoted to a long exploration of Scythia and its people. In it, he describes a city to the north called Gelonus, a place many archaeologists have associated with Bilsk specifically. According to Herodotus, Gelonus was built by the Budini, a people who lived beyond the lands of Scythia, in a region that was thickly overgrown with trees and woodland.[3] Their city is described with an air of wonder and amazement:

> They have a city of their own built of wood, it is named Gelonus. Each side of its large wall is thirty stades long and made entirely of wood, so too are their houses wooden, and their temples. For they have temples dedicated to Greek gods there, equipped in the Greek style with statues, altars and shrines of wood.[4]

If Herodotus is describing Bilsk here, then his informant has grossly underestimated the size of the site; thirty stades only equates to just under six kilometres. But, assuming that Herodotus never actually saw the settlement, we can give him the benefit of the doubt in that regard. More confusing is his attempt to reconcile this seemingly Greek city, with its high walls, houses and temples made from wood, being located out beyond the furthest reaches of the known world. He explains that the people of Gelonus were in fact Greek in origin; that they had departed from their trading ports of origin and settled with the Budini. In turn, they built this city of wood. Herodotus claims that this is further evidenced by the fact that the local dialect was a combination of Greek and Scythian.

His confusion is understandable. He describes the Budini in much the same way as he does the Scythians and associates the two groups very closely, even though he is adamant that they were not the same people. The Budini were *autochthones*, people from the earth – a description usually given to indigenous groups of people who lived in the same lands from where they originated – but they were also nomads who lived off the wildlife in the dense forests and marshy lake lands in the area. Herodotus, like many scholars who have followed him, struggled to reconcile this culture with having built an enormous, permanent wooden city. His solution was simple: the Budini could not have done this. It must have been some Greeks.

Archaeologists have been excavating the site of Bilsk for decades, and with each new season comes new information about the history of the fort and the people who built it. Scholars are gaining more and more evidence that Herodotus' description fits Bilsk almost perfectly, but perhaps more importantly they are also highlighting the misconceptions in his account. What Herodotus did not know, what he could not know, was that Bilsk did not start out as this mega-fort. By the time Herodotus was writing in the late fifth century BCE, Bilsk had been inhabited for over two centuries. The earliest settlements were built in the late eighth or early seventh centuries BCE, not by Scythians to the east but by migrants from the western banks of the Dnieper. It was not until the late sixth century BCE that the beginnings of the fort emerged, in the guise of two smaller forts. The first was built on the western part of the site, the second to the east. It was only at the turn of the fifth century BCE that the Great Fortification was built by connecting the various forts with a single continuous wall.[5]

* * *

The ancient world was full of converging points of interaction: areas or routes where numerous cultures intersected, interacted and interjected into each other's worlds. The most famous example would be the Mediterranean Sea itself, which was home to a multitude of cultures, and enabled a transference of material goods, people and, importantly, ideas. It was of course not unique: the same could be said of the Black Sea, or even the Indian Ocean during the ancient period. But what is perhaps less appreciated are the areas and routes on land. Barring the Silk Road, it is quite difficult to think of a location or route that served this function in human history. Perhaps this is in part due to the viciously territorial approach many cultures have had to land, as opposed to the sea – a place that is notoriously difficult to control and claim as your own. However, the location in which Bilsk was situated was such a place.

Located on the border between the open, flat plains of the steppes, and the forest steppes to the north, it sat between two different worlds. On the plains, the horse could reign supreme, producing cultures that were fast-moving, often migratory, relying on their livestock for the majority of their goods. In contrast, the horse was of less importance to the way of life in the forest steppes, where many more sedentary cultures focused on agriculture, which required the building of urban settlements. Equally, Bilsk was situated at the western end of the steppe, where eastern Europe meets western Asia. While our written sources focus on the cultural interactions coming from the south, i.e. the Greeks and Persians coming into the region, the archaeology shows a clear cultural exchange between east and west as well.

The site was originally settled by indigenous migrants from the forest steppe. Their material culture shows a connection with the so-called Zhabotin culture, based on archaeological finds at a site across the Dnieper to the south of Bilsk. Ceramic finds in the earliest layers at the fort reveal a characteristic, black-glazed tableware, with decorative patterns formed with geometric shapes inlaid with a white paste.[6] These migrants were also skilled metalworkers. While bronze and copper make up the majority of early metal objects found, there is evidence of iron work being done at the turn of the seventh century BCE and iron tools becoming commonplace soon after.[7]

While we cannot pinpoint exactly where these people originally moved from, what is revealing is how quickly they were able to establish key trade routes both westward and south. Indeed, it has been speculated that the migrants had most probably brought a well-developed knowledge of the western land routes from the Dnieper into central Europe.[8] Add to this the spread of Greek traders into the northern Black Sea at places such as Olbia, as well as the beginnings of nomadic Scythian movements into the same region at the turn of the seventh century BCE, and Bilsk was destined to become a melting pot of culture, language and technology. As a result, we see three clear cultural spheres present in Bilsk, alongside their own: Greek, Scythian and a culture from central and western Europe, Hallstatt.

Hallstatt culture is most commonly associated with proto-Celtic peoples in Europe, and their influence can be seen as far east as the Danube and modern Romania. It would later be replaced by the La Tène culture, which is what we think of when we visualise the Celts of western Europe. However, in Bilsk the influence is clear to see. From everyday items fitting the so-called 'Hallstatt type' such as tweezers, hatchets, razors and clothing pins, to decorative items such as pendants and earrings, we see not only the presence of trade; there is also clear evidence that the people at Bilsk began to produce their own copies, in house, so to speak.[9]

One of the most important finds has been, of all things, Hallstatt-style tweezers. While these tweezers will never be the star attractions in any museum and were quite commonplace throughout Hallstatt Europe, they are unique to this fortification in the northern Black Sea region. This may not sound like much, but sometimes the most innocuous of objects can shed light on the unknown. We may have been tempted to explain their presence as a common cultural adoption in the area, but their so far unique presence here suggests otherwise.

Other items, such as a lovingly shaped double-axe pendant made from bone, suggest a deeper connection to this Hallstatt culture than one simply forged through trade and prevailing fashions. The small pendant is very smooth and worn on its surface, suggesting prolonged use or at least intensive touching. A logical explanation is that it served as some sort of amulet or charm, one that would be touched or rubbed regularly for luck or to ward off evil. These are commonly found in the Balkans from this period, but their personal and ritual character leads us to assume that these were not traded in Bilsk. Rather, they must have been brought into the area by people who continued to use them.

In fact, one of the most interesting aspects of the Hallstatt-type items at Bilsk is that many seemingly elite cultural items, such as worked metal and even swords, were not found in the burials in or around the site. That is not to say there are no

Hallstatt items found in the burials: there are bronze plaques decorated with a distinctive pattern of three concentric circles, and female headdresses have also been found. However, it does suggest that some of these high *value* items were not considered the highest *social* markers; that their presence would not imbue the deceased with any sense of elevated status. All this paints a picture of people moving to Bilsk with strong cultural ties connected with central Europe.[10]

The same cannot be said of Greek culture, which appears at Bilsk almost exclusively as a result of long-distance trade. Despite its separation from the Greek world, Bilsk is notable for not only the number of Greek objects that have been found, but also the variety of locations that these objects came from. Since the seventh century BCE, a clear trade link existed between the people of Bilsk and the Greeks to the south. Originally, this was channelled through the island of Berezan, next to Crimea, and then, following its later foundation, the city of Olbia took control. Greek pottery such as decorated wine jugs, cups and plates were high-status items, no doubt a reflection of their exorbitant costs, and are not only found in the main fortifications but also in the burial mounds as well. We also know that they traded in wine. As time passed and the trading relationship grew ever stronger, we see more variety in the Greek objects. These include Greek mirrors, lidded bowls and larger vases such as amphorae. As a result, Bilsk was part of the great trade network of the Aegean and beyond. Pottery types have been identified as coming from Asia Minor, and famous trade and production centres such as Lesbos and Miletus.

As we have seen through our explorations of both Olbia and Naucratis, a place in the Greek trade network connected any site with dozens of different markets, different lands and different cultures. Nowhere is this clearer than in a burial site discovered just outside Bilsk, where the extraordinary remains of a wealthy young woman were discovered. The burial chamber was typical of the region, formed of a wooden vault measuring four by five metres. Even the floor was made of wooden planks resting on logs, which were themselves set in pre-prepared grooves. The chamber would have been just over a metre below the ground surface when it was first covered with a mound measuring fifteen metres in diameter.

The buried woman was clearly a person of great social standing, perhaps a priestess or something similar. Her body was found with a variety of important and symbolic items, such as the remnants of an ornate headdress, a bronze mirror, jewellery, a knife, and even the remains of a sacrificed goat, to name but a few. But most intriguing of all is a small decorative bead, a part of a much larger necklace, made of faience. Next to it was an amulet in the shape of a scarab. This scarab, which would have originally been covered in a striking blue glaze, is inscribed on the bottom with two hieroglyphs inside an oval outline: a cobra and a scorpion.[11]

The discovery of an Egyptian amulet is remarkable. Dating from the middle of the sixth century BCE, it is the earliest known example in the region, some 2,000 kilometres away from Egypt. Inevitably, its presence raises more questions than it answers. Neither the cobra nor the scorpion is indigenous to the Black Sea region, so did the wearer or even the buyer have any idea what these symbols represented? Did they know that these were real creatures, or did they absorb them into their own fantastical world of myth and monsters? Did the people of Bilsk know of Egypt at all? But also, we are left to wonder: where did this amulet actually come from? Was it made in Naucratis, like those found in Olbia, or was it Egyptian-made? If the latter, then is it safe to assume that the Greeks were the ones who traded it, rather than, say, the Persians or maybe even the Scythians? We cannot know for certain, not yet at least, but what we do know is that the cultural reaches of Bilsk stretched much further than the Black Sea.

* * *

One of the biggest mysteries surrounding Bilsk has been its relationship with the nomadic Scythians. It is not only Herodotus who has wrestled with this question; it is in fact still common to see Bilsk described in the history books as a 'Scythian' city but, as we have clearly seen, this was not the case. No: the problem comes not in whether the Scythians formed the settlement, but, rather, in what their relationship with the site actually was. Some scholars have argued that the Scythians were the reason it was fortified in the first place, from fear of these marauding nomads. Others have argued that the Scythians used the site but allowed the inhabitants to stay there permanently as well. The truth behind this, or indeed the order of events in which things occurred, are near-impossible to figure out based on the evidence we have. However, one thing is clear: the Scythians exerted a great influence over Bilsk.

Identifying the presence of Scythian culture at any site is, in equal measure, both very simple and very complicated. The material culture is defined by the discovery of certain items, what archaeologists call the Scythian triad: a type of horse bridle; similar weapons (most commonly a short composite bow, and a three-edged arrowhead); and a very distinctive style of art called animal-style, which focuses on animal motifs often contorted into unusual positions, and uses swirls and whirlpools for decoration and embellishment. If a combination of these items, or ideally all three, are found in a burial or around a settlement, then the presence of Scythians can be clearly noted. The complication arises from judging what the presence of these items actually means: does it mean that Scythians lived there? Does it mean that Scythian items were traded there? Does it mean that the people who had these items were the same as other people using these same items elsewhere (the triad can be found as far east as Siberia)? It is not always possible to answer these questions, but the presence of the triad is always pertinent to understanding the Scythian way of life.

All the hallmarks of Scythian culture appear in the archaeological record at Bilsk from a very early period. By the latter half of the seventh century BCE, we find the presence of animal-style art on objects made from metal, bone and horn, and there are also iron bridles, as well as the distinctive arrowheads. So, with regard to the triad, that is three for three. Furthermore, we find evidence that many of these objects were being made on-site as well. The arrowheads were made with a cast, and examples of these moulds have been found in the fort. Workshops have also been identified where researchers have discovered blanks of bone and horn products, which were either never used or only partially completed.[12] This does not suggest that the Scythians were bringing their cultural objects with them, or that they were selling them to locals at Bilsk; rather, it suggests that there was a permanent demand for them because the Scythians were also living there.

These Scythians do not resemble the romantic warrior nomads from popular history. In fact, recent scientific studies of skeletal remains at Bilsk show that they were living a completely different way of life. The recent work by a team of researchers has conclusively shown that inhabitants of Bilsk were not travelling vast distances during their life. The researchers selected burials which contained items from the Scythian triad and attempted to gauge the distances these people may have travelled using a strontium isotope analysis, a method which measures the concentration and isotopic ratio of the element strontium in the bone and enamel. As strontium is present in rock, soil and water, different areas of the world have something akin to a strontium signature, with their own specific balance of the four strontium isotopes that occur naturally. Humans and animals who live in that area will inherit that signature through the food they eat and the water they drink, allowing researchers to place an historic individual into the geological landscape in which they lived, and track any large-scale movements they made during their life as well.

For the bodies at Bilsk, the estimated radius of movement during their lifetime was only fifty kilometres: this short distance would not even allow you to travel from the fort to the Dnieper River, let alone the Black Sea. In addition to these Scythians' lack of mobility, archaeologists have also found that their diet resembles that of agro-pastoralists, that is people who practised a mixture of agriculture and pastoralism. Domesticated grains, such as millet, were an important staple for many, alongside local plants, wildlife and dairy products.[13]

All this information comes together to paint a rather confusing picture. At this enormous fort in north central Ukraine we have indigenous people, who shared strong cultural ties to western and central Europe, living alongside Scythian nomads, who neither travelled nor ate like nomads. All the while, elite members of these groups were importing cultural items from the Greeks and absorbing them into their own way of life.

On the surface, this is a confusing mishmash of cultures and identities that cannot be made sense of. However, Herodotus had warned us of this. In fact, if we return to his account of Gelonus and the Budini people, we find his description is remarkably accurate:

> The Budini are indigenous nomads, and the only people in these parts that eat pine seeds; the people of Gelonus work the land, eating grain and cultivating orchards; they are unlike the Budini either in form or in complexion.[14]

Herodotus knew that there was more than one cultural group associated with Gelonus, as there clearly was at Bilsk. He knew that these groups had almost completely opposite ways of life. But what he perhaps did not appreciate, and is actually the source of much of his confusion, is the fact that the nomads may have adapted their way of life over time, travelling less and engaging more with agriculture.

* * *

The plateau at Bilsk did not begin life as a fortified position. The first settlements were unprotected, and the waves of migration into the area between the eighth and early sixth centuries BCE, from both the east and the west, did not bring with them any direct evidence of conflict. That is to say, we do not find evidence of burning or major destruction, nor of battle-worn bodies and expended weapons, to suggest otherwise. However, this began to change within the sixth century, firstly with the construction of the Western Fort and then a few years later with the Eastern Fort.

The Western Fort started out as one of these early, unprotected settlements on the slope of the plateau. The area has offered up some of the oldest finds from the site and was undoubtedly inhabited by the earliest migrants. Its fortification in the second half of the sixth century BCE reveals a stark change in fortune. The need to further protect a site, considering the natural protection offered by the high vantage point, suggests the introduction of a new threat. Of course, without any written evidence to elucidate the situation we are left to wonder what that threat might have been. It could possibly have been due to a shift in the relationship between the settled people and the nomadic groups in the area, but this would fly in the face of almost 200 years of relative harmony. More likely is the idea that a new group of people had entered the area, and that this migration was the reason for the discontent.

The Eastern Fort was built only a short time later, but the remains show a very different cultural fingerprint. People living in the Western Fort practised animal sacrifice, built ornamental altars for their rituals, lived in large dugout houses and scattered ash mounds (called *zelinks*, they contain much of the material evidence we have been looking at) on abandoned houses. The new people living in the Eastern Fort did none of these things. The distinction is so clear between the two camps that the situation reveals itself immediately. Two tribal groups cohabited the same space atop the plateau and each built a defensive structure to protect themselves, or at least distinguish themselves, from the other group.[15]

Who this new group was has yet to be answered. Why there was this change in circumstance is perhaps more easily reconciled. This period we are talking about, the last quarter of the sixth century BCE, saw the rise and expansion of the largest empire seen in or around the Mediterranean, under the Achaemenid dynasty of Persia. According to Herodotus, the Persians had expelled the Scythians from Asia at the turn of the sixth century, forcing them north and back into their homelands. Apparently, the Scythians had themselves entered Asia Minor in pursuit of another nomadic people: the Cimmerians.

Unfortunately, all this occurred during a period of absolute chaos in the region when the Assyrian Empire was collapsing, the Neo-Babylonians were just establishing themselves and the Persians were growing as a power (though nothing like the force they would become under Cyrus the Great). As a result, our evidence is scanty, but it does give the impression of large movements of nomadic groups. If we visualise this as not so much a mass migration, but, rather, a domino effect where one group is moved into another's territory, forcing those people to move into someone else's, and so on, we can at least understand how a new cultural group came to arrive at Bilsk.

Shortly after the two forts were built, the large enveloping ramparts of the Great Fortification were built. Dating the sequence of events has proven difficult, so scholars are split between two explanations: one, that the two forts and large rampart were built gradually, without any grand plan in place; or two, that this was a synchronised building programme, and the end result of a mega-fort was always the aim.[16] No matter which explanation is correct, the Great Fortification appears towards the end of the sixth century and remained in use until the fourth century BCE.

To build this fort required a lot of worker hours, a lot of wood and resources and the ability for a community to provide and supply both of these elements. A dry moat was originally dug, with the excavated earth being used to form a rampart, upon which was built a simple wooden wall. With an overall perimeter of more than thirty-three kilometres, the amount of wood alone is astronomical: more than 84,000 logs, or the equivalent of a small forest. It is not just the wood itself, but the time it took to cut the wood, move it and build the palisade. Add to this the time it took to dig out the moat and we can begin to imagine how much of an undertaking this was for a small community.[17]

Commitment to an endeavour like this would require a powerful and secure leadership which had the resources necessary to facilitate it. As a result, it is believed that the fortress may at this point have been under the protection of a powerful nomad group. In this context the large fort makes a lot of sense. The walls and ramparts are actually quite poor in terms of their defensive capabilities, and the inner space has been found to be predominantly empty – so why would people enclose such a large space if they did not use it? The answer is, presumably, that they did use it, but not just to home their buildings. Perhaps the space was used by nomads and pastoralists who could bring in their livestock during times of crisis and danger. Or maybe, as one theory advances, the space was used by royal Scythians as a temporary site when they were in the region, for the yurts and tents of their court and army.[18]

The fort, for all its grandeur, was designed to be abandoned; this became particularly useful when the lands of Scythia were invaded in 513 BCE by the now dominant forces of Persia under the command of Darius I. We saw in Chapter 4 that the Persian invasion was unsuccessful but still had a lasting impact on the Greek cities around the Black Sea. For the Scythians, the defence of their lands was a masterclass in Fabian strategy – they mobilised all their people, and the surrounding neighbours willing to fight alongside them, and drew the Persians further and further into their land by abandoning their towns and staying on the move. The Persians were trying to wage a war which relied on the control of urban centres and to incite a decisive set of battles. But the Scythians did not play ball. To ensure a truly hostile environment for Darius' army, the Scythians also implemented a scorched-earth policy, leaving little for their enemies to either plunder or forage from.

Among the list of Scythian allies, both the Budini and the people of Gelonus (Bilsk) are named. During the campaign, all the women and children were sent north as the men harassed and tormented the Persians, and it is possible a site such as Bilsk was where they were sent. However, if we take Herodotus at his word, Bilsk was not safe either:

> But when [the Persians] entered the land of the Budini, they found themselves before the wooden walls [Bilsk]; the Budini had abandoned it and left nothing behind, so the Persians set it ablaze.[19]

The defences at Bilsk do show signs of minor destruction, possibly corroborating this story. They also show evidence of remodelling and reinforcement afterwards. This tells us that these walls were never meant to stop an actual army; they were a useful perimeter which served as a corral for the livestock and a deterrent to any raiders. They were never meant to offer protection against a siege.

The Scythian plan was successful: the Persians ran out of steam chasing shadows and inevitably retreated from the region with their tail suitably between their legs. It was a brutal dressing down for the most powerful military force in the world. In a slightly later account of the invasion, given by the Greek physician Ctesias, who worked at the Persian court, we hear about the underlying panic of the Persian commanders during their retreat. He tells us that Darius ordered the destruction of his bridge across the Danube before all his men had crossed it, such was his concern that the Scythians would follow him. Ctesias claims that 80,000 men were cut off as a result and taken captive by the Scythians, later to be put to death.[20]

Having survived Darius' invasion, Bilsk underwent its final evolution. The people living in the Western Fort abandoned the site in the fifth century BCE, and it is predominantly in the Eastern Fort that the last centuries' remains have been found. The Scythian identity of the site became more established at the elite level, with a proliferation of burial mounds (*kurgans*) beginning to appear in the wider region. However, it never became a Scythian town; the majority of people living within the walls were still farmers and cattle breeders. In fact, there was a clear hierarchy between the various groups at Bilsk which reveals that a mixed, heterogeneous society was in place. The most culturally unified group were the elite military aristocracy, alongside the priests and other influential people, who appear on the surface of it all as rather Scythian. The general populace, however, do not. So we can still see that Bilsk is a culturally eclectic place with various identities living alongside one another.

Even during this period where there was a clear Scythian ruling class, there is also an evident shift in the use of the site, with many scholars referring to fifth- and fourth-century BCE Bilsk as an urban centre rather than merely a fort. The reasons for this are manifold. Bilsk did not exist in isolation: it was in fact the largest of many mega-forts in the Dnieper region. The size and prominence of Bilsk led to it becoming something of a cultural and economic centre within this larger network. It may even have been something of a political centre as well, bringing together the various tribal groups across the forest steppe.[21] Bilsk also becomes quite a production centre, with numerous artisan workshops having been identified in the fort.

The Eastern Fort must have been a hive of activity. Surveys show that the settlement had a clear road layout that separated clusters of housing and other buildings. During the fifth century BCE, the inhabitants also built two sanctuaries, the largest of which was a temple built with wooden columns and five clay altars, one of which was found inside the footprint of the temple while the other four were found outside. The unusual shape of the building, and the presence of the altars, make this a very unusual find. It has been suggested that the temple could have been used for astrological observations, but who or what this temple was dedicated to is thus far unknown.[22]

Alongside the domestic and civic architecture, there were also numerous workshops which show clear signs of industry, such as smelting furnaces for working in bronze and iron, kilns for firing pots and the tell-tale weights used for weaving on looms. While many of the objects made in these workshops show clear cultural influences from Scythia, Greece and eastern Europe, it is also clear that they are, in their own way, unique to Bilsk in many of their designs. This was not simply a factory complex churning out replicas like those in Naucratis: it was an artistic focal point where traditions met and merged.

We cannot as yet connect examples to Bilsk itself, but we know that this merging of artistic culture was prevalent in the Black Sea region with the appearance of the so-called Greco-Scythian art style, which combined the Scythian mastery of gold and metalwork with the Greek obsession with realism and the human form. But perhaps more intriguing is the possibility of Scythian and Celtic art styles merging through interactions at sites like Bilsk.

As the Hallstatt culture became superseded by the La Tène in the fifth century BCE, we begin to find conventionally 'Celtic' objects showing very multicultural influences. Perhaps the clearest example comes in the form of two flagons found at Basse-Yutz in eastern France. Their shape clearly imitates Etruscan vases, their geometric banding was popular in Hallstatt art, and the small duck on the spout was a common image in La Tène decorations as well. The handle, however, is notably Scythian in its look. The elongated body of a dog or a wolf stretches from the rim down to the main body of the flagon and it evokes the 'predatory ferocity' of animal-style art.[23] More specifically, the ears and shoulder joints of the canine animal are embellished with the swirls which are most prevalent in steppe art rather than in western European art. Examples such as this are rare, suggesting that ideas, designs and motifs, rather than people, were moving around the Eurasian continent and beyond, influencing artists who acted like magpies. This leaves us with only echoes and fleeting shadows to notice, looking at an object that appears both unique but also strangely familiar.

While it is unlikely that production at Bilsk specifically catered for a western European market, archaeologists have found very unique workshops which betray the Scythian clientele of its artisans. One in particular has been identified through the discovery of several processed human skulls. The skulls had been scalped, as shown from markings on the bone, and turned into drinking bowls which used the temple bones as handles.[24] Such a discovery would usually be quite shocking, but for a description of the head-hunting traditions of the Scythians, given by Herodotus:

> The heads themselves, not all of them but those of their enemies, they process in this way. Each saws off the part of the skull beneath the eyebrows and cleans it out. If he is a poor man, then he covers the outside with a piece of raw hide and makes use of it accordingly; but if he is rich, he covers the head with the raw hide, lines the inside of it with gold, and uses it as a cup. A Scythian would also make these cups from the heads of family members with whom he had been feuding and subsequently defeated in single combat in front of the king. If guests are visiting, he will serve them with these heads and explain how they once belonged to his relatives, who brought war against him but were bested by him; this they describe as the height of masculine virtue.[25]

This description reads like the fantasy writing of a man who knows nothing of a world beyond his own, who is merely inventing horrific stories to shock his audience. However, the discovery at Bilsk is the first archaeological evidence to back up his claims.

The combination of this local industry and the continued trade with the Greeks on the Black Sea made Bilsk a very desirable place for merchants and tradesmen alike. Right through to the fort's final years, we have continued evidence of Greek trade including a few coins, gold rings and, of course, more wine. We also have some rather anomalous items which are in need of explanation, including gems, spindles and a fish dish, all of which are either etched or graffitied with Greek writing. Add to these the presence of Greek lamps, which were not used by locals, and we can tentatively conclude that there were Greeks actually living at Bilsk, at least on a temporary basis.[26]

By the end of the fourth century BCE, Bilsk was a thriving centre of art, industry and cultural exchange. It was a central focal point which connected three disparate cultural worlds. It was also resilient, withstanding widespread changes coming from migration as well as invasion. It not only absorbed other cultures, but maintained its own sense of identity, one that clearly attracted a lot of interest from the Greeks in particular. And yet, at the end of the fourth century BCE, it all just stopped.

For our imagined fourth-century Greek merchant who opened this chapter, we can only wonder how he would have reacted. Was he even aware of what was going on in Bilsk? Is it possible that one year, unsuspectingly, he began his semi-regular journey north only to find the site abandoned and his trade prospects disappeared along with the people? Perhaps he was lucky, and news had already reached him in Olbia of the shifting tides among the Scythian people, news that would have caused misery not only to him but to many other merchants, who relied on key trading sites like Bilsk to make their living. In mainland Greece, seismic events such as these did not even cause a ripple, at least not if our sources are anything to go by, but for the Greeks that shared their lives with these foreign communities it would have been felt very deeply.

We do not know how or why, but the site of Bilsk was simply abandoned. There is no evidence of any damage to the site, no signs of burning or layers of destruction which could help us visualise a cataclysmic event to explain this change. It is, for want of a better word, a mystery. In fact, it is part of a much broader mystery from the Scythian world more widely. Around this time, the classical Scythian culture also begins to disappear from the record, but again the reasons for this are not clear. Perhaps Bilsk is simply one of many casualties of a broader change in Eurasian nomadic politics, or maybe the thriving trade market that Bilsk had forged was beginning to dissipate. Whatever the cause, Bilsk soon faded into obscurity. With it went an important chapter of world history.

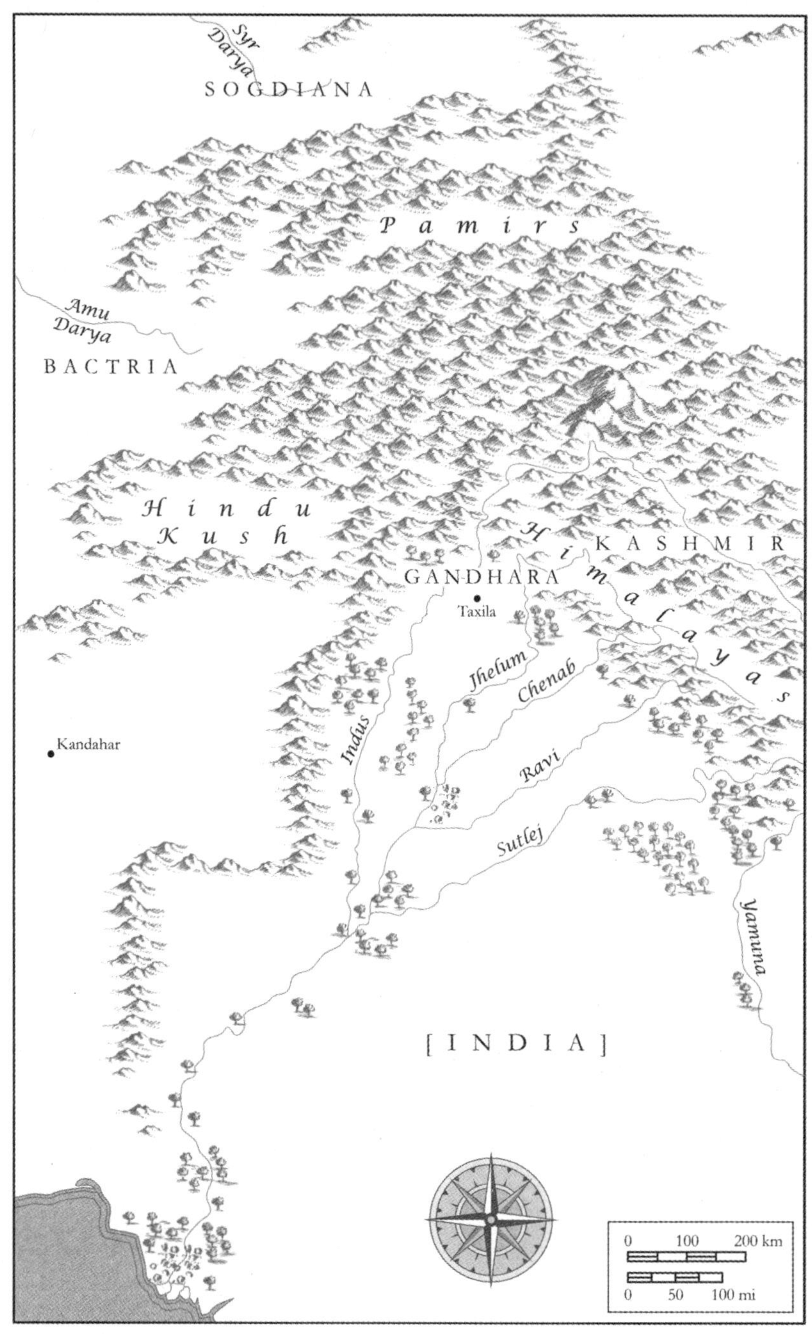

Syr Darya
SOGDIANA
Pamirs
Amu Darya
BACTRIA
Hindu Kush
Himalayas
KASHMIR
GANDHARA
Taxila
Jhelum
Chenab
Indus
Kandahar
Ravi
Sutlej
Yamuna
[INDIA]
0 100 200 km
0 50 100 mi

11

# Taxila, Pakistan

The further we remove ourselves from the cultural centres of the ancient Mediterranean, the more we come to realise how flexible and malleable, adaptive even, the people of the ancient world truly were. We have already seen how classical perceptions of the Scythians misrepresented what was a multifaceted culture, and how the Greeks saw themselves as superior to most other cultures. When we ignore the perspectives of other cultures, we risk internalising this perception and growing to believe it ourselves. Why else do you think we refer to their work as part of the classics?

In spite of this sense of superiority, the Greeks were able to adapt and include foreign people in their everyday lives, as we saw in all three of our Greek examples. But there was still a persistent sense that the Greeks would never abandon core facets of their identity and adopt another. This, we are often told in history books, is something *other* cultures do when they interact with Greek culture – they Hellenise and adopt many of the ways of the Greeks. And if we focus on the usual narrow remit of the Greek world, perhaps this idea can be rationalised and validated. Out beyond the edges of the classical world, however, we have evidence which raises some serious questions. One monument in particular has caused no end of debate.

In the modern state of Madhya Pradesh, in central northern India, lies the village of Bais. With a population of over 1,200 people and positioned just on the northern outskirts of the city of Vidisha, the village is bisected by the State Highway 19, giving Bais the feeling of a very busy place. But amid the rush of modern life, a quiet solitude can usually be found somewhere. In Bais, one such place is a small fenced-off area to the east of the highway. It is not usually busy, except for the children often found playing there and the occasional tourist on the hunt for its ancient treasures. The crowning jewel among the rather modest archaeological collection is a tall pillar monument, set atop a platform that is a metre above the ground level, standing over five metres in height.

The pillar dates from the second century BCE, and was designed with a refined, geometric beauty. For the first three metres or so from the ground it is shaped octagonally, then it morphs into sixteen distinct sides for a further two metres before it changes once more, becoming thirty-two-sided for only a short distance before it becomes a smooth, cylindrical pillar towards the top. This trunk holds up an ornate bell capital, upon which is the ruined remains of the abacus – a platform that is usually wider than the pillar and takes the weight of something above it, often an arch or the lintels of a roof. This pillar was not part of a larger building; in fact, the abacus's role was to hold a small statue of Garuda, a bird-like being considered the vehicle (*vahana*) to Vishnu. While the pillar is a fascinating object in its own right, one that has survived in a remarkably good condition over two millennia, our interest lies in the rather humble-looking inscription towards the bottom.

Written in Brahmi script, the inscription uses a Middle Indo-Aryan dialect (or Prakrit) typical of the time. It was originally hidden from the earliest scholars, as it was covered in a vermilion-coloured paint; but when they finally decided to remove the paint and reveal the words hidden beneath, they were confronted with something of a surprise:

> This Garuda-pillar of Vāsudeva, the god of gods, was constructed here by Heliodorus the Bhagavata, the son of Dion, from Taxila, the Greek ambassador who came from the Great King Antialkidas, to King Kasiputra Bhagabhadra, the Saviour prospering in the fourteenth year of his reign.[1]

Heliodorus was a Greek ambassador (the word he uses in Prakrit is *yona*) from the Greco-Bactrian ruler Antialkidas, whose kingdom stretched across north-western India, modern Pakistan and parts of Afghanistan. There are a few elements of real interest here, and the first is, of course, the language being used. The Greeks were not afraid of using their own language and alphabet, no matter where in the world they found themselves. So, the decision to use an Indian script, and a local language as well, is important. This is a message Heliodorus wants to be read by the locals, not his Greek peers back home. The second element is also something of a little mystery. He describes himself as a Bhagavata, a devotee of Vishnu in his form as Lord Krishna. In fact, the name Vāsudeva and the reference to the Garuda bird are both related to Vishnu and the early worship of Krishna – making this monument one of the earliest references we have to a growing popular form of Hinduism called Vaishnavism.[2] Vaishnavism challenged certain elements of the established tradition of Vedic Brahmanism without abandoning it outright. In particular it rejected animal sacrifice, a ritual that was, coincidentally, central to Greek religious practices as well.

So how has this monument come to be? Why is there a Greek man, commissioning an Indian-script dedication to a local god far beyond the boundaries of any Greek or Roman empire? Empires, it should be noted, which never crossed the Indus River. The answer lies not in Greece but in the place where Heliodorus was born: Taxila in modern Pakistan. This was a city that lay at the crossroads between three different worlds: Europe, central Asia and the Indian subcontinent.

The city of Taxila enters the European histories in a rather dramatic fashion during the expedition of Alexander the Great as he attempted to push his empire out beyond the Indus Valley. Following his crushing defeat of the weakened Persian empire of Darius III, Alexander had marched east to subdue its final remnants. While in Sogdiana, in modern Uzbekistan, Alexander achieved his aim with the suppression of the rebel leader Spitamenes in 328 BCE, but his ambitions went beyond the limits of the Persian Empire. He planned to move south into the land our ancient sources call 'India', but on a modern map also covers parts of Afghanistan and all of Pakistan.

As he planned his next move, Alexander received an envoy from Taxiles, the ruler of Taxila, inviting him south and offering his own forces in support of the Macedonian king's invasion. Perhaps Taxiles was driven by pragmatism, seeing how successful Alexander's army had been and knowing that resistance was futile; or perhaps he intended to use Alexander to settle his own scores against local rulers. For Taxila lay on fertile land between the Indus and Hydaspes rivers. Plutarch describes the kingdom as being the size of Egypt with abundant pastureland and growing the finest fruit.[3] But Plutarch exaggerates the size of Taxila's domain, for its reach did not exceed the river boundaries. Across the Hydaspes lay a rival kingdom ruled by a man called Porus.

Our sources inform us that there were in fact two Taxiles; the first, the father, is presented as a wise man who earned the respect of Alexander. But, by the time Alexander reached Taxila, Taxiles had died and been succeeded by his son, who also took the name of Taxiles. Taxiles the younger is presented as a more ambitious man, trying to assert his own authority in the region; it may well have been he who suggested reaching out to Alexander in the first place. The young king marched out with his army to meet Alexander and join him in a new campaign against Taxiles' rival, Porus. In addition to large sums of money, Taxiles gave Alexander twenty-five war elephants and 700 cavalrymen. He also offered Taxila as a base for his expedition.[4]

The generosity and unequalled support from the rulers of Taxila did not go unnoticed. Alexander rewarded them with equal generosity, a gesture that did not go down well with his loyal Macedonian commanders:

> So, after receiving many gifts and giving many himself, finally he lavished upon Taxiles a thousand talents in coins. Alexander's actions greatly upset his friends, but it undid much of the hostility felt by the barbarians towards him.[5]

And that is it, really, for the story of Taxila in the European tradition. Taxiles helped Alexander defeat Porus, but the Macedonian king soon realised that subjugating India was beyond even his military capabilities. He headed towards the coast, massacring many people as he went, and departed, leaving behind a very weak arrangement of vassalage where Taxiles maintained his kingship, while being overseen by a Greek governor in the region. But there is so much more to the story of Taxila that our Greek and Roman sources do not tell us, both before and after Alexander's invasion.

* * *

The history of Taxila (Sanskrit: Takkasila) is, in effect, the history of three areas of the world converging. Goods from south Asia came in abundance via the royal highway that stretched across India, down through the imperial capital of Pataliputra and towards the Bay of Bengal. Central Asian goods flowed in from the north of the Himalayas, linking Taxila with what was to become the Silk Road and a route to eastern China. The city also saw large numbers of traders come and go from western Asia and the eastern Mediterranean. Due to its location, Taxila served as a gateway to India and, as empires rose and fell, and trade routes expanded, it sat at one of the largest crossroads in the ancient world.[6]

The region in which Taxila sat, Gandhara, was a coveted part of the world. No doubt its allure was enhanced by Taxila's great reputation. Taxila was said to have been founded by the hero Bharata, brother to Rama himself, giving it a long and distinguished mythological pedigree. It appears by name in the two great Sanskrit epics, the *Ramayana* and the *Mahabharata*; in fact, there is one tradition that the *Mahabharata* was first recited in Taxila itself. The respect and reverence this tradition bestows upon Taxila should not be understated; if we were to imagine that there was a single city in Greece that could lay claim to have first heard the *Iliad* of Homer, this would still not come close to the religious and cultural importance of Taxila's relationship with the *Mahabharata*.

The archaeological work done at the site of Taxila goes some way to support this literary tradition. While it had been inhabited since the Neolithic period, the first major settlement appears at the turn of the first millennium BCE. By the late sixth century BCE, it had established itself as an affluent city. At the same time, a new imperial power came into the region, the Achaemenids of Persia. Forming the most easterly point of the Persian Empire, Gandhara offered the Persian court unprecedented wealth and resources. According to Herodotus, this new province of 'India' held the largest population in the empire, and its tribute of gold dust made up one-third of all their revenue from Asia.[7] As a result, we see in a collection of Persian administrative documents known as Persepolis Fortification Texts regular mention of people going to India, and indeed of Indians coming to one of the Persian capitals at Persepolis, in modern Iran.[8] The province of India was no far-flung place which bore no direct relevance to the Persian Empire, barring its revenue stream; it was an important and integral participant in Persian domination. We hear of Indian forces in the armies of Xerxes I during his invasion of Greece in 480 BCE and in the armies of Darius III during his battles with Alexander.

It was not just the imperial power of Persia that was beginning to spread its influence over Taxila. The late sixth and early fifth centuries BCE also witnessed the rise of another powerful and influential person whose impact on history would supersede that of Darius: Siddhartha Gautama, the Buddha. Taxila appears in early Buddhist stories – the *Jakatas* which detail the previous lives of the Buddha – and is described as a place of learning and contemplation. The city is presented as almost a university town, with 'world famed teachers', and a place where the Bodhisattva (the Buddha in his former lives) learned the principles of science, philosophy and theology.[9] Taxila was also famous as a centre for learning medicine; one of its alumni was the famous physician Jivaka who is said to have healed the Buddha himself.[10] This characterisation of a town out on the edges being an innovative centre of learning is one we have seen before in both Naucratis and Massalia, so perhaps we are seeing once again the intellectual benefit of being removed from the more traditionalist eyes of the cultural centres, this time in India.

Interestingly, Taxila's reputation as a centre of learning also existed outside of the Buddhist tradition. Perhaps the most famous scholar to be associated with the city was the grammarian Panini, who wrote the first formal grammatical work of Sanskrit. His work is considered to be the foundation of modern linguistics, offering a scientific and, one must say, comprehensive survey of the Sanskrit language. In fact, his genius spread beyond the study of language: his use of abstract symbols to denote groups of words and letters that could be replaced has been linked to the origins of algebra, and his creation of a generative grammar has led many to claim Panini's work as the original or at least the forebear of modern computing languages.[11] It is no exaggeration when scholars of Panini claim his work as 'one of the greatest monuments of human intelligence'.[12]

When the Greeks met these Indian intellectuals, they often described them simply as philosophers, which does not really do justice to their achievements. The most famous of these were a group known as the *gymnosophists*, the naked thinkers – a very Greek description for what was clearly a group of religious adherents. The descriptions of these sophists, of which we have many, show that the Greeks did not understand the difference between the various religious sects; whether they were Hindu, Buddhist or Jain ascetics, they were all described as if they were one group.[13] One of our eyewitness accounts comes from Onesicritus, a cynic philosopher and companion of Alexander, who the king sent to meet with a group of *gymnosophists*. His description, which comes to us through a retelling by Strabo, betrays the shock and admiration he clearly felt on meeting these men:

> Onesicritus found, at the distance of 20 stadia from the city, fifteen men standing in different postures, sitting or lying down naked, who continued in these positions until the evening, and then returned to the city. The most difficult thing to endure was the heat of the sun, which was so powerful, that no one else could endure without pain to walk on the ground at mid-day with bare feet.[14]

* * *

It is easy for us to overly fixate on what was happening west of Taxila, bringing the city into an extra-European narrative, but this would be grossly misguided. For as much as there were political and imperial movements to the west, there were equally dominant imperial powers to the east.

Alexander's focus on the relatively minor Indian ruler Porus highlights just how little the Greeks knew about the political landscape of India. For all the beauty and majesty that Gandhara offers, the central focal point of the Indian subcontinent during this period was around the River Ganges. Porus was but a small fish when compared to the Nanda kings of the Magadha Empire, who ruled from the royal city of Pataliputra. The Nanda dynasty had a horrible reputation for their despotic rule, but their power was unmatched in the south Asian subcontinent. It is said that when Alexander's army heard rumours of the Nanda's military strength they refused to march on, forcing him to turn back on his plan to cross the Ganges.

Alexander never actually set foot in the land of modern India and yet, if his biographer Plutarch is to be believed, he may have met a young man at Taxila who would go on to change the shape of the Indian world:

> Androcottus, when he was a young man, saw Alexander himself, and would often say later in life that Alexander missed an opportunity to take control of the country.[15]

Androcottus, a Hellenised form of the name Chandragupta, was the man who would go on to start the Mauryan dynasty that would rule most of India for the next 140 years.

Chandragupta Maurya began life in a rather sorry state. Part of an elite lineage which some traditions connected to the family of the Buddha himself, Chandragupta's father was killed before he was born, leaving his mother destitute and alone. On the move with nowhere to belong, his mother headed to Pataliputra and gave birth to her son, Chandragupta. Whether for his safety, or simply due to a lack of means to raise the boy herself, she left the baby at a cow pen, to be found and raised by a cowherder. This foster father had no paternal instincts and sold Chandragupta to a local hunter who raised the boy as his own.

As Chandragupta grew older, he showed himself a born leader, inventing games of kingship where he would order the other local boys around, and even hold a mock court to administer justice. His actions and demeanour soon caught the eye of the great Indian philosopher Chanakya. Chanakya was not only a great teacher but also a shrewd political thinker, a Machiavelli of his time, and it was prophesied that he would one day raise an emperor of his own, guiding him to rule the land. As he watched the young Chandragupta playing, who was no more than perhaps ten years old, he identified the regal attributes on display and saw his chance. He went to the boy's father and offered him 1,000 *kashapanas* (silver coins). Having now bought Chandragupta, Chanakya returned to his own hometown of Taxila where he ensured the child received the best education in the humanities, sciences and arts, as well as more practical subjects such as law, military science and medicine.[16] Perhaps it was during these years that he met Alexander.

Once he came of age, Chanakya encouraged Chandragupta to raise an army and take control of Magadha, the centre of the Nanda Empire. Without a kingdom of his own, Chandragupta was forced to rely upon the fiercely independent tribal groups living in the wider Punjab region, beyond the reaches of the Nanda king, for support. Even in the face of powerful rulers such as Taxiles and Porus, many communities were considered 'king-less' in our Indian sources. Rather dismissively described as robbers and bandits in our Greek sources, these 'king-less' men came to form the bulk of Chandragupta's forces, aided in turn by an alliance made with a king in the Himalayas.[17] But even with this groundswell of local support, the rebel army was not strong enough to take on the might of the Nanda forces. This is where the foresight and intelligence of Chanakya came into play.

There is no account of the invasion and conquest of the Ganges Basin, however a legend survives which gives an indication of what may have happened. One source tells the story of a mother who scolded her son for the way he was eating his meal. The child was impatient and thrust his hand straight into the middle of the piping-hot porridge, instead of eating from around the edges first. She compared this to Chandragupta and Chanakya's invasion:

> Dim-witted Chanakya rendered himself defenceless when he began to besiege Nanda's capital, without securing the outlying districts. In the same way, this child did not begin by gradually eating his way in from the edges, but put his hand in the middle, and got his fingers burnt.[18]

There are variants of this tale: sometimes the boy is eating bread but discarding the crusts, yet the message remains the same: the first invasion did not go well. Perhaps this reflects early, faltering attempts undertaken by the rebel army to invade the heart of the Nanda kingdom. Or perhaps it is simply an apocryphal story to highlight the adaptability of Chanakya and his young charge in the face of defeat. Either way, the army regrouped and chose to take control of the outlying lands of the empire first, securing their control before moving closer and closer to the beating heart of the empire. The strategy worked, and the Mauryan Empire was founded with its capital at Pataliputra, with Chandragupta as its first emperor in 321 BCE. Not one to rest on his laurels, Chandragupta consolidated his new empire and looked at a growing unrest in the north-western region of Gandhara.

When Alexander retreated from India in 325 BCE, he left behind him something of a political quagmire. Both Taxiles and his rival Porus were allowed to keep their kingdoms, while a Greek regent was given nominal command of the region and a small garrison force. In reality, the region had always been fiercely independent and, in turn, it had now become an open target for anyone hungry for power. By the year of Chandragupta's accession, any sense of Greek control had completely unravelled. The Greek regent to whom Alexander had given command of the region had been assassinated by his own troops. Alexander had promised a replacement, but this never materialised.

Alexander died in 323 BCE, causing a huge succession crisis for his newly forged empire. This crisis encouraged the Macedonian regent Antipater to relinquish the lands of Porus and Taxiles back to them, without Greek oversight. By 321 BCE, the last local presence of Alexander's original authority, Eudamus the Thracian, decided to leave and join the Seleucid faction in the so-called War of the Successors. Before his departure from India, he left a lasting impact on the political landscape by assassinating Porus, a king who was considered to be the most powerful in all of northern India.[19]

Without a powerful or united force in the north-west, Chandragupta invaded with a very large army – one source claims it was 600,000-strong – and he must have taken control of the region swiftly, but our sources' silence on the topic is somewhat deafening.[20] While we cannot be certain, his authority along the Indus must have been established by 306 BCE because it prompted an aggressive reaction from the newly founded Seleucid kingdom of Seleucus Nikator. Unfortunately for Seleucus, any hopes of defeating a disunited and fractured India were sorely misguided.

We are not told how the war played out. It is possible that the Indians won decisively in battle, but it is also likely that Seleucus aborted his mission after he crossed the Indus and realised just how large an army Chandragupta had under his command. Strangely, the only part of this war we know about in any detail is the agreed terms of peace. Strabo gives us the greatest amount of detail, describing Seleucus' ceding of the Indus Valley, as well as parts of the Hindu Kush and Afghanistan. He also describes a marriage agreement between the Greeks and Indians, suggesting a formal arrangement of intermarriage. Finally, Chandragupta gifted Seleucus 500 war elephants, a paltry price for just how much land he had received in return.[21] (Though Seleucus did in fact use those elephants to great effect during the battle of Ipsus (301 BCE) in his war against the Antigonids in western Asia.)

Even at this point of imperial expansion under the Mauryans, the impression we have been given by the sources from all traditions is that Taxila was something of an outlier in both the European/west Asian and the Indian context. The city maintained an independent reputation, aided by its peripheral position to the various empires it served as a buffer to. It obviously was not a Greek city, but it did not abide by all the customs of India either. One clear example comes from the account of Strabo, whose own source describes the seemingly strange customs he witnessed in Taxila. Perhaps the most intriguing concerns a marriage custom, whereby poorer families would take the daughters to a marriage market, a custom condemned in Indian law:[22]

> Aristobulus relates also some strange and unusual customs of the people of Taxila. Those, who through poverty are unable to marry their daughters, expose them for sale in the marketplace, in the flower of their age, to the sound of shell trumpets and drums, with which the war-note is given. A crowd is thus assembled. First her back, as far as the shoulders, is uncovered, then the parts in front, for the examination of any man

> who comes for this purpose. If she pleases him, he marries her on such conditions as may be determined upon.[23]

Taxila's reluctance to accept Mauryan control was once attributed to a closer affinity with Persian and Greek culture, but this does not seem to be the case. During the reign of Bindusara, the son of Chandragupta, the city of Taxila had a reputation for rebelling. To quell one particularly large uprising, Bindusara sent one of his own sons with a large army that included cavalry, elephants, chariots and infantry, to put Taxila to siege. Much to the prince's surprise, as he neared the region of Gandhara he did not encounter any hostility, but instead found his road to Taxila lined with vases filled with offerings stretching for thirty kilometres. On his arrival he met no resistance but instead received an explanation. The Taxilians told him that it was never their intention to rebel against the young prince, or indeed his imperial father. It was the oppression they felt under the local ministers, people they described as evil; these were the target of the rebellion. Instead, the prince was embraced and welcomed into the city, bringing the rebellion to a swift and bloodless end.[24]

That prince's name was Ashoka Maurya, and he would grow up to become possibly the most important and powerful ruler in all ancient India. For our purposes here, the importance of Ashoka and his reign comes not in his internal political reforms, but, rather, in his religious ones. Often dubbed the 'Constantine of India', Ashoka reformed the Buddhist faith and became patron to its evangelical spread across the world.

* * *

Although Buddhism had already established itself as a religious movement in India by the third century BCE, it was beset with internal division and theological debate. Under the rule of Ashoka, Buddhism was transformed into a state religion for the

Mauryan Empire and, similar to Christianity in the third century CE, held numerous councils to solidify the Buddhist teachings in the face of growing differences.

This whole process is interesting in and of itself, but what makes it all the more pertinent is that Ashoka was a man invested in the wider world around him. Growing up in the court of Bindusara, he would have met or at least seen and heard of the emissaries and envoys coming from distant, foreign lands, such as the Greek author Megasthenes, who served as a diplomat to Seleucus following his withdrawal from the Indus. Megasthenes would go on to write a book based on his time in India, his *Indika*, the surviving snippets of which offer us an amazing insight into Indian culture and life in Pataliputra where he was based. But Ashoka's interest went beyond the simple intrigue of foreigners in the court.

During his reign, Ashoka emulated the Persian royal tradition of inscribing his achievements and pronouncements on either rocks or pillars. These edicts are indicative of his view of the wider world. The one furthest north – thus far identified – has been found in Kandahar, Afghanistan. His edicts are written in various languages, the majority of them in Prakrit, but two of them in Greek and Aramaic – in fact, the Kandahar edict is written bilingually in Greek and Aramaic, pointing us directly to his intended audiences. A later rock edict commemorating Ashoka's victory in war over Kalinga, an independent kingdom on the east coast of India, mentions five Greek kings who have been identified as Antiochus II of Syria, Ptolemy II of Egypt, Magas of Cyrene, Antigonus Gonatus of Macedonia and Alexander of either Corinth or Epirus. The importance of this particular edict is twofold: it shows that Ashoka had an understanding of, and a possible diplomatic relationship with, numerous Mediterranean kings; and it was the first monument that allowed historians to tie the reign of Ashoka to a known series of dates in history. For a long time, Indian history lacked firm dates because western scholars could not align Indian chronology with European traditions; the identification of kings that historians could name and compare the reigning dates of allowed for the accurate dating of an Indian ruler.

When Ashoka convened the Third Buddhist Council in c.250 BCE, it concluded with the decision to send nine missionaries, Buddhist monks of the highest reputations, to the corners of the Indian world to spread the faith. One monk, Majjhantika, was sent to Kashmir and Gandhara, either establishing or cementing the Buddhist presence at Taxila. Another by the name of Maharakkhita was sent to the land of the Yona, the Greeks.

We have already seen how Taxila quickly became a hallowed place of learning in the Buddhist traditions. Gandhara more generally is the location of the oldest known Buddhist texts ever found, dating from as early as the first century BCE, so the region's importance cannot be overstated.[25] But, of course, Taxila was not situated in an entirely Indian cultural sphere, so where Buddhism found a home it also found other cultures to interact with. In the first century CE, long after the reign of Ashoka and the later collapse of the Mauryan Empire, an important development occurred in the region which had not been seen before. Craftsmen began to make realistic images of the Buddha, following the Indo-Greek style of sculpture which had established itself in the region. Up until that point, the Buddha was never shown in his physical, human form; Buddhist art and sculpture used symbols such as a footprint, or a wheel, or sometimes simply a vacant space to represent him. In fact, the earliest Buddhist traditions suggest that there were widespread concerns and debates about whether it was appropriate or indeed even possible to depict the Buddha in his physical form. While it is not common in this literature, there is one tradition, preserved in Chinese, which suggests some sects may have banned the use of his image outright:

> [The body of the Buddha] transcends all class of gods and contains the seven riches of Law, which is beyond the stages of men, gods and other natural living beings, and cannot be made an image.[26]

Notwithstanding this potential cause of controversy, suffice it to say that the Greeks left an indelible mark on Buddhism, especially in the north-west hinterland. Not only did their artistic style encourage the human depiction of the Buddha, but he is also sometimes depicted with the Greek hero Hercules as his protector. Such a deep cultural influence could only be achieved at places like Taxila, where intellectual and artistic freedoms met with a merging of multicultural ideas and expressions.

It was not only a matter for Greek artistic styles; we also see Greek individuals appear in Buddhist history, such as the Greco-Buddhist monk called Dharmaraksita, who was one of the missionaries sent out by Ashoka. Dharmaraksita would later go on to be the teacher of another important monk by the name of Nagasena who, in turn, would famously convert the Greco-Bactrian king Menander I to Buddhism. This conversion is described in the Buddhist text *Milinda Pañha* (The Questions of King Menander), which depicts a fictional dialogue between the king and his teacher.

As the Mediterranean transformed under the Roman Empire at the turn of the Common Era, we know that both Indian culture and Buddhism had spread to the region through trade, missionary activities and cultural envoys. While the Buddhist faith did not spread prolifically through the empire, Clement of Alexandria describes a group of Indian philosophers in the Egyptian city who followed the teachings of the 'Boutta' (Buddha).[27] His claim has been all but verified by the recent discovery of the Berenike Buddha, a third-century CE statue of the Buddha brought to light in the temple grounds of Isis in the ancient Egyptian town of Berenike on the Red Sea coast.[28]

We also know that during a visit to Athens, the first emperor of Rome, Augustus, received an Indian delegation which included a Buddhist monk. That monk decided to prove his faith by setting light to himself and burning to death, and in doing so he left an unprecedented impression on the Athenian people. They erected a tomb to house his remains and, in the accompanying inscription, bestowed upon him the highest honours – they acknowledged his transition to immortality. It read:

> Zarmanochegas the Indian, from Bargosa, having immortalized himself according to the customs of his homeland of India, here lies.[29]

While this offers us a fascinating insight into the global nature of the ancient Mediterranean during this period, it is, of course, the relationship between Buddhism and eastern Asia which was the more significant. In the absence of an interconnected road network, the eastern spread of Buddhism was quite slow. One place that certainly facilitated its expansion north and east of the Himalayas was Taxila, with its prime location connected to the emerging Silk Road.

Taxila had undergone numerous regime changes by the time Buddhism spread east into Han China. The Mauryans had been supplanted by the Greco-Bactrian kingdom, which in turn had been replaced by Scythian rulers, Parthian rulers and then, by the mid-first century CE, Taxila was controlled by a nomadic group called the Kushan. The earliest mention of Buddhist teachings in China date to this first century, and specifically refer to an envoy from the king of the Kushan (Yuezhi in Chinese) teaching the sutras.[30] While it is thus far impossible to say with absolute certainty, all the evidence suggests that Buddhism spread from its stronghold in Taxila, north through Bactria and then east along the Silk Road into China.

It would be fair to state that the importance of Taxila in this religious dissemination is based slightly on conjecture. It was in the right place at the right time and had long-standing Buddhist connections and monuments. But there is later evidence which suggests its importance was never forgotten. For long after the city's fall from grace, Buddhist pilgrims would still visit the site. One such man, the Chinese travel writer Faxian, recorded his visit to Gandhara in the fifth century CE and, in turn, tells us one tradition for how Taxila got its name:

> Seven days' journey from this to the east brought the travellers to the kingdom of Taxila, which means 'the severed head' in the language of China. Here, when Buddha was a Bodhisattva, he gave away his head to a man; and from this circumstance the kingdom got its name.[31]

Heliodorus' inscription at the beginning of this chapter now begins to make a lot more sense. While the monument originally seemed to be one of jarring contradictions, with its Greek patron inscribing in Prakrit his devotion to Vishnu, it can now be seen to represent a wider picture of life at Taxila. This was a city filled with learning and cultural exchange, where religious innovation and novelty was embraced and given space to thrive. It was a place where no one language superseded another, but where different languages sat side by side – whether it was Ashoka's edict in Aramaic and Greek, or another in Prakrit. Heliodorus was raised in this unique cultural tradition, much more than he was raised in a purely Greek one. He was a man of Taxila, and his monument is testament to all that that means.

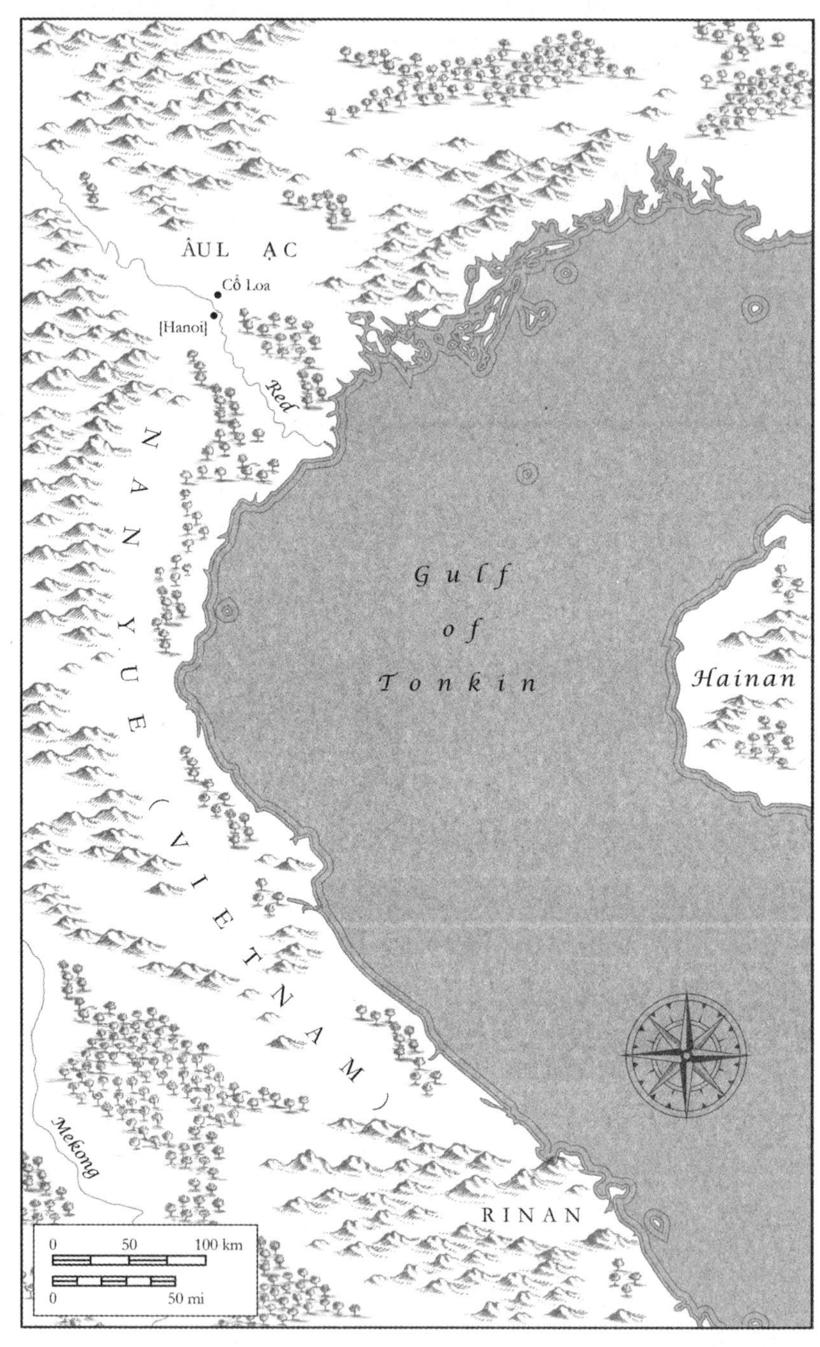
ÂU LẠC
Cổ Loa
[Hanoi]
Red
NAN YUE (VIETNAM)
Gulf of Tonkin
Hainan
Mekong
RINAN
0 50 100 km
0 50 mi

12

# Co Loa, Vietnam

Unlike the previous two chapters, our next example takes us as far away from Greek and Roman influence as possible. It is arguably the furthest point in the world of which the Romans had a vague knowledge. Beyond the lands of India, Roman geography became very speculative, but they knew that there was more and that people lived out there. It was another world just beyond their reach, but one they knew was real, if only because of the trade goods that came from there. It was known as Sericae, the land of silk. Roman geographers amalgamated all that they knew about east continental Asia, which included parts of modern China as well, into one poorly defined area. They also talk about the lands of the Sinae, which were reached by sea and roughly correlate with the south-east Asian peninsula which includes modern Vietnam.

In terms of the Greco-Roman world map, this would be the very furthest point from the centre. Over 9,000 kilometres away, the Romans could exert no influence over it, nor have its influence thrust upon them, but they were both a small part of each other's stories. Vietnam also serves as the location for one of history's biggest 'what might have beens', where Rome and the powerful empire of Han China almost made direct contact with each other. The role of ancient Vietnam in the story of the ancient European world is not one of elite interaction but of ordinary merchants travelling between two worlds, connecting in ways that modern scholarship is only starting to reveal. Yet Vietnam deserves to be more than a footnote to the history of ancient Rome. It has its own important story to tell.

Ancient Vietnam is not a common topic in our history books, but it should be. Surrounded by powerful cultures in India to the west and China to the north and east, and tapping into a growing global trade network via the Indian Ocean, Vietnam was a melting pot of ideas and technologies. Its history offers many parallels to much we have seen already, but also presents new narratives that resonate into the modern day. Ignoring the historic tensions and influences between Vietnam and the rest of south-east Asia, or between it and China, would be like ignoring the influence of Rome on Britain. This dichotomy of cultural independence and interdependence with other societies is epitomised by Vietnam's oldest city, Co Loa, which sat between two worlds.

According to ancient Vietnamese legend, the Red River Valley in northern Vietnam had been ruled over by a religious dynasty known as the Hung kings. Their founding king is said to have used illusion and magic to take control, and his successors ruled for eighteen generations into the third century BCE. However, political movements to the north in modern-day China brought their dynasty to a swift and decisive end. The growing empire of Qin was spreading south, forcing thousands of people to flee or else be subsumed into what would later become Imperial China. In the face of such an indomitable power, the ruler of Shu permitted his son, Thuc Phan, to take a force of 30,000 people south towards the Red River to find a new home for themselves.[1] His arrival in the valley was not well received, and the Hung king relied on his ancestral tactics of fear and mysticism to win the day. He asked Thuc Phan, 'Do you not know of my magical powers? Are you not afraid?', but his bluster did little to aid his armies, which were crushed under the might of the invader. Having lost his land, the Hung king took his own life by throwing himself down a well, leaving Thuc Phan to establish a new kingdom, which he called Au Lac, and proclaim himself An Duong Vuong (or King An Duong).

To cement his rule, An Duong Vuong began building a new capital, Co Loa, a place that would not only give his people a focal point, but also offer the outside world a demonstration of his power. He ordered the construction of his new citadel immediately, but it was beset with problems from the start. For it is said that the building project was constantly thwarted by a group of demons living on a nearby mountain. Each day the men would start the construction work but, at nightfall, out these spirits would come and destroy all that had been achieved. An Duong Vuong was at a loss as to what he could do until he was approached by a divine Golden Tortoise, who informed him that these demons were led by a thousand-year-old White Chicken working on behalf of the son of the former king. The Golden Tortoise subdued the evil White Chicken, and the defences of Co Loa were finally completed. Before it departed, the Golden Tortoise gave An Duong Vuong a claw as a gift, which came with a set of very specific instructions. He was to make a large crossbow, using the claw as its trigger, which would give him the power to defeat all his enemies.[2]

From here the story continues in a similar vein to many global myths of kingship. A holy man by the name of Cao Thong made the weapon for the king, and pronounced: 'He who is able to hold this crossbow rules the realm; he who is not able to hold this crossbow will perish.'[3]

This story of a new king trying to unite a disparate group of people against the forces of chaos around them, who is approached and aided by a divine presence from the water, which brings with it the key to power in the form of a magical weapon, has very clear comparisons with the stories of Arthurian legend.

Indeed, An Duong Vuong would later be betrayed by those closest to him, lose the crossbow and end up meeting with the Golden Turtle once more to be taken away to the watery realm – his own Avalon.

Much like the legend of King Arthur, the 'truth behind the myth' of An Duong Vuong has been the subject of a centuries-long debate. Traditionally, his invasion of the Red River Valley is dated to 257 BCE, but Chinese annals show that his father's kingdom of Shu was brought under Qin control as early as 316 BCE, which contradicts this oral history somewhat. The problem originates from the evidence itself.

Much of this story comes to us from fourteenth- and fifteenth-century CE works which relied heavily on earlier Chinese sources for the detail. This becomes clear when we consider the more mythological imagery in the story: the battle between two supernatural animals. The chicken was an ancient indigenous symbol in the region, whereas the tortoise represents the Chinese god of war, Chen Wu.[4] Suddenly the story takes on a rather clear symbolic meaning, with the 'Chinese' An Duong Vuong besting the valiant but inferior indigenous people who still rely on mysticism and magic, rather than skill, ingenuity and intellect. As the story has been retold, the themes and ideals it represents have been moulded to fit the political and social context of those time periods. In fact, you can trace the growing thread of Vietnamese identity, as well as Sino-Vietnamese relations, through both the later versions of this tale and the academic study of it.[5]

This tussle between Chinese and Vietnamese identity, embodied by the figure of An Duong Vuong, is ever-present in the study of ancient Vietnam. For many years it has been believed that the Chinese brought civilisation to the Red River Valley, thus making all later Vietnamese history and culture reliant on this early Sinification. That is certainly another clear theme within the legend, which ends with the usurpation of An Duong Vuong by another ruler to the north by the name of Zhao Tuo. Zhao Tuo had established a new kingdom in southern China in 204 BCE, following the fall of the Qin dynasty, and his invasion of Au Lac in the early second century BCE would have a lasting impression on the land and its people as they became part of Nan Yue – or, as it is written in Vietnamese, Nam Viet.

This story of Chinese superiority and early colonialism, imbued as it is with an air of cultural superiority on behalf of our sources, is exactly that: a story. For Zhao Tuo did not find a people inferior to himself in any way, nor did he find a disparate group of tribes who lacked any central leadership. This is not only implied in the written evidence; the excavations at Co Loa have proven this unequivocally.

Away from the myths and the legends, Co Loa is not another fictional Camelot: it was a real town built and lived in by real people. Ideally located in the fertile Red River Delta, about ten miles north of modern Hanoi, Co Loa had been inhabited since the Neolithic era, but the earliest dating of its earthen ramparts – of which there are at least three – suggests that the fortification of the site began at the turn of the third century BCE, a dating which incidentally is corroborated by the oral history surrounding An Duong Vuong.

The outer rampart runs along a five-mile perimeter, enclosing an area of approximately 600 hectares, and still stands at ten metres in height and up to eighteen metres wide. It is surrounded by a moat, fed to the south by the Red River, which punctuates the rampart to the east, allowing the waterway to come all the way through into the city itself. A slightly smaller inner rampart follows a similar layout, forming two irregular concentric circles and, once more, encircled by a moat. A third and final rampart was built in the centre of Co Loa, roughly rectangular in shape, the walls of which run for only one mile.[6] These formed the earliest defences and are contemporaneous with the earliest constructions of similar earth-packed defences further north that would later form part of the Great Wall of China.

In total, the fortifications at Co Loa would have required the excavation of nearly 1,000,000 cubic metres of earth, and the making of over ten miles of ramparts. Archaeologists have estimated that this construction would have required 10,000 people working every single day for one and a half years without interruption, or three years if we assume they worked for 175 days in a year. In terms of labour requirements, this is comparable in scale to the great Pyramid of the Sun of Teotihuacan in Mexico.[7] When we consider that these people would not only need to be fed, but also to be relieved of their normal daily duties of farming and the like, it is easy to see why it has been strongly argued by one scholar that the construction could only be achieved if facilitated by a central state-like authority.

Co Loa's location and design rather crucially offered its rulers control over both agriculture and trade in the region. The control of agriculture allowed them to exploit the highly fertile surroundings in which the city was located: an area that still, to this day, accounts for 70 per cent of crop production in northern Vietnam. The main agricultural activity was wet-rice production, a system of agriculture that utilised the abundant water supply and rainy seasons during the year through the formation of enclosed, level paddy fields, the advent of which predates Co Loa by many centuries.[8] Co Loa's control of trade, on the other hand, was not only reliant on the local geography but was actually built into the very sinews of the city. The outer moats converged and entered through the eastern part of the fortifications, passing through water gates in the middle rampart where it then splits into five channels shaped like a grasping hand. The thumb and index finger of the 'hand' form a U-shaped mini peninsula on which archaeologists have discovered the remains of a dockyard. This plugged Co Loa directly into the Red River highway, both inland and towards the coast, which in turn would have taken ships to and from the Gulf of Tonkin and beyond, to the South China Sea.

This city and its people drew upon ideas, technologies and building techniques from their neighbours to the north, aided no doubt by small movements of people coming south, but they were not reliant on the Chinese for their culture or identity, a balancing act that they were only able to perform because of Co Loa's unique position. Culturally, Co Loa shares the hallmarks of the Dong Son culture, an indigenous Bronze Age culture dating between 600 BCE and 100 CE, the artefacts for which have been found throughout northern Vietnam and are associated with the Lac Viet people. Two particularly distinguishing markers of this culture come from the bronze they used in their metalwork. First, the bronze itself had a remarkably high lead content (about 20 per cent) which makes it easier to identify against Chinese bronze, which had a much higher tin content. Second, they produced large and distinctive bronze drums that were possible to make thanks to this high lead content, which allowed for smelting to occur at a much lower temperature. Leaded bronze also increases the plasticity of the alloy, allowing for greater precision and a more delicate design.

These drums, in particular, are impressive for their size if nothing else; one found in Co Loa is half a metre high and just over seventy centimetres wide. Weighing seventy-two kilograms, it would have required the smelting of maybe as much as seven tons of copper ore alone. Scholars are not sure what these drums were used for, and it is likely they were used on a multitude of different occasions including war; but their intricate artistic decorations often have an aquatic theme which depicts a form of ritual such as praying for rain, so it is assumed they are linked to some sort of ceremonial, cult activity.[9]

The impression we receive from the archaeological material is that Co Loa was a sophisticated polity with a central organisation that was able to fund and support ambitious projects, as well as patronising artisans to become masters of their craft. What is more, there is evidence that the people of northern Vietnam were literate, or at least their social elite were. Imperial Chinese reports from the second century BCE mention that local population records existed that were written in an unidentified writing system. If it is true that there was an indigenous Lac Viet written language of some description – and there is little reason to question this – that is a clear indication of the political and social sophistication on display at important cultural centres like Co Loa. It does, however, also make it likely that anything written in that language, especially historical records and chronicles, was destroyed as we know that the first emperor of Qin, Qin Shi Huang, ordered the destruction of all books and materials pertaining to the history of states other than his own.[10]

This is the city that Zhao Tuo found when he arrived. It was a thriving urban centre that dominated the trade and agricultural landscape of northern Vietnam – one that exploited the waterways to perfection and that used its surplus of goods and produce to support a large population capable of exquisite artwork. It was also a military and naval centre, capable of offering resistance to even the greatest military forces in the region. Zhao Tuo did not make Co Loa his capital for the region, but nor did he destroy such an important city. He chose to use local Lac Viet chiefs to help organise the territory, one of whom took Co Loa as their court. Under their guidance, the kingdom of Nan Yue was stabilised, even in the face of a new and growing power in China.

The void in China that had been formed by the collapse of the Qin dynasty was subsequently filled by the equally ambitious Han dynasty. Their own need for political stability in the wake of such upheaval meant that Zhao Tuo was able to use diplomacy to keep them at bay and maintain his own independence. Their relationship was fraught with difficulties, not helped by Zhao's early insistence on calling himself an emperor – something that did not go down well in the Han court. Up to his death in 137 BCE, Zhao Tuo was able to keep the Han out of the Red River Valley, but it was not to last.

* * *

Under both the Qin and early Han dynasties, Chinese dealings with the Red River Valley were characteristically indirect. As a result, their knowledge and understanding of the region and its people is filled with generalisations and generic stereotypes, much as we have seen in our Greek and Roman sources. The Lac Viet were lumped together with the many other 'barbarian' peoples to the south of the imperial heartland, who the Chinese called the Yue.[11] Indeed, the name of Zhao Tuo's kingdom, Nan Yue (Nam Viet), translates to mean the southern Yue, as does the modern name of Vietnam.

The Yue were supposedly a barbaric and backward people who failed to uphold any Chinese sense of civility, order or organisation – something that was regimented by Confucian ideals and principles. During the period following the death of Zhao Tuo, one member of the Han imperial court specifically counselled against an invasion. His reasoning reveals a lot about how the Yue, and specifically the southern Yue, were perceived:

> Yue is a land beyond this world, with a people who shear their hair and tattoo their bodies. It cannot be regulated by the laws of civilized nations.[12]

What is particularly striking here is that, if you simply changed the name of the subject in this sentence, this could comfortably be mistaken as a Greek description of the Scythians or the Thracians, or an Egyptian description of the Kush. The driving beliefs of cultural superiority and exceptionalism live in the heart of all imperial and colonising missions.

In 111 BCE, the armies of the Han commander Lu Bode had successfully subdued the southern Yue, but he stopped short of the Red River Delta. Instead, the Han court implemented a similar political tactic to Zhao Tuo by allowing the ruling Lac Viet elite to maintain their positions of authority, as long as they supplicated to the emperor. Some men tried to take advantage of this new political order by taking up new positions in place of established chiefs. One such man was named Huang Tong, a commander of the Lac Viet who held the title 'General of the Left of Old Au Lac'. Huang Tong decided to show his newfound loyalty to the Han court in the most brutal of ways, by beheading one of the local vassals of Nan Yue. His plan was successful and in 110 BCE he was elevated to the position of marquis in the new Chinese world order. The man he killed so ignominiously, without regard for loyalty or honour, was the last Lac Viet ruler to reign from Co Loa.[13]

Once the dust had settled, life for the Lac Viet remained pretty much the same. Even after the administrative reorganisation of the region, to bring it in line with the rest of the Han Empire, it was local administrators who were left in charge. We also know that the region was exempt from taxes, so there were few added burdens placed upon them. More interestingly, local customs were tolerated, meaning that there was no attempt to 'civilise the barbarian'. All this suggests that the Han wished to control the region, but not incorporate it into their cultural sphere, at least not yet. In truth, the regions of south-west China and northern Vietnam were considered most important for their control of access to the south seas, and this seems to have been the motivating factor in the Han court's decision-making.[14]

Even with the region under their control, Chinese writers still considered the land of Lac Viet exotic, wild and dangerous, with dense forests and fierce, wild animals like tigers and elephants. But nothing was as wild as the people themselves, with their tattoos and blackened teeth, who it was believed would eat snake meat, and also use poisoned arrow tips in war.[15] The behaviour and manners of these people were considered a direct result of their living conditions. Based in the tropical region, the constant heat was thought to be the cause of their impetuousness and passion. It was said that this transformed them into venomous people, in turn revealing to us just how blurred the lines were between myth and reality when it comes to these accounts:

> When they talk with others, and a drop of their saliva strikes the interlocutors, the arteries of the latter begin to swell and ulcerate ... When the people there curse a tree, it withers, and when they spit on a bird it drops down dead.[16]

But the most striking cultural difference between the Chinese and the Lac Viet was the role and position of women. In China, Confucian ideals of law, order, structure and hierarchy influenced almost all aspects of their culture and were replicated everywhere: a man was obedient to his ruler, as a son was to his father, and in marriage a wife was to her husband. Within this clear hierarchical system of patriarchal order as seen through the family, the court and the state, women had little influence. Among the Lac Viet, this was certainly not the case. We know that some unwedded couples would live together, with marriage not occurring until after the birth of the first child. We also know that marriage cemented the matrilineal bonds of a family, with the new bridegroom moving in with his wife's family. What is more, women could inherit from their parents, so their economic status was equally secured externally from their husband or male family member. It would be a stretch to describe this society as matriarchal, but the importance placed on the female line did mean that it was possible for some women to hold equal influence over men, especially within the home.

However, this cultural and political autonomy was not to last. By the turn of the first century CE, there were rumblings of a civilising mission by the Han administrators, who were growing more and more concerned by what they considered immoral customs by the Lac Viet. This cultural clash became all the more apparent when the Han dynasty was overthrown in 9 CE by a usurper to the throne, Wang Mang. His rule was only short, and he was replaced by what is called the Later Han dynasty, which was established in 25 CE, but during those intervening years thousands of refugees fled south into the region of Lac Viet.

This influx of people not only brought cultural friction, as many of them were highly educated within Confucian systems of learning and administration, it also put further pressure on a densely populated region. Local officials looked to the Han court for more support and investment in the infrastructure, which did come, but at a frightful cost. The specific details are not clear in the records, but it seems that an investment in agriculture, in particular, made the region one of the primary grain suppliers for all of southern China. It also facilitated greater trade traffic to and from the South China Sea. This resulted in the hitherto semi-autonomous Lac Viet lords losing their autonomy, and there is even a strong suggestion that they, like other regions in the south of Han China, lost their tax-exemption status at this time.[17]

This environment of cultural conflict, political imbalance and enforced taxation created a very volatile situation, one that would need handling deftly and with understanding, preferably by an experienced administrator. Unfortunately, what the region received instead was Su Ting, a cruel, greedy, power-hungry man whose approach to the situation was to try and enforce new laws and quell any opposition in the most brutal manner possible. According to the Vietnamese tradition, he identified one Lac Viet leader named Thi Sach as a particular upstart who may or may not have been planning a rebellion. Su Ting did not care to find out the truth and had him executed, and in doing so he unwittingly unleashed a force of such power and ferocity as he could never have anticipated. For Thi Sach's wife, Trung Trac, alongside her younger sister Trung Nhi, used this as a catalyst to unite all the disgruntled Lac lords in revolt in 40 CE.[18]

Their revolt began in the Red River Valley, but quickly spread both north, into former Nan Yue lands, and south into the most southern region under Han control, Rinan, in what is now central Vietnam. Trung Trac, as the leading figurehead of the revolt, drew great support from both the aristocracy and the peasantry in the region, which swelled the ranks of her army. According to Chinese accounts, Su Ting refused to go out and fight the rebels, consumed as he was by his own fear and innate cowardice. As his forces were swept aside by the formidable Trung sisters, whom later traditions depicted riding tandem atop a giant war elephant, Su Ting quickly fled back into China, leaving Trung Trac to take control of sixty cities and crown herself queen, setting up her court in her homeland of Me Linh, just to the west of Co Loa. To try and compare this achievement in its scale and success is nigh on impossible, but the obvious choice is the famous revolt of Boudicca of the Iceni tribe in Britain against the Romans. Only twenty years later than the Trung sisters, the female ruler Boudicca took on an equally powerful army in rebellion and defeated them in battle. Her rebels took control of only three cities.

The rebels' swift action and unmitigated success would have invoked shock, if not necessarily panic, among the Han courtiers. The Han had already faced their fair share of uprisings and insurrections – this was par for the course – but the fact that this was being spearheaded by two independent and powerful women was particularly jarring for the Chinese. Ironically, this is best summed up in a thirteenth-century CE Vietnamese source which, at the time it was written, was strongly influenced by Chinese Confucian ideals of gender norms and roles. It emphasises the genders of all involved to make a clear moral statement:

> All the male heroes bowed their heads in submission;
> Only the two sisters proudly stood up to avenge their country.[19]

The Trung sisters' revolt was emphatic, ferocious and inspired, but it was not to last. Trung Trac's main support base was in her homeland, while other lords led regional revolts further afield. Their early success relied on the element of surprise and was fuelled by a shared rage against a symbolic individual, Su Ting. But with him gone, and the glowing embers of revolt beginning to dim, it would only take a brief test of commitment to put a stop to the uprising, the job of which was given to a very experienced Han commander named Ma Yuan, the 'Wave-Calming General'. With an army 10,000-strong, supported by 2,000 tower ships, he headed south in 41 CE along the coastline where he chose a further 12,000 local men to swell his ranks. His advance was stalled as he entered the lands around Co Loa, the traditional stronghold of Lac Viet resistance since the earliest Han invasion. He initially set up camp in the hills just east of the city, giving him a dominant position overlooking the entire delta.

The following year fighting commenced, and the forces of Ma Yuan were fiercely contested by Trung Trac and her rebels. We are told that, in one battle alone, Yuan faced and defeated 20,000 men, and then later went on to fight another battle where he killed and captured a further 5,000. It was not just the rebels that his men were fighting, it was the tropical weather as well, as he later recalled:

> [The] rain fell, vapours rose, there were pestilential emanations, and the heat was unbearable; I even saw a sparrowhawk fall into the water and drown.[20]

Against such a disciplined army as Ma Yuan's, the rebels stood little chance. Indeed, the sources suggest that Trung Trac was forced into action as her men grew concerned about the constant presence of the Han army. She knew that her men were not disciplined or experienced enough to face off against this Chinese army, but equally she was aware that her authority relied on action and success; if she stalled, her army would disperse, and the revolt would be over. Unfortunately for her, she was correct, and her forces were no match for Ma Yuan's.

Following his military success, Ma Yuan spent the remainder of the year quelling the last remnants of resistance in the region. The task relied on the capture of the Trung sisters, something he is said to have achieved by the end of 42 CE. There is a multitude of different traditions about the deaths of the two women. According to some, they died heroically in battle. According to others, they were captured and beheaded by Ma Yuan. One tradition has them choosing death by suicide, jumping into a river and drowning; another has them dying of illness. One even suggests that they ascended into the clouds in the vein of an apotheosis. It is likely they were captured and killed, but we cannot be certain.[21]

While this would not be the final rebellion in the region – far from it – the suppression of the Trung sisters' rebellion had two important repercussions for both the history of the Han and the history of Vietnam. For the Han, it confirmed their overall control of the region, not only administratively but in its entirety. The Lac lords lost what little autonomy they had left, and the Chinese invested heavily in transport and trade links through all of Vietnam. The demand for exotic goods from in and around the region made it a valuable asset to the Han Empire. In time, they would also introduce more and more Chinese cultural ideals into the region without fully replacing all indigenous identity.

For the history of Vietnam, the Trung sisters' uprising became a beacon of hope, of resistance against oppression, and in effect it was a founding moment in Vietnamese identity. They would later be called upon in spirit to aid against imperial and military aggression, including Chinese dynasties, during the French rule in the nineteenth and early twentieth centuries, and during the war against the United States. The Trung sisters became objects of admiration, but also weapons of shame. As one thirteenth-century writer shows, the shame was directed at the memories of those who allowed imperial rule to continue:

> What a pity, for a thousand years after this [the rebellion], men of our land bowed their heads, folded their arms, and served the northerners; how shameful is this in comparison with the two Trung sisters, who were women![22]

* * *

The story of Co Loa is, rightly or wrongly, defined purely by its location. The city existed in a 'chokepoint for cultural interaction and the movement of people and goods', and as a result it is easy to zoom into that small, but intensely fascinating, socio-political environment and assume that what we are seeing is the whole story.[23] However, Co Loa should not be simply defined by these Sino-Viet tensions; it existed in a much bigger world than that.

As a settlement, Co Loa was only one within a large pattern of moated settlements arising in south-east Asia during the Bronze and Iron Ages. Similar sites have been identified in modern Thailand, in the Thai-Malay peninsula, Cambodia and Myanmar, but Co Loa is undoubtedly the largest in scale compared to the others.[24] So it is fair to assume that Co Loa was but one part of a large social movement in the region. In fact, at a time when these modern national boundaries did not exist, south-east Asia was an area of cultural exchange and interchange between a large number of different societies. They were also linked by a shared linguistic family, Austroasiatic, of which modern Vietnamese and Khmer are both members.[25]

It is impossible to know whether these cultural links facilitated trade, or if trade was the catalyst for greater cultural exchange, but the major river systems in the region made trade both simple to maintain and highly profitable. In modern Vietnam there are two major river deltas, the Red River to the north and the Mekong in the south. The Red River Delta was, as we have seen, important for its links to the South China Sea. The Mekong similarly offered a means of trade that utilised the Gulf of Thailand and its links west towards the Indian Ocean. The river was equally a transportation system that stretched for more than 3,000 miles, originating in the Tibetan Plateau, passing through the modern western China, Myanmar, Laos, Thailand and Cambodia before emptying into the gulf in Vietnam. This course only focuses on the main body of the river; if we are to consider its many tributaries as well, the Mekong begins to appear like the venal system on the map of south-east Asia.

We can see the effectiveness of this watery highway through the wide distribution of a single, important cultural artefact – the large bronze drums that we read about earlier. Almost 300 of these drums have been found in Vietnam itself, but some have also been discovered in Laos, Cambodia, Thailand and

Malaysia.[26] They have even been discovered as far as the island of New Guinea, nearly 3,000 miles away.[27] While it is, of course, possible that some of these may have been the result of singular exchanges for their novelty or exotic value, this cannot be assumed. Indeed, we know that between the third and first centuries BCE, drums made in northern Vietnam were being traded to Indonesia rather consistently, with fifty examples so far discovered.[28] When we remember that these drums were used in ritual and ceremony, the wide distribution does imply some commonalities between the people buying them and those selling.

Still further afield, the southern links to the Indian Ocean opened a much wider world of trade networks to bring global cultural artefacts to Vietnam. For, long before the famous Silk Road which linked eastern Europe and China through a network of trade routes through mainland Asia, these trade routes were already established by sea – as we saw clearly at the site of Megiddo. In fact, by the time the Han took control of Vietnam they entered a trading network which linked western Europe, the Mediterranean and Black Seas, East Africa, the Indian subcontinent, south-east Asia, right through to east Asia.

Much of this trade was indirect; items entered into a system of exchange, travelling thousands of miles, but it cannot be assumed that people at one extreme of the network were actually aware of those at the other end. However, when we consider the size, power and wealth available to two specific empires living synchronously with one another, the Han in China and the Romans in Europe, there is a tantalising possibility that they knew more about each other than is often acknowledged by modern histories.[29]

What is clear is that Roman authors knew very little about the regions in east Asia. Their name for what we think of now as China was Seres, from the Greek word for silk; for that is all that was really understood about this far-flung place beyond the known world: it produced silk. Many of our sources are not even sure how the silk was made, with some claiming it grew on trees, but it was enough to earn the region its name.[30] One much later source claims that a Chinese envoy was received by the Roman emperor Augustus in the first century BCE, but there is no other corroborating evidence that this was the case, and our Chinese sources date their first failed attempt to send an envoy to 97 CE.[31] So it is clear that our Roman writers knew very little about east Asia in any meaningful way, but that does not mean that all Romans were equally ignorant.

We know that the Romans inherited a geographic and trade-based knowledge of the Indian Ocean from the Greeks and Persians before them. By the second century CE, Claudius Ptolemy wrote his *Geography*, in which he utilised the accounts of sailors and traders to describe the sea and lands to the east of India, places that he had never visited himself. This work was so influential, and Ptolemy's authority so accepted, that *Geography* was still being used and modified as a reference work by the likes of Marco Polo and Christopher Columbus during the Middle Ages and early Renaissance. Within it, Ptolemy describes a place called the Golden Peninsula, which scholars have recently claimed relates to the Thai-Malay peninsula. He also mentions a town called Cattigara, whose name most likely comes from a Sanskrit word meaning 'strong city' or possibly 'renowned city'.[32] The location of this elusive place, beyond the farthest eastern reaches of the known world, beguiled explorers and geographers for centuries, and still no firm consensus has been formed; but the town has been tentatively identified with the southern Vietnamese site of Oc Eo, in the Mekong Valley. Such an identification is, of course, a matter of speculation, but the site of Oc Eo is a strong candidate.

Oc Eo is considered to have been an important and influential port in the Funan kingdom, which was centred around the Mekong Valley. There is clear evidence of extensive trade coming in and out of the town, but the items that capture the imagination more than any others are two Roman medallions and coins minted during the reigns of Antoninus Pius, and the philosopher-emperor Marcus Aurelius. Alongside these are other Roman items such as glass ornaments and beads, suggesting that the medallion and coin were not simply novelty items passing from hand to hand, but part of a sustained trading network between south-east Asia and the Roman Empire, facilitated through the middle ground of India. This is also corroborated by the presence of Vietnamese beads found at Berenike, along the western shore of the Red Sea in Egypt.[33]

The presence of coins during the reign of Marcus Aurelius is particularly exciting because it correlates with the only direct piece of evidence we have in the written record, which suggests that the Romans actually travelled to the lands of present-day Vietnam. No surviving Roman writer tells us this tale, but it comes from the late Chinese source the *Book of the Later Han* which reveals a fascinating outside perspective on the Romans. It describes a supposed envoy sent from the king of Da Qin, the Chinese name for Rome that translates literally as the Great Qin:

> In the ninth *yanxi* year [166 CE], during the reign of Emperor Huan, the king of Da Qin, Andun, sent envoys from beyond the frontiers through Rinan [Commandery on the central Vietnamese coast], to offer elephant tusks, rhinoceros horn and turtle shell. This was the very first time there was direct communication between the two countries. The tribute brought was neither precious nor rare, raising suspicion that the accounts [of the 'envoys'] might be exaggerated.[34]

The date of 166 CE allows us to safely identify the Roman emperor as Marcus Aurelius; the Chinese name 'Andun' could possibly be a rendering of his cognomen Antoninus. The Chinese tradition surrounding this event is imbued with great scepticism. They do not seem to believe the claims of the envoys and the paltry offerings of tribute did little to help their cause. As the fourteenth-century historian Mǎ Duānlín put it: 'Their tribute contained no precious stones whatever, which fact makes us suspect that the messengers kept them back.'[35]

The Chinese account betrays a lack of in-depth knowledge about the Roman Empire that mirrors the Roman ignorance of China. Scholars generally believe that Da Qin refers more specifically to Roman Syria, or more generally the Eastern Roman Empire or Byzantium, depending on the time period. We know that the Han attempted to send envoys to the Roman emperor; the earliest was an envoy called Gan Ying who only made it as far as the Persian Gulf before he was convinced to turn back by locals who claimed the next leg of the journey would take months – little did he know he was only a few days from entering the eastern end of the Roman Empire. Considering his failure to reach Rome, the Chinese assessment is still quite even-handed. It describes the Romans as fair in trade, offering a single price to all, and presents them as a wealthy state with a wide array of valuable items available for trade including jewellery and fine clothing. This may go some way to explaining the disappointment of this first direct interaction described in the *Book of the Later Han*. Ivory, turtle shells and rhino horn were neither novel nor exotic to the Chinese court, and certainly not a tribute or trade worthy of Da Qin.

What the literary evidence does not make abundantly clear is that the Romans and Chinese were trading with each other, and the lands of modern Vietnam were central to this. We know that the Romans coveted Chinese silk, but we also know that

Roman objects were equally coveted in China, such as glass, embroidery and silver tableware. Interestingly enough, Roman silk was also highly prized. Ultimately, the links between Rome and China were predominantly ones of trade, not cultural or political interaction. Neither empire knew of the other in any detail; they both existed in a 'twilight realm of fable and myth'.[36]

There is also a suggestion that the Roman slave trade may have reached as far as south-east Asia, although maybe not to China itself, but the Chinese records do seem to make reference to it. In 121 CE they record an embassy to the Han court from a ruler in what is now the modern state of Myanmar. Within this retinue there were entertainers for the court who, when questioned, identified themselves as being Roman.[37] The selling of enslaved people, assuming that this was what happened with these performers, or else economic migration might possibly explain a recent discovery in the archaeological site of Roman London, where two east Asian men have been tentatively identified from their skeletal remains.[38] DNA testing has not yet been published to give slightly firmer confirmation, but a similar find in Vagnari, Italy, has confirmed the presence of at least one person of east Asian ancestry dating from the second to the third century CE.[39]

These exchanges and trades were not achieved through direct contact between Roman and Chinese craftsmen or politicians, but through traders travelling between these different cultural worlds at two ends of the known map. They were made possible through sites like Oc Eo and Co Loa, places that sat between cultural spheres and facilitated their exchange. Over time, Co Loa lost its primacy even within the Red River Delta itself, replaced by newer capitals chosen by Han rulers. It would be easy to see this as the end of the city, quietly left by the wayside to dissipate into the shadows of history; but this is not strictly true. For Vietnam did not remain under Chinese rule for ever. The Red

River Valley would free itself of imperial control during the tenth century, under the leadership of Ngo Quyen. After defeating the Chinese, the Ngo dynasty needed a capital city, somewhere they could position themselves most ideally not only to rule over the valley but also to offer strong opposition to any future Chinese invasion. They chose the traditional seat of power at Co Loa and in so doing aligned their rule with a pre-Sinitic past and a historic identity going back over 1,000 years.

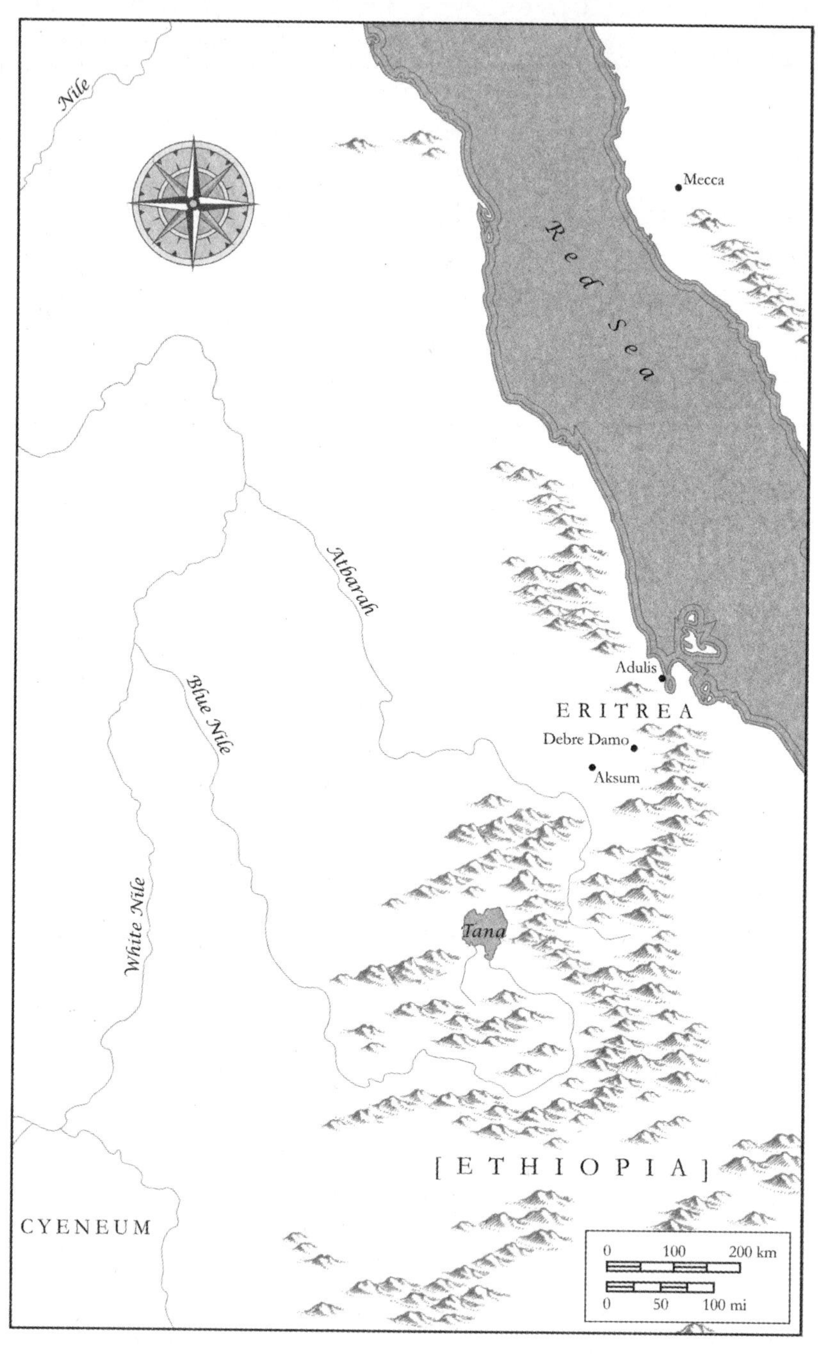

Nile
Mecca
Red Sea
Atbarah
Blue Nile
Adulis
ERITREA
Debre Damo
Aksum
White Nile
Tana
[ ETHIOPIA ]
CYENEUM
0 100 200 km
0 50 100 mi

# 13

# Aksum, Ethiopia and Eritrea

Our final site brings us full circle, back to north-eastern Africa. Unlike our other sites, this was not a small place overshadowed by a dominant cultural power – quite the opposite, in fact. By the sixth century CE, the European status quo had been shattered into a million pieces. The Roman Empire was dead and gone, with the Western Empire breaking up into a multitude of smaller kingdoms while the Eastern Empire now existed independently from its seat in Byzantium. The Christian faith had taken hold but was beset with theological conflict, disagreement and popular heresies. This was no Dark Age, contrary to how this period has long been portrayed in the history books, but it was one of turmoil and instability for many communities throughout the Mediterranean and wider Europe. It was during this time of change and fluctuation that a man from Alexandria, known only as 'Cosmas who sailed to India', entered a very different situation indeed.[1] He entered a land that was unaffected by the fall of Rome; a kingdom that was flourishing, and where the Christian faith was one of cultural cohesion. But to find it he had to leave Europe behind him.

Cosmas was originally a merchant trading in spices and possibly silk but, as his moniker suggests, he is remembered by history not for his entrepreneurial skills but for his travels.[2] For once he gave up his life of haggling and bartering around the world, Cosmas embraced his Christian faith more deeply and became a monk, during which time he decided to use his experiences of travel to support what he believed to be the Bible's true teachings about the nature of the earth in a work he dubbed *The Christian Topography*. Chief among his theories was his ardent belief that the world was flat.[3] This is particularly noteworthy for a few reasons: firstly, he is one of the very few medieval writers that we know of who lays out this claim; secondly, this theory was counter to all the accepted scientific and geographic work at that time; and, thirdly, his theory was not a popular one and never really caught on.

In spite of the misguided underpinning to *The Christian Topography*, it offers us an amazing insight into Cosmas' experiences beyond the world of his contemporaries. For the subject of this chapter we are particularly interested in his time spent at the near-coastal town of Adulis in modern-day Eritrea where, so he tells us, he was trading some twenty-five years before he wrote his account. This would have been around the start of Justin I of Byzantium's reign as emperor, so approximately 518–520 CE.

Adulis was a wealthy town with an adjacent port on the coast of the Red Sea and had long been known to Roman authors; writing four centuries earlier, Pliny the Elder described it as the principal port used by the Troglodytes (literally 'Cave Dwellers') and the Aethiopians, and states that it traded in ivory, rhinoceros horn and hippopotamus hides, as well as live animals and enslaved humans.[4] While Cosmas was there, he found himself in the midst of a new wave of imperial expansion. Adulis was, at this time, under the control of the kingdom of Aksum, a city over 100 miles west in the Ethiopian highlands. Their king, a Christian by the name of Kaleb, was planning an invasion of southern Arabia, possibly to help support a Christian population that was suffering at the hands of a local ruler called Yusuf As'ar Yath'ar (the chronology of events at this time is notoriously difficult to piece together).

Kaleb made a request to the governor of Adulis who, in turn, passed it on to two foreign traders, one of whom was Cosmas:

> [Kaleb], who was then King of the Aksumites, and was preparing to start on an expedition against the Homerites on the opposite side of the Gulf, wrote to the Governor of Adulis directing him to take copies of the inscriptions on the Chair of Ptolemy and on the tablet, and to send them to him. Then the Governor, whose name was Abbas, applied to myself and another merchant called Mênas . . . and at his request we went and copied the inscriptions.[5]

We do not know what Cosmas actually thought about the assignment or what Kaleb needed these inscriptions for. What we do know is that he made an error. Cosmas believed that both sets of inscriptions were made on behalf of Ptolemy III, the powerful Egyptian ruler of the third century BCE, but this was not the case. The tablet was indeed propaganda for the Ptolemaic king, in which he claimed to have taken control of vast swathes of land from Ethiopia up to Bactria, which was not strictly true. However, the inscription on the chair was not actually about Ptolemy but, rather, a local ruler dating from around the third century CE, whose name did not survive on the inscription.

The confusion was perhaps understandable. Cosmas spends a long time describing the ornate chair itself, made from white marble and decorated in a Hellenistic style, with slender pillars and the identifiable figures of Hercules and Hermes on the back of the seat. He was clearly impressed with what he saw, perhaps not expecting to see something so familiar to him so far from home. As if to reinforce his misconception, the inscription was done bilingually – one in Greek, the other in the local language of Ge'ez. Finally, and perhaps a little speculatively, we might consider that the inscription discouraged him from thinking it was about any local ruler:

> I first and alone of the kings of my race made these conquests . . . I reduced all the nations bordering on my own country, on the East to the country of frankincense, and on the West to Ethiopia and Sasu. Of these expeditions, some were conducted by myself in person, and ended in victory, and the others I entrusted to my officers. Having thus brought all the world under my authority to peace, I came down to Adulis and offered sacrifice to Zeus, and to Ares and to Poseidon, whom I entreated to befriend all who go down to the sea in ships.[6]

This chair was inscribed with victory on a very grand scale. The king had defeated a long list of rivals in the wider region, both towards the Red Sea in the east and beyond the Nile in the west. The inscription also describes his successful campaigns into southern Arabia, where he forced the local rulers to pay him tribute. This may well answer our question about the interest Kaleb had in the inscription, as he was planning a similar expedition of his own.

Kaleb's own invasion was a success: his army effectively removed Yusuf and installed a new ruler in his stead, one who was both Christian and sympathetic to Aksum's aims. His success in the region brought the kingdom onto the radar of the Byzantine emperors, not simply as part of a large trade network, but as an imperial power in its own right. The emperor Justinian is said to have asked the Aksumites for their support in fighting the Persians, but we do not know if they did send any men.[7] Yet, this was not all down to the work of Kaleb; indeed, Aksum's reputation was such that the third-century CE Persian prophet Mani famously remarked that during his time there were four great kingdoms on earth: the kingdom of Babylon and Persia, the kingdom of Rome, the kingdom of Aksum and the kingdom of China.[8]

Unlike so many of the sites in this book, which are mostly obscure places spread throughout the ancient world, the question needs to be asked: why is ancient Aksum not more well known? Aksum is not only regularly omitted from the history of the ancient world, but also ignored in the history of Christianity. It is a kingdom that sits as a chronological bridge between two worlds often kept separate in history: the ancient and medieval periods. Ultimately, it does not fit the modern historical narratives. Beyond the edges of the Roman Empire, beyond the reaches of Christendom, and beyond the memory of the European historical tradition, Aksum has become a victim of historical amnesia. As Edward Gibbon, the eighteenth-century historian, rather ominously put it: '[E]ncompassed on all sides by the enemies of their religion the Ethiopians slept near a thousand years, forgetful of the world, by whom they were forgotten.'[9]

* * *

The foundation of Aksum is rather hard to pinpoint. Even the archaeological evidence in and around the ancient site does not offer much in the way of clarity; scholars talk about a variety of local historical cultures including pre-Aksumite and proto-Aksumite, as well as Aksumite proper. Confusion comes from a lack of contemporary narrative history. The earliest mention of the city comes from an anonymous source called the *Periplus of the Erythraean Sea*, a Greek work most likely written in the first century CE that lays out the trading routes, towns, markets and opportunities for merchants from the Red Sea through to the Indian Ocean. The passage in question gives more information about Adulis than it does about Aksum and describes the port town as a 'fair-sized village', one established by law. As for Aksum, we are told that there was a 'city of the people called Auxumites . . . to that place all the ivory is brought from the country beyond the Nile through the district called Cyeneum [southern Sudan], and then to Adulis'.[10]

In what seems a rather innocuous reference to but one town among many, the mention of Aksum here draws our attention for a few reasons. The first is that it was clearly part of a trade network linking the Red Sea with the African interior. The reference to the Nile does not in this instance mean Egypt, nor does it really relate to Nubia, but, rather, it refers to the branches of the Nile further up river that lay due west and south-west of Aksum.[11] Second, we can see from the start that the city held a key role in the trading of ivory, a material with which it will regularly be associated throughout its time as a major trading power. Thirdly, and perhaps most importantly, Aksum is one of only two towns in this entire work that is named from the African interior.[12] Any others are to be found exclusively on the coastline, which is, of course, where Greek and Roman traders would have spent most of their time. For Aksum therefore to be so pivotal within the trade network that it warranted inclusion is in itself worthy of note and suggests that it was founded before Rome anointed its first emperor.

Our sources talk of Aksum as an exporter of many luxury items. As mentioned above, ivory, rhino horn and live animals were only a few of their specialities. During the height of Aksumite power, they were able to draw upon more resources to trade from their empire including gold, spices, incense and even sugar cane to sell to Rome, Persia and India.[13] They also benefited from a road established during the third century CE which directly linked Aksum with Egypt, bypassing Kush-controlled trade routes through Nubia.[14]

In return, Aksum imported cloth, lace and robes, as well as glassware, pottery, gold items and raw iron, especially that from India.[15] This is not just the hearsay of our written evidence: Indian gold coins dating from the third century CE have been found at a sixth-century monastery between Aksum and the coast called Debre Damo.[16] The incongruence in dates between the monastery's foundation and the age of the coins might suggest a value for the coins that goes beyond simply one of currency. Researchers have also identified Aksumite coins and ceramics in the Arabian peninsula, northern and southern India, and even as far afield as Sri Lanka.[17]

The story of Aksum is closely tied to its place within this wider trade network. By the turn of the Common Era, Aksum was transforming from a small settlement into a large town of maybe eighty-five hectares, housing large, palatial buildings, no doubt for elite families, and cemeteries that contained expensive tombs and large stelae. It was clearly accumulating excess wealth for at least some of its community members. While Aksum was never walled, and perhaps the word 'city' would be a little misleading here, it continued to grow, with some estimates suggesting it was over 180 hectares at its peak between the fifth and seventh centuries, making it larger than Roman London and pre-Islamic Damascus, and around the same size as ancient Athens.[18]

The manifestation of wealth is perhaps most keenly seen, by modern tourists at least, in the great Stelae Field that still stands in the modern town of Aksum. With the purpose of marking elite (maybe even royal) burials, these enormous monuments were carved from a single piece of rock that had been cut and transported from quarries a few miles west of the town. On arrival, some were more finely carved and decorated with patterns and sometimes military symbols, and a distinctive design reminiscent of Aksumite domestic architecture. These tall obelisk-like monuments were made to look like multi-storey buildings, with their own door and windows. The tallest measures a phenomenal thirty metres in height and weighs as much as 520 tonnes, putting into perspective how much effort and dedication was needed to erect just one of these. This tradition had been in place in north-east Africa for millennia, long before Aksum, and while Aksum took their size and design to a whole new level, there is something distinctly local about their presence. For it has been noted that even when Aksum was building monuments inscribed in various languages, projecting a worldly image of itself as not only literate but polyglot, these stelae do not have any script written on them. It was not until the adoption of Christianity that this long tradition finally came to an end in the fourth century CE.[19]

Aksum was a place that could both maintain local traditions and incorporate new trends from overseas. The true extent of its international cultural network is not yet fully understood. If one theory is correct, Aksum – or perhaps Adulis – was the original location of Huang Chi, an important trading centre located twelve months' sailing from China, as recorded by Han dynasty chroniclers.[20] The idea is an exciting one, but thus far there is only one object found at Aksum that has been identified as *possibly* being of Chinese origin, so we will just have to wait for further proof.[21] According to the *Periplus of the Erythraean Sea*, the Aksumite trade network would have stretched as far south as the town of Rhapta, the site of which has been convincingly placed in Tanzania, thanks to the discovery of Roman traded items in the region.[22] But we also have items found in the United Kingdom from Anglo-Saxon burials in Lincolnshire dating from the fifth to sixth centuries, which show just how far ivory from Aksum was travelling.[23]

Early cultural influences in Aksum came predominantly from southern Arabia, as can be seen linguistically, artistically and also religiously. So when Aksumite rulers began to exert pressure over Arabia, culminating in their imperial control over some parts in the sixth century, it really highlights the shift in balance between the two cultural spheres.

The important position of Aksum in this global trade network meant that it would attract more cultural influences. While Arabian cultural trends influenced the early shape of Aksum, the Hellenic culture from much further afield made an equally lasting impression. We cannot be sure when the adoption of Greek cultural markers began in the region; it may go back as far as the early Ptolemies. But it is interesting that the *Periplus of the Erythraean Sea*, the first mention of Aksum in the historical record, gives this small titbit of information about a local ruler in the surrounding region of Adulis:

> These places, from the Calf-Eaters to the other Berber country, are governed by Zoscales, who is miserly in his ways and always striving for more, but otherwise upright, and acquainted with Greek literature.[24]

The presence of Greek inscriptions in and around Aksum merely works to cement this portrayal of a Greek-loving king otherwise unknown to scholars. For Aksum used the Greek language on many of its official inscriptions as part of multilingual monuments, often put alongside two different scripts of Ge'ez. Scholarship has long favoured any object, big or small, found with either Greek or Latin on it, not just in Ethiopia and Eritrea but indeed throughout the world. These two languages were prioritised over the objects they were written on, so much so that many ancient objects with these scripts on them were destroyed or broken up after the writing had been recorded. So, too, with Aksum: inscriptions or objects with Greek writing have seen the most academic focus shone upon them. But this centres what was a peripheral language, one that spoke to the world beyond the edges of Aksum.

Greek was a language for the Aksumite elite, but it was one of practicality, a language that enabled them to talk, negotiate and trade with the wider world using the lingua franca of their main trading partners.[25] We also see Greek used on early Aksumite coinage, emulating the coins they would have most readily seen. Over time, the inscribed Greek becomes less consistent, often presenting with spelling mistakes or even garbled nonsense by the fifth and sixth centuries, as the knowledge of Greek clearly receded among the die-engravers, suggesting that the influence of the Mediterranean had waned as it became politically unstable.[26] While the Greek alphabet continued to be used on gold coins, probably because they were intended to be used with foreign traders, silver and copper coins were inscribed in Ge'ez – without, it should be added, the same linguistic errors.

One of the reasons why they selected Greek as their foreign language of choice may also have been because of the number of Greek-speaking expatriates who chose to live around Aksum and Adulis. As they were mostly traders, it is perhaps easy to dismiss them as ephemeral to the day-to-day life of the Aksumites, but a recently uncovered tombstone of a ten-year-old boy whose name, along with the inscription itself, was Greek, points to a different story: one of family, settling down and integration in one form or another. The headstone is decorated with a single motif, an image indicative of perhaps the largest 'Greek' import into Aksum, one that would leave a lasting impression on the history of the entire region: a small Christian cross.

* * *

There are two very different cultural traditions that link Christianity with Aksum. The first and perhaps most famous comes not from the ancient evidence but from a fourteenth-century Ethiopian text called the *Kebra Nagast.*

It describes the renowned Queen of Sheba, Makeda, meeting with the Israelite King Solomon and eventually having a son by him called Menelik. Menelik would later transport the Ark of the Covenant, the famous chest that houses the original tablets of the Ten Commandments, from Jerusalem to Aksum where – it is believed by many – it continues to reside to this very day.

Scholars debate the origin of this story, with some believing that it may have existed in some form during the sixth century when Aksum was a Christian nation, while others have pointed out that this story was as much about legitimising Aksumite royalty as it was about religious legacies. It appears in the fourteenth century to validate the so-called Solomonic dynasty, who claimed their lineage from the Aksumite kings and, through them, to Solomon. If early Aksumite kings believed that they were descended from Makeda and Solomon, these scholars argue, we would expect to see this in their royal titles and inscriptions, but we do not.[27]

The second tradition comes from near-contemporary Christian writers from around the Mediterranean; people who, it should be said, had never set foot in Aksum. The story goes that two young men from Syria named Frumentius and Aedesius were travelling to India when their ship was wrecked and they were captured and taken to the king of Aksum. The king took a shine to them and offered employment in his palace, one as a cupbearer and the other as treasurer and secretary. When the king died, his wife became regent for her young son, during which time she increased the influence of the two Syrian men in the kingdom. Frumentius in particular used this time to help the small Christian community around Aksum. When the young prince came of age and became the new Aksumite king Ezana, the two men left with royal blessings. Aedesius went back home to Syria, while Frumentius went instead to Alexandria in Egypt to speak with the bishop Athanasius, who then consecrated him as the first bishop of Aksum, where he swiftly returned.[28]

The study of early Christianity and its initial spread in the ancient world is often characterised by what we call a bottom-up approach. Within the Roman Empire, Christianity was a popular religion, by which I mean it was driven by the people themselves, not the social or political elite. In Aksum we see the reverse. Christianity began as a religion among the foreign traders and the local elite, possibly beginning with Ezana while he was a child.

We cannot be certain when Ezana embraced the new faith. Early in his reign he minted coins that still exhibited the symbols of local religious traditions, in particular the disc and crescent. We also have early inscriptions in which he continued the long-standing tradition of his ancestors of describing himself as the son of Mahrem, a local deity often compared with Ares, the Greek god of war. As Ezana grew older, many of these allusions disappear; but, even then, his Christian faith was not proclaimed candidly. His royal inscriptions stop referring to specific gods of Aksum's polytheistic pantheon, but they are not replaced by the god of Abraham nor with the name of Jesus. At least, not in the Ge'ez inscriptions.

There is one intriguing example where we can see the interplay between Ezana's faith and the power of language very clearly in a pair of inscriptions. The pair both record a military campaign that Ezana conducted in Nubia, and in the Ge'ez form of the inscription there are vague references to God, but it is never made clear which god. However, in the corresponding Greek inscription, it makes a very clear statement:

> [T]o the power of the Father, Son and Holy Spirit who saved for me the kingdom by the faith of his Son, Jesus Christ, who has helped me and will always help me.[29]

Ezana was similarly bold on his gold coins, which replaced the pagan disc and crescent symbol with that of the cross, making them the first known royally minted coins to show the Christian cross anywhere. It would be easy to view these developments through a political lens: that he was using Christianity as a way of connecting with the wider Christian world and their trading network. Hence the plainest declarations are in Greek, and on coins used to trade with foreign merchants. However, scholars have also noted how this could be indicative of issues closer to home.[30] While the king may have been Christian, his people still predominantly followed a polytheistic religion. One, it must not be forgotten, that had been used by previous generations of Aksumite kings to legitimise their own right to rule. Ezana was walking a fine line between keeping his people happy and embracing his new faith.[31]

From these tentative first steps, Aksum would come to fully embrace the Christian faith. Monasteries and churches were built, supporting thriving intellectual communities and producing some of the most exquisite examples of illustrated gospels, known as the Garima Gospels. Written in a Ge'ez script, the oldest of the Garima Gospels' parchment has been carbon-dated to between 330 and 650 CE, making them some of the oldest surviving examples in the world.[32] The influence of Christianity was not so much coming from Rome or Byzantium as it was from Alexandria in Egypt. But, even then, being separated from Egypt and the rest of the Christian world allowed the Ethiopian Church to take on its own distinct identity, away from the squabbling synods and ecclesiastical councils. It was not ignorant or impervious to them, but, equally, it was not dictated to in any direct manner.

Yet Christianity did not drive Aksum to become some insular kingdom. We have already seen in the actions of the sixth-century king Kaleb that the Christian faith, or at least the protection of other Christian communities, was used to justify expansion into southern Arabia. While the Aksumite imperial presence in the region was short-lived – it would not last the century – it made a lasting impression. According to later Arabic sources, following their successful invasion of the modern lands of Yemen, the Aksumites came north and even attempted to besiege Mecca itself. The story is first recorded in the Qur'an:

> Have you not seen how your Lord dealt with the companions of the elephant?
> Did He not make their stratagem go awry?
> And He sent upon them birds in flocks,
> Pelting them with stones of petrified clay,
> Thus, He made them like straw eaten up.[33]

Islamic tradition dates this event to the year of the Prophet Muhammad's birth in 570 CE and it is a story that is told repeatedly, remembered as the 'Year of the Elephant'. While the miracle of the birds attacking the Aksumite army is evocative in its own right, later writers give more information about the elephants, or one elephant in particular called Mahmud. This giant of an animal was brought by the Aksumite general Abreha with the explicit role of destroying the sacred Ka'ba, which held deep religious significance even in pre-Islamic Arabia. They planned to attach chains to the pillars of the Ka'ba that would then be placed around the neck of Mahmud, all with the intention of pulling them out and bringing the roof crashing down. But, of course, a miracle occurred and Mahmud would not march against Mecca; so whenever he was made to face that direction he would instead bow his head out of respect, ending their plan before it had even started.

Ironically, the Ka'ba was later destroyed after a rather careless individual dropped incense and set the temple alight. It was duly rebuilt in 608 CE by the local Quraysh community with the help of a foreigner by the name of Baqum al-Rumi, a name that some scholars believe derives from an Ethiopian name Habakkuk. Indeed, there is an Ethiopian tradition that tells of an architect travelling to Mecca and helping with the rebuild, and Aksumite designs have been noted in the descriptions of the architectural redesign, suggesting that this may be more than some tall tale.[34]

The irony that Aksum would come to help rebuild a temple it had intended to destroy only a few decades before should not be lost on us. But Aksum was not rigid in its diplomacy. The kingdom would soon open its doors in 615 CE to a group of political exiles from Mecca escaping persecution as followers of the new religious movement of Islam. The Quraysh leaders offered gifts in exchange for their return, but Armah, the king of Aksum, refused, choosing instead to keep them safe before they were ready to return of their own accord. The final exile would not return until 628 CE.[35]

This period of inter-religious collegiality, at a time when Islam was not being acknowledged by other Christian powers, forged a strong relationship between Aksum and its lands with the rising Islamic powers. It was so important that, even as the star of Aksum began to fade during the seventh century, the lands of Ethiopia and Eritrea were considered neutral to Islamic expansion. In other words, the lands of Ethiopia were exempt from *jihad* and Muslim armies were effectively banned from attacking unless the Ethiopian kingdom attacked first. This ruling came straight from Muhammad himself, when he is alleged to have said: 'Leave the Ethiopians in peace, so long as they leave you alone.'[36] The authenticity of this *hadith* was not without its detractors even in the medieval period, but true to its word the region did not become part of the Islamic world until the sixteenth century, when most of what is now Eritrea was annexed by the Ottoman Empire.

As for Aksum, the rise of Islam was one large global shift too many to contend with, having witnessed and adapted to the spread of Greek cultural and economic power in the Red Sea, Roman dominance and a globalised trade network, Rome then splitting in two before the demise of the Western Empire, the rise of Persia, the spread of Christianity, and then the discourse and schisms within Christianity. When Aksum first rose to prominence, Britain had not yet been colonised by the Romans; by the time Aksum had come to an end, we find their ivory products in Anglo-Saxon graves. Aksum persevered and thrived while the rest of the ancient world (in the Mediterranean at least) was in disarray. As European antiquity faded, and the medieval world was being born, Aksum was in its own classical period.

The demise of Aksum did not occur with a bang; there was no large-scale invasion or uprising to overthrow the royal family. It was a long, drawn-out affair possibly stretching back to before the emergence of Islam in the Arabian Gulf. But, by the mid-seventh century CE, Aksum had lost its control over important trade routes both inland and at sea, greatly reducing its income as a result. Aksum itself was abandoned, but the cultural pillars of its heyday still stood strong. The Ethiopian church, the royal lineage and the Ge'ez language held firm, each one nurtured in a world connected to, but distinctly separate from, the cultural powers of Europe and Asia. Aksum would not be the last powerful kingdom of Ethiopia, but its decline – more so than Rome's – does bring an end to the ancient world.

# Conclusion

When the Greek writer Herodotus decided to set down the first recorded history, he knew he had to travel. To understand the world, he wanted to see as much of it as he could. He passed through many of the lands covered in this book. He set foot in the lands of the Scythians, travelled to the Levant, walked through the temples of Egypt and headed west to the Greek cities in Italy. His studies of cultures beyond his own make up the majority of his history. The theme of his work, the Persian Wars, actually makes up less than half of the finished book. By taking this approach, Herodotus established the core tenets for the study of history.

History is not a narrative, but an inquiry. This is, in fact, what the word history actually means in the original Greek: *historia*, an inquiry. Herodotus understood that any inquiry is built upon a multitude of narratives, of stories and different perspectives, each one helping us make greater sense of the whys, hows and what fors. So he set out to record as many as he could, no matter if they contradicted each other. Even with this valiant effort, we learn from his work that any inquiry must, through necessity, be limited to a particular area of interest, whether that be political, cultural, military or simply geographical. The questions we ask limit the narratives we draw upon.

The most common historical inquiries focus on the cultural and political centres of society which, in turn, give us a very one-sided perspective of that historical period. It is, in essence, like visiting London for a week and claiming to have seen the United Kingdom or going to New York and claiming to have visited all of the United States. Yes, these cities are vibrant and invigorating cultural centres, but they do not equate to the lived experiences of most British or American people. And so it is with history: we must look beyond the centre and out to the periphery.

In the sites we have focused on in this book, we have seen that those central influences were strong – whether it be Egyptian culture influencing a town like Megiddo, Chinese building techniques appearing in Co Loa, or even the coming together of numerous strong traditions as we saw in the blending of Indian and Greek culture in Taxila. Language played an important role in the distribution of cultural identities and the dominance of scripts, such as Latin, Greek and Sanskrit, can often hide the equally influential languages of power such as Prakrit, as we saw in India, or Ge'ez in Aksum. Language was used to control narratives but also to express messages, and so the choice of language for rulers and commoners alike is revealing – from the inscriptions left by Roman soldiers around the empire, to the Hebrew inscription found in Volubilis; from the Gallic language recorded in the Greek alphabet in Massalia, to the trilingual inscriptions found around the ancient world. Languages mattered and, away from the city centres, those languages could not be taken for granted.

This approach, however, is simply to look at these sites through the lens of the cultural centres and what they add to our understanding of 'Egyptian' or 'Roman' culture as a whole. We can, and should, also appreciate them for what they were: unique expressions of cultural identity that were shaped by their position at the edges. Without the scrutiny of cultural policing, every one of these sites became a small melting pot of different influences including indigenous cultures.

These were not necessarily big cultural movements, but in terms of language we see regional dialects appear and linguistic blending, all through the eyes of critical observers such as Dio Chrysostom at Olbia and Ovid at Tristia (both of whom were unimpressed with the style of Greek spoken around the Black Sea). But it is in these small divergences of cultural norms that we see what was important to the people themselves. Even seemingly trivial objects hold significance when we try and understand their contextual relevance. These are often smaller elements of everyday life that meant a lot more to the people themselves than perhaps translates into the modern day. For instance, at the Egyptian fort of Askut, even during a period of Egyptian domination in the region and an Egyptian garrison stationed there, we saw, perhaps surprisingly at first, that Nubian cooking pots were the most commonly used.

As a direct result of these unique blends of lifestyle and culture, it is at the edges of the world that we find quite radical ways of life and of thinking. Is it any surprise that we saw unique religious expressions at places like at Megiddo even in the wake of Judaism's spread, or the unique expression of Christianity formed at Aksum? And what of Taxila? The birth and spread of Buddhism may have begun elsewhere, but its beating intellectual and spiritual heart was in Taxila. It was also there that Greek influence gave rise to the Buddha's honorific human form, creating the artistic style we are so used to seeing today. But we also know that this influence was not one-way, with the discovery of Buddhist statues in Greco-Roman Egypt, and Buddhist monks appearing in our Greek and Latin sources. It is not frequent, but it is enough to show that they made a lasting impression.

So many of these sites were pivotal points in trade networks, bringing together land and sea routes from all over the world. They enabled the interaction of cultures that had no real concept of one another. If we did not look to the edges of the world, we would not see how Han China and Imperial Rome actually did interact (albeit not directly). They came together in the lived experiences of people in Vietnam and India, maybe even Aksum, which served as enormous global marketplaces. If we focus solely on Egyptian empire-building, we will miss out on the trade links between Canaan, Cornwall and Indonesia. If we obsess over the collapse of the Western Roman Empire, we ignore the continued trade links from Aksum to Britain during that same time period. And if we focus solely on literate societies, we would not see the amazing blending of Celtic and Scythian art styles.

Exploring life at the edge of the known world challenges our own historical preconceptions. It forces us to look beyond the Mediterranean and our main sources' very blinkered view of the world around them. It is no longer permissible to accept the civilised-barbarian dichotomy adored by our elite sources. Whether it be the mixed marriages we saw at the Egyptian–Nubian frontier and again at Olbia and Massalia, or the takedown of cultural stereotypes at Bilsk and Co Loa, we can see that our sources' blinkered view of the world cannot be trusted. Equally, we find that our own tendency to over-generalise becomes a problem. Dissent and rebellion were born at the edge of empire, as we saw towards the end of Roman rule of Britain, but also in Taxila and Co Loa; while other places like Massalia and Volubilis displayed an almost zealous loyalty. We believed that monuments and large building projects required sedentary, agricultural societies to facilitate the resources and manpower necessary to execute them, but the pillar sites around Lake Turkana and the enormous fort at Bilsk suggest otherwise. We thought that the ancient world ended with the fall of Rome in the fifth century CE, but Aksum continued to flourish for another two centuries.

As we explored the periphery, we did not find a utopia away from the 'evils' of social conformity and homogeneity; at times, in fact, we saw an overcompensation by people clinging to their heritage. But the greatest tensions seem to have come from the expectations of visitors more than anything else: not only invaders, but equally travellers bringing with them preconceptions and misunderstandings of what they were seeing. The experiences of the Roman poet-in-exile Ovid, stuck as he saw it in the wastelands at the far edges of the empire, exemplifies the tensions we have seen throughout this book between cultural centres and their peripheries.

In a collection of letters, written in verse, Ovid laments the uneducated state of the people he is surrounded by in Tomis, and yet they in turn paid him great respect as a poet. He tells us that they made him exempt from tax and praised him for his work, in spite of the fact that they knew he hated it there and wanted to leave.[1] Similarly, he bemoans his own intellectual deterioration, claiming that he was getting worse at Latin. This claim is contrasted somewhat with another, where he describes his own innovative poetic development:

> I am almost a Getic poet. Ah! it brings me shame! I have even written a poem in the Getic tongue, setting barbarian words to our measures: I even found favour – congratulate me – and began to achieve among the uncivilised Getae the name of poet.[2]

Much of Ovid's letter writing is filled with pleas to his family and friends to help him appeal to the man responsible for his exile, the emperor Augustus, and ensure his return to Rome. As such, he paints the starkest of pictures of life in Tomis. It was a means to an end, one designed to elicit empathy on his behalf. But ultimately he failed in his quest; the poem he claims to have written in the 'Getic tongue' was one dedicated to the recently deceased and now deified Augustus who died in 14 CE, during Ovid's sixth year of exile. Any hopes he may have had of restarting his petitions with the newly crowned Tiberius or other powerful individuals in Rome were dashed during a particularly harsh winter two years later. Ovid died in Tomis, most probably as a result of the deteriorating health he describes in his letters. His greatest fear was to die and be buried at the edge of the world, and his fears came to fruition. However, he would have taken solace in the fact that his reputation as a poet, ahead of all his peers back in Rome, would survive intact. It is his work that has influenced writers and painters for over 2,000 years, even if he did end up living at the farthest edges of the known world.

A study of the far edges serves as a reminder that cultural barriers exist only when people refuse to interact. Ovid's refusal to embrace his situation and accept the community around him as his own led to some very miserable final years for the poet. He was clinging to an idea of what culture was, what being Roman should mean. What he never learned was that, away from the sheltered lives at the centre, multiculturalism was necessary for survival. It did not eradicate individual identity or cultural pride but enhanced it – keeping the best bits and embracing new ideas that added to it. In some ways, we in the modern day fall foul of the same errors as Ovid as we look at the ancient past. By focusing our minds on the narrow, traditional narratives of history we do not appreciate just how many stories, innovations and shared histories we inadvertently eradicate. Rather than using history to reinforce division, these sites clearly show that it has the power to bring different people together.

# NOTES

## INTRODUCTION: BEYOND THE KNOWN WORLD

1 Euripides, *Medea* 539–41, translation my own.
2 Herodotus, *Histories* 2.104.
3 Strabo, *Geography* 7.3.6, translation my own.
4 Appian, *Mithridatic Wars* 3.15.
5 Xenophon, *Anabasis* 4.8.23–24, translation from Carleton L. Brownson, *Xenophon: Xenophon in Seven Volumes*, Vol. 3, Harvard University Press, Cambridge, MA, 1922.
6 Peter Green, *The Poems of Exile: Tristia and the Black Sea Letters*, University of California Press, Berkeley, 2005, p. xxi.
7 For a brief overview of his life story see Peter E. Knox, 'A Poet's Life', in *A Companion to Ovid*, ed. Peter E. Knox, Wiley-Blackwell, Oxford, 2009, pp. 3–7.
8 Ovid, *Tristia* 5.7.43–4.
9 Ibid., 3.10.
10 Ibid., 3.9; Apollodorus, *Library* 1.9.24.
11 Vincent Gabrielsen, 'Profitable Partnerships: Monopolies, Traders, Kings, and Cities', in *The Economies of Hellenistic Societies, Third to First Centuries BC*, eds Zosia H. Archibald, John K. Davies and Vincent Gabrielsen, Oxford University Press, Oxford, 2011, p. 224; Eric C. De Sena and Pia Guldager Bilde, 'Tomis', in *The Encyclopedia of Ancient History*, 1st edn, eds Roger S. Bagnall, Kai Brodersen, Craige B. Champion, Andrew Erskine and Sabine R. Huebner, Blackwell Publishing, Oxford, 2013, pp. 6,782–3.
12 Ovid, *Tristia* 5.2.63–70.
13 Ibid., 4.1.71–76, translation from Arthur Leslie Wheeler, *Ovid: Tristia, Ex Ponto*, Harvard University Press, Cambridge, MA, 1939.

## 1 LAKE TURKANA, KENYA

1 'Importance of the Turkana Basin', Science & Research, Turkana Basin Institute, accessed 29 June 2023, https://www.turkanabasin.org/research/turkana-basin

2 M. Mirazón Lahr et al., 'Inter-group violence among early Holocene hunter-gatherers of West Turkana, Kenya', *Nature* 529, no. 7,586 (2016): 394–8.

3 Ibid.: 396.

4 Isabelle Crevecoeur, Marie-Hélène Dias-Meirinho, Antoine Zazzo, Daniel Antoine and François Bon, 'New insights on interpersonal violence in the Late Pleistocene based on the Nile valley cemetery of Jebel Sahaba', *Scientific Reports* 11, no. 9,991 (2021).

5 Lawrence H. Robbins, 'Lake Turkana Archaeology: The Holocene', *Ethnohistory* 53, no. 1 (2006): 79.

6 Elizabeth A. Sawchuk, Steven T. Goldstein, Katherine M. Grillo and Elisabeth A. Hildebrand, 'Cemeteries on a moving frontier: Mortuary practices and the spread of pastoralism from the Sahara into eastern Africa', *Journal of Anthropological Archaeology* 51 (2018): 190.

7 Elisabeth A. Hildebrand et al., 'A monumental cemetery built by eastern Africa's first herders near Lake Turkana, Kenya', *PNAS* 115, no. 36 (2018): 8,942–7; Sawchuk et al., 'Cemeteries on a moving frontier': 195–6; Katherine M. Grillo and Elisabeth A. Hildebrand, 'The context of early megalithic architecture in eastern Africa: the Turkana Basin c. 5000–4000 BP', *Azania: Archaeological Research in Africa* 48, no. 2 (2013): 193–217.

8 Sawchuk et al., 'Cemeteries on a moving frontier': 195.

9 Grillo and Hildebrand, 'The context of early megalithic architecture in eastern Africa': 201–2.

10 Hildebrand et al., 'A monumental cemetery built by eastern Africa's first herders near Lake Turkana, Kenya': 8,945.

11 Ibid.: 8,944.

12 Geoff Emberling, 'Pastoral States: Toward a Comparative Archaeology of Early Kush', *Origini* 36 (2014): 134.

13 Ibid.: 130–1; Matthieu Honegger, 'The Holocene Prehistory of Upper Nubia until the Rise of the Kerma Kingdom', in *Handbook of Ancient Nubia*, ed. Dietrich Raue, De Gruyter, Berlin, 2019, pp.

224–6; Matthieu Honegger, 'Kerma et les débuts du Néolithique africain', *Geneva* 53 (2005): 242.

14 Honegger, 'The Holocene Prehistory of Upper Nubia until the Rise of the Kerma Kingdom', in *Handbook of Ancient Nubia*, p. 226.

15 Emberling, 'Pastoral States: Toward a Comparative Archaeology of Early Kush': 131; F. Geus, 'Pre-Kerma storage pits on Sai Island', in *Nubian Studies: Proceedings of the Ninth Conference of the International Society of Nubian Studies, 1998*, ed. T. Kendall, Department of African-American Studies, Northeastern University, Boston, 2004, pp. 46–51.

16 Honegger, 'The Holocene Prehistory of Upper Nubia until the Rise of the Kerma Kingdom', in *Handbook of Ancient Nubia*, p. 226.

17 Emberling, 'Pastoral States: Toward a Comparative Archaeology of Early Kush': 130–3.

18 Louis Chaix, Jérôme Dubosson and Matthieu Honegger, 'Bucrania from the Eastern Cemetery at Kerma (Sudan) and the Practice of Cattle Horn Deformation', in *Prehistory of Northeastern Africa: New Ideas and Discoveries*, *Studies in African Archaeology*, Vol. 11, eds J. Kabacinski, M. Chlodnicki and M. Kobusiewicz, Poznan Archaeological Museum, Poznan, 2012, pp. 189–212.

19 P. Iacumin, H. Bocherens and L. Chaix, 'Keratin and N stable isotope ratios of fossil cattle horn from Kerma (Sudan): a record of dietary changes', *Il Quaternario* 14, no. 1 (2001): 41–6.

20 Emberling, 'Pastoral States: Toward a Comparative Archaeology of Early Kush': 134.

21 James Henry Breasted (ed.), *Ancient Records of Egypt*, Vol. 1, University of Chicago Press, Chicago, 1906, pp. 247–50.

22 [Adapted] translation from Breasted (ed.), *Ancient Records of Egypt*, Vol. 1, p. 247.

23 *Wadi Halfa Inscription of Mentuhotep*, translation from Breasted (ed.), *Ancient Records of Egypt*, Vol. 1, p. 249.

24 Garry J. Shaw, *War & Trade with the Pharaohs: An Archaeological Study of Ancient Egypt's Foreign Relations*, Pen & Sword, Barnsley, 2017, p. 52.

## 2 THE GREAT CATARACT, SUDAN

1 Laurel Bestock, 'Egyptian Fortresses and the Colonization of Lower Nubia in the Middle Kingdom', in *The Oxford Handbook of Ancient*

*Nubia*, eds Geoff Emberling and Bruce Beyer Williams, Oxford University Press, Oxford, 2020, pp. 277–8.

2 Ibid., p. 277.

3 The relationship between these pharaohs is not entirely clear due to the lack of explicit evidence remaining, but it is presumed by scholars that these two were related.

4 *The Teaching of King Merikare*, translations from William Kelly Simpson (ed.), *The Literature of Ancient Egypt: An Anthology of Stories, Instructions, Stelae, Autobiographies, and Poetry*, Yale University Press, New Haven, 2003, p. 162.

5 *The Teaching of King Amenemhat* 12, [adapted] translation from R. B. Parkinson, *The Tale of Sinuhe and Other Ancient Egyptian Poems, 1940–1640 BC*, Oxford University Press, Oxford, 1997.

6 Although such a connection is far from clear and may very well reflect an identification driven by a preconceived conclusion – having seen the Egyptians mention the Medjay, early Egyptologists went on the hunt to find them in the archaeological record regardless of any inconsistencies in the evidence. However, a clear Medjay identity in Lower Nubia does begin to appear during the later Middle Kingdom. Kate Liszka, ' "We have come from the well of Ibhet": Ethnogenesis of the Medjay', *Journal of Egyptian History* 4, no. 2 (2011): 164–5.

7 While I will simplify here and continue discussing Nubian culture, as opposed to Egyptian, it is important to note that Nubia was not home to simply one single society.

8 Stuart Tyson Smith, 'Askut and the Role of the Second Cataract Forts', *Journal of the American Research Center in Egypt* 28 (1991): 128.

9 *Boundary Stela of Senusret III*, translation from Alan B. Lloyd, 'The Late Period (664–332 BC)', in *The Oxford History of Ancient Egypt*, ed. Ian Shaw, Oxford University Press, Oxford, 2003, p. 368.

10 Herodotus, *Histories* 2.102–103.

11 K. W. Crawford, 'Critique of the "Black Pharaohs" Theme: Racist Perspectives of Egyptian and Kushite/Nubian Interactions in Popular Media,' *African Archaeological Review* 38 (2021): 704–5.

12 M. Lichtheim, *Ancient Egyptian Literature: A Book of Readings*, Vol. I, *The Old and Middle Kingdoms*, University of California Press, Berkeley, 1973, p. 119, as quoted in Stuart Tyson Smith, *Wretched Kush: Ethnic Identities and Boundaries in Egypt's Nubian Empire*, Routledge, Abingdon, 2003, p. 1.

13 Tyson Smith, *Wretched Kush*, p. 117.

14 Ibid., p. 118.
15 Stuart Tyson Smith, 'Pharaohs, Feasts, and Foreigners Cooking, Foodways, and Agency on Ancient Egypt's Southern Frontier', in *The Archaeology and Politics of Food and Feasting in Early States and Empires*, Springer, Boston, 2003, pp. 51–2.
16 Tyson Smith, *Wretched Kush*, pp. 119–24.
17 Solange Ashby, 'Dancing for Hathor: Nubian Women in Egyptian Cultic Life', *Dotawo: A Journal of Nubian Studies* 5 (2018): 69–72.
18 Ibid.: 66–7.
19 Geoffrey J. Tassie, 'Identifying the Practice of Tattooing in Ancient Egypt and Nubia', *Papers from the Institute of Archaeology* 14 (2003): 89–93; Ashby, 'Dancing for Hathor: Nubian Women in Egyptian Cultic Life': 72–4.
20 *Semna Dispatch* 8, translation from Bryan Kraemer and Kate Liszka, 'Evidence for Administration of the Nubian Fortresses in the Late Middle Kingdom: The Semna Dispatches', *Journal of Egyptian History* 9 (2016): 45.
21 *Semna Dispatch* 1, translation from Bryan Kraemer and Kate Liszka, 'Evidence for Administration of the Nubian Fortresses in the Late Middle Kingdom: The Semna Dispatches', *Journal of Egyptian History* 9 (2016): p. 23.
22 Kraemer and Liszka, 'Evidence for Administration of the Nubian Fortresses in the Late Middle Kingdom: The Semna Dispatches': 47–8.
23 *Semna Dispatch* 3, [adapted] translation from Paul C. Smither, 'The Semnah Despatches', *Journal of Egyptian Archaeology* 31 (1945), 7–8, taking consideration of comments from Kraemer and Liszka, 'Evidence for Administration of the Nubian Fortresses in the Late Middle Kingdom: The Semna Dispatches': 35.
24 *Semna Dispatch* 4, translation from Bryan Kraemer and Kate Liszka, 'Evidence for Administration of the Nubian Fortresses in the Late Middle Kingdom: The Semna Dispatches', *Journal of Egyptian History* 9 (2016): p. 32, 44.
25 *Semna Dispatch* 5, Paul C. Smither, 'The Semnah Despatches', *Journal of Egyptian Archaeology* 31 (1945): p. 9. The evidence for an actual famine in the desert area during this period is non-existent, barring this one statement, so it is worth considering that this could be a lie in an attempt to curry favour and sympathy: B. J. Kemp, 'Old Kingdom, Middle Kingdom and Second Intermediate

Period', in *Ancient Egypt: A Social History*, eds B. G. Trigger, B. J. Kemp, D. O'Connor and A. B. Lloyd, Cambridge University Press, Cambridge, 1983, pp. 179–81; Georg Meurer, *Nubier in Ägypten bis zum Beginn des neuen Reiches: Zur Bedeutung der Stele Berlin 14753*, Abhandlungen des Deutschen Archäologischen Instituts Kairo 13, Achet Verlag, Berlin, 1996, p. 127; Kraemer and Liszka, 'Evidence for Administration of the Nubian Fortresses in the Late Middle Kingdom: The Semna Dispatches': 45.

26 Josef W. Wegner and Josef Wegner, 'Regional Control in Middle Kingdom Lower Nubia: The Function and History of the Site of Areika', *Journal of the American Research Center in Egypt* 32 (1995): 153.

27 Adela Oppenheim, Dorothea Arnold, Dieter Arnold and Kei Yamamoto (eds), *Ancient Egypt Transformed: The Middle Kingdom*, Yale University Press, New Haven, 2015, p. 264.

28 Kerry Muhlestein, 'Execration Ritual', *UCLA Encyclopedia of Egyptology* 1, no. 1, 2008; John Coleman Darnell and Colleen Manassa, *Tutankhamun's Armies: Battle and Conquest During Ancient Egypt's Late 18th Dynasty*, Wiley, Hoboken, NJ, 2007, p. 133.

29 I am indebted to the public history work of Kyle Lewis Jordan for this reconstruction, and his patience with my numerous enquiries.

30 Tyson Smith, *Wretched Kush*, pp. 79–80.

31 *Stela from Buhen*; T. Säve-Söderbergh, 'A Buhen Stela from the Second Intermediate Period (Kharṭūm No. 18)', *Journal of Egyptian Archaeology* 35 (1949): 50–58, as quoted by Tyson Smith, *Wretched Kush*, p. 78.

32 László Török, *Between Two Worlds: The Frontier Region Between Ancient Nubia and Egypt 3700 BC–500 AD*, Brill, Leiden, 2009, pp. 106–8.

33 Ellen Morris, *Ancient Egyptian Imperialism*, Wiley Blackwell, Chichester, 2018, pp. 100–1.

34 *Carnarvon Tablet*, translation from Tyson Smith, *Wretched Kush*, p. 56; Alan H. Gardiner, 'The Defeat of the Hyksos by Kamōse: The Carnarvon Tablet, No. I', *Journal of Egyptian Archaeology* 3, no. 2/3 (1916): 95–110.

35 Josef Wegner and Kevin Cahail, *King Seneb-Kay's Tomb and the Necropolis of a Lost Dynasty at Abydos*, University Museum

Monograph 155, University of Pennsylvania Museum of Archaeology and Anthropology, Philadelphia, p. 370.

36 Vivian Davies, 'Sobeknakht's Hidden Treasure', *British Museum Magazine* 46 (2003): 18.

37 *Tombos Stela* as quoted in Tyson Smith, *Wretched Kush*, p. 84.

38 Török, *Between Two Worlds*, p. 184.

## 3 MEGIDDO, ISRAEL

1 A. J. Spalinger, *War in Ancient Egypt: The New Kingdom*, Blackwell Publishing, Oxford, 2005, p. 83.

2 Eric Cline, *The Battles of Armageddon: Megiddo and the Jezreel Valley from the Bronze Age to the Nuclear Age*, University of Michigan Press, Ann Arbor, 2000, pp. 2–3.

3 David Ussishkin, *On Biblical Jerusalem, Megiddo, Jezreel and Lachish*, Divinity School of Chung Chi College, The Chinese University of Hong Kong, Hong Kong, 2011, pp. 42–3.

4 David Ussishkin, *Megiddo-Armageddon: The Story of the Canaanite and Israelite City*, Israel Exploration Society, Jerusalem 2018, pp. 173–4.

5 *Annals of Thutmose III*, translation from James B. Pritchard (ed.), *The Ancient Near East: An Anthology of Texts and Pictures*, Princeton University Press, Princeton, 2011, p. 229.

6 Cline, *The Battles of Armageddon*, pp. 18–19.

7 *Annals of Thutmose III*, translation from Cline, *The Battles of Armageddon*, pp. 20–1.

8 Jared Miller, 'Political interactions between Kassite Babylonia and Assyria, Egypt and Hatti during the Amarna Age', in *Karduniaš: Babylonia Under the Kassites 1*, Vol. 1, eds Alexa Bartelmus and Katja Sternitzke, De Gruyter, Boston/Berlin, 2017, p. 95.

9 Armana Letter, EA 244, [adapted] translation from W. L. Moran, *The Armana Letters*, Johns Hopkins University Press, Baltimore, 1992, p. 298.

10 Armana Letter, EA 253 and 254, Moran, *The Armana Letters*, pp. 306–7.

11 Armana Letter, EA 252, [adapted] translation from Moran, *The Armana Letters*, p. 305.

12 Armana Letter, EA 245, Moran, *The Armana Letters*, pp. 299–300.

13 Ashley Scott et al., 'Exotic foods reveal contact between South Asia and the Near East during the second millennium BCE', *PNAS* 118, no. 2 (2021): 1–10.

14 Vanessa Linares et al., 'First evidence for vanilla in the old world: Its use as mortuary offering in Middle Bronze Canaan', *Journal of Archaeological Science: Reports* 25 (2019): 77–84; Melissa S. Cradic and Vanessa Linares, 'Vanilla in the Middle Bronze Age: New Findings from Megiddo', *ANE Today* 8, no. 1 (2020); Andrew Lawler, 'In Biblical City of Armageddon, Signs of Early Vanilla and Elaborate Medical Care', *Science.org*, DOI: 10.1126/science.aaw2095.

15 Daniel Berger et al., 'Isotope systematics and chemical composition of tin ingots from Mochlos (Crete) and other Late Bronze Age sites in the eastern Mediterranean Sea: An ultimate key to tin provenance?', *PLOS ONE* 14, no. 6 (2019), DOI: 10.1371/journal.pone.0218326.

16 Ussishkin, *On Biblical Jerusalem, Megiddo, Jezreel and Lachish*, p. 55.

17 Ibid.

18 Judges 5.

19 Matthew J. Adams, Jonathan David, Robert S. Homsher and Margaret E.Cohen, 'The Rise of a Complex Society: New Evidence from Tel Megiddo East in the Late Fourth Millennium', *Near Eastern Archaeology* 77, no. 1 (2014): 34–5.

20 Ibid.: 35–6.

21 Ibid.

22 David Ussishkin, 'The Sacred Area of Early Bronze Megiddo: History and Interpretation', *Bulletin of the American Schools of Oriental Research* 373 (2015): 89.

23 Ussishkin, *Megiddo-Armageddon: The story of the Canaanite and Israelite City*, p. 171.

24 Ibid., pp. 217–20.

25 Uzi Avner, 'Sacred Stones in the Desert', *Biblical Archaeology Review* 27 (2001): 30–41.

26 2 Kings 23:6–13.

27 This inscription is open to some debate regarding translation, but the meaning ultimately remains the same. This translation is taken from the suggestion in Judith M. Hadley, 'The Khirbet el-Qom Inscription', *Vetus Testamentum* 37, no. 1 (1987): 51.

28 Jeremiah 7:17–19. For a full list of similar instances, see Francesca Stavrakopoulou, 'Popular Religion and Official Religion', in

*Religious Diversity in Ancient Israel and Judah*, eds Francesca Stavrakopoulou and John Barton, T&T Clark, London, 2010, p. 43.

## 4 OLBIA, UKRAINE

1 Herodotus, *Histories* 4.100.
2 Pseudo-Hippocrates, *On Airs, Waters, and Places* 17.
3 Herodotus, *Histories* 4.105.
4 Pausanias, *Description of Greece* 8.2.1–6. For a collection of lycanthropic stories from across the Greek and Roman world, I strongly recommend: 'Lycanthropy in Greek and Roman Culture', Sententiae Antiquae, last modified 31 October 2016, https://sententiaeantiquae.com/2016/10/31/lycanthropy-in-greek-and-roman-culture
5 Pindar, *Pythian* 10.41–4.
6 Herodotus, *Histories* 4.18.1. For an overview of Herodotus' account of Olbia and the surrounding region, see Stephanie West, 'Herodotus and Olbia', in *Classical Olbia and the Scythian World: From the Sixth Century BC to the Second Century AD*, eds David Braund and S. D. Kryzhitskiy, British Academy/Oxford University Press, Oxford, 2007, pp. 79–92.
7 Dio Chrysostom, *Discourses* 36.1, translation from J. W. Cohoon and H. Lamar Crosby (eds), *Dio Chrysostom: Discourses 31–36*, Harvard University Press, Cambridge, MA, 1940.
8 Dio Chrysostom, *Discourses* 36.4.
9 Herodotus, *Histories* 4.53.2–3, translation from A. D. Godley, *Herodotus: The Persian Wars*, Vol. 2, Harvard University Press, Cambridge, MA, 1920.
10 For the wider context of Greek and Egyptian trade around the Black Sea, see Christopher S. Parmenter, 'Egypt on the Steppe: A Gazetteer of Sixth Century *Aegyptiaca* from the North Black Sea', *Bibliotheca Orientalis* 76, no. 1–2 (2019): 13–24.
11 Gocha R. Tsetskhladze, 'On the Earliest Greek Colonial Architecture in the Pontus', in *Pontus and the Outside World: Studies in Black Sea History, Historiography, and Archaeology*, ed. C. J. Tuplin, Brill, Leiden, 2004, p. 266.
12 S. D. Kryzhitskiy, 'Excavations at Olbia in the Past Three Decades', in *Classical Olbia and the Scythian World. From the Sixth Century BC to the Second Century AD*, eds Braund and Kryzhitskiy, p. 9.

13 Polybius, *Histories* 4.38.
14 Diogenes Laertius, *Lives of Eminent Philosophers* 4.7.46.
15 C. P. Jones, 'Stigma: Tattooing and Branding in Graeco-Roman Antiquity', *Journal of Roman Studies* 77 (1987): 148.
16 Athenaeus, *The Deipnosophists* 13.61.
17 Diogenes Laertius, *Lives of Eminent Philosophers* 4.7.55–7.
18 Plutarch, *Solon* 5.2, translation my own.
19 Diogenes Laertius, *Lives of Eminent Philosophers* 1. 101–5.
20 Herodotus, *Histories* 4.76.
21 Ibid., 4.78–9.
22 Ibid., 4.79–80.
23 Franco Ferrari, 'Orphics at Olbia?', in *Submerged Literature in Ancient Greek Culture*, Vol. 2, *Case Studies*, eds Giulio Colesanti and Laura Lulli, De Gruyter, Berlin, 2016, pp. 177–86.
24 Edith Hall, *Inventing the Barbarian: Greek Self-Definition Through Tragedy*, Clarendon Press, Oxford, 1989.
25 Herodotus, *Histories* 4.17.
26 See Margarit Damyanov, 'On the Local Population around the Greek Colonies in the Black Sea Area (5th–3rd centuries BC)', in *Ancient West & East*: Vol. 2, no. 2, ed. G. R. Tsetskhladze, Brill, Leiden, 2003, pp. 253–64.
27 *Sylloge Inscriptionum Graecarum*: 495.
28 Plato, *Menexenus* 245c-d, translation from W. R. M. Lamb, *Plato in Twelve Volumes*, Vol. 9, Harvard University Press, Cambridge, MA.
29 Joseph Skinner, *The Invention of Greek Ethnography: From Homer to Herodotus*, Oxford University Press, Oxford, 2012, p. 155.
30 Alcaeus Fr. 14 D, D. Page, *Lyrica Graeca Selecta*, no. 166, Oxford, 1968, p. 89.
31 Philostratus, *Heroicus* 54.3–13; Guy Hedreen, 'The Cult of Achilles in the Euxine', *Hesperia: The Journal of the American School of Classical Studies at Athens* 60, no. 3 (1991): 320.
32 Skinner, *The Invention of Greek Ethnography*, p. 166.
33 A. S. Rusyayeva, 'Religious Interactions between Olbia and Scythia', in *Classical Olbia and the Scythian World: From the Sixth Century BC to the Second Century AD*, eds Braund and Kryzhitskiy, pp. 93–103.
34 Hippocrates, *On Airs, Waters and Places* 22, translation from W. H. S. Jones, *Hippocrates Collected Works I*, Harvard University Press, Cambridge, MA, 1868.

35 Dio Chrysostom, *Discourses* 36.7, translation from Cohoon and Lamar Crosby (eds), *Dio Chrysostom: Discourses 31–36*.

36 Herodotus, *Histories* 4.28.

37 Dio Chrysostom, *Discourses* 36.9.

38 Balbina Bäbler, ' "Long-Haired Greeks in Trousers": Olbia and Dio Chrysostom (Or. 36, "Borystheniticus")', *Ancient Civilizations* 8, no. 3–4 (2002): 321–2.

39 Athenaeus, *Deipnosophists* 11.427a, translation my own. For more on the drunk Scythian trope, see Joanna Porucznik, 'The Image of a "Drunken Scythian" in Greek Tradition', *European Scientific Journal* 9, no. 19 (2013): 710–13.

40 Herodotus, *Histories* 6.84.

41 This is a very abridged version of what Herodotus tells us: Herodotus, *Histories* 4. 118–43.

42 Joanna Porucznik, 'Heuresibios Son of Syriskos and the Question of Tyranny in Olbia Pontike (Fifth–Fourth Century BC)', *Annual of the British School at Athens* 113 (2018): 407.

43 Thucydides, *The History of the Peloponnesian War* 2.65.

44 Plutarch, *Pericles* 20.1.

45 Porucznik, 'Heuresibios Son of Syriskos and the Question of Tyranny in Olbia Pontike (Fifth–Fourth Century BC)': 408.

46 Macrobius, *Saturnalia* 1.11.33, [adapted] translation from Robert A. Kaster, *Macrobius: Saturnalia*, Vol. I, Harvard University Press, Cambridge, MA, 2011.

## 5 NAUCRATIS, EGYPT

1 Herodotus, *Histories* 2.53; Plato, *Timaeus* 22b.

2 Aristotle, *Politics* 1329b.

3 Herodotus, *Histories* 2.58.

4 Plato, *Timaeus* 22b.

5 *The Naucratis Stela*, 380 BCE.

6 Myrto Malouta, 'Naucratis', *Oxford Handbooks Online*, July 2015, DOI: 10.1093/oxfordhb/9780199935390.013.114

7 Ross I. Thomas, 'Roman Naucratis and its Alexandrian context', *British Museum Studies in Ancient Egypt and Sudan* 22 (2014): 195–9. For an overview of the site and the most recent excavation material there is no better starting place than the British Museum's research

catalogue: Alexandra Villing et al., 'Naucratis: Greeks in Egypt', National Archives, archived 1 August 2019, https://webarchive.nationalarchives.gov.uk/ukgwa/20190801114017/https://www.britishmuseum.org/research/online_research_catalogues/ng/Naucratis_greeks_in_egypt/topography.aspx

8 Herodotus, *Histories* 2.135.5.

9 Plutarch, *Why the Pythian Priestess No Longer Gives Oracles in Verse*, 14.

10 Herodotus, *Histories* 1.135 (although he dismisses the story as false); Diodorus Siculus, *Library* 1.64.11; Pliny the Elder, *Natural History* 36.17.2; Strabo, *Geography* 17.1.33.

11 Aelian, *Varia Historia* 13.33; Strabo, *Geography* 17.1.33. On the issue of her name change, there is an excellent online article which offers a convincing explanation: Gregory Nagy, 'Herodotus and a courtesan from Naucratis', Classical Inquiries, last modified 1 July 2015, https://classical-inquiries.chs.harvard.edu/herodotus-and-a-courtesan-from-naucratis

12 Heliodorus, *Aethiopica* 2.25, translation from J. R. Morgan, 'Heliodorus. An Ethiopian Story', in *Collected Ancient Greek Novels*, ed. B. P. Reardon, University of California Press, Berkeley, 2019, pp. 407–686. My thanks to Dr Mai Musié for pointing me towards this reference.

13 Ovid, *Epistles (Heroides)* 15, translation from Grant Showerman, *Ovid: Heroides and Amores*, Harvard University Press, Cambridge, MA, William Heinemann Ltd, London, 1931.

14 Sappho fr. 5.5; Maarit Kivilo, *Early Greek Poets' Lives: The Shaping of the Tradition*, Brill, Leiden, 2010, pp. 168–9.

15 Herodotus, *Histories* 2.135.6.

16 Ibid., 2.179.

17 Strabo, *Geography* 17.1.33.

18 A. Möller, *Naucratis: Trade in Archaic Greece*, Oxford University Press, Oxford, 2000, pp. 211–12.

19 John Boardman, *The Greeks Overseas: Their Early Colonies and Trade*, Thames & Hudson, London, 1980, p. 128.

20 Toby Wilkinson, *The Rise and Fall of Ancient Egypt: The History of a Civilisation from 3000 BC to Cleopatra*, Bloomsbury, London, 2011, p. 182.

21 Alexandra Villing and Udo Schlotzhauer, 'Naucratis and the Eastern Mediterranean: Past, Present and Future', in *Naucratis: Greek Diversity in Egypt: Studies on East Greek Pottery and Exchange in the*

*Eastern Mediterranean*, eds Alexandra Villing and Udo Schlotzhauer, British Museum, London, 2006, p. 2.

22 Herodotus, *Histories* 2.91.1.

23 Boardman, *The Greeks Overseas*, p. 143.

24 Plato, *Phaedrus* 275a–b, translation from Harold N. Fowler, *Plato in Twelve Volumes*, Vol. 9, Harvard University Press, Cambridge, MA, 1925.

25 Plato, *Phaedrus* 274c.

26 Diogenes, *Lives of the Eminent Philosophers* 3.6.

27 Plutarch, *Solon* 2.4.

28 Plutarch, *Solon* 26; Aristotle, *Constitution of the Athenians* 11.1; see also Herodotus, *Histories* 1.29; Maria Noussia-Fantuzzi, *Solon the Athenian: The Poetic Fragments*, Brill, Leiden, 2010, p. 299.

29 Athenaeus, *The Deipnosophists* 6.16.

30 Herodotus, *Histories* 2.29.

31 Ibid., 2.35.3.

32 Ibid., 2.71.

33 It would be remiss of me not to note that the site of Naucratis was originally identified by one of the earliest pioneers of Egyptology, William Flinders Petrie, in 1883.

34 Boardman, *The Greeks Overseas*, p. 142. I will admit to buying into the romantic notion that this possibility conjures. For a more cynical analysis see D. W. J. Gill, 'Two Herodotean Dedications from Naucratis', *Journal of Hellenic Studies* 106 (1986): 184–7.

35 Philostratus, *Lives of the Sophists* 2.12.2.

36 Athenaeus s.v. *Oxford Classical Dictionary Online*.

37 Athenaeus, *The Deipnosophists* 13.69.

38 Ibid., 11.61.

39 Arrian, *Anabasis* 2.11.8; Curtius, *History of Alexander* 3.11.10; Stephen Ruzicka, *Trouble in the West: Egypt and the Persian Empire 525–332 BCE*, Oxford University Press, Oxford, 2012, pp. 204–5.

40 Curtius, *History of Alexander* 4.7.1–2, translation from John C. Rolfe, *Quintus Curtius*, Vol. I, Harvard University Press, Cambridge, MA, 1946.

41 Pseudo-Aristotle, *Economics*, 2.1352a–b.

42 Demosthenes, 56.7.

43 Pseudo-Aristotle, *Economics*, 2.1352b.

44 Ibid., 2.1352a.

45 Dominic Rathbone, 'Villages, Land and Population in Graeco-Roman Egypt', *Proceedings of the Cambridge Philological Society* 36, no. 216 (1990): 114. See also Chapter 9.

46 Ross I. Thomas, 'Roman Naucratis and its Alexandrian context', *British Museum Studies in Ancient Egypt and Sudan* 22 (2014): 201.

47 Ibid.: 202.

48 Young Kim (ed.), *The Cambridge Companion to the Council of Nicaea*, Cambridge University Press, Cambridge, 2021, p. 369.

49 Thomas, 'Roman Naucratis and its Alexandrian context': 202.

## 6 MASSALIA, FRANCE

1 Cicero, *For Flaccus* 26.

2 For an excellent overview of all of the available accounts, see Martin Mauersberg, 'The Ktisis of Massalia Revisited: What to do with Contradictory Ancient Sources', *Ancient West & East* 14 (2015): 145–68.

3 Justin, *Epitome of Pompeius Trogus' Philippic Histories* 43.3.

4 As referenced in Athenaeus, *The Deipnosophists* 13.36.

5 See also Chapter 10.

6 Xenophon, *Hellenica* 7.1.20.

7 Plutarch, *Camillus* 22.2–3.

8 Ibid., 22.3.

9 W. M. Freeman Philip, 'The earliest Greek sources on the Celts', *Etudes Celtiques* 32 (1996): 24–5, 30–4.

10 Aristotelian Corpus, *On Marvellous Things Heard* 27.87.

11 Strabo, *Geography* 4.1.5.

12 Athenaeus, *The Deipnosophistae* 10.33.26; Kathryn Lomas, 'Hellenism, Romanisation and Cultural Identity in Massalia', in *Greek Identity in the Western Mediterranean: Papers in Honour of Brian Shefton*, ed. Kathryn Lomas, Brill, Leiden, 2004, pp. 480–1.

13 Valerius Maximus 2.6.7.

14 Strabo, *Geography* 4.1.5.

15 Tacitus, *Agricola* 4, translation my own.

16 Ibid.

17 Seneca, *Natural Questions* 4.2.22, [adapted] translation from Thomas H. Corcoran, *Seneca: Natural Questions*, Vol. I, Harvard University Press, Cambridge, MA, 1972.

18 M. Carey and E. H. Worthington, *The Ancient Explorers*, Methuen & Co., London, 1929, p. 46.
19 Hanno, *Periplus* 18, translation my own.
20 Diodorus, 5.21.3.
21 Strabo, *Geography* 2.5.8; 7.3.1.
22 Ibid., 3.2.9.
23 Ibid., 4.1.5.
24 Julius Caesar, *Gallic Wars* 1.29.
25 Justin, *Epitome of Pompeius Trogus' Philippic Histories* 43.4, translation from John Selby Watson, *Justin, Cornelius Nepos and Eutropius*, George Bell & Sons, London, 1876.
26 Patrick E. McGovern et al., 'Beginning of viniculture in France', *Proceedings of the National Academy of Sciences of the United States of America* 110, no. 25 (2013): 10,151.
27 Anthony King, *Roman Gaul and Germany*, University of California Press, Oakland, 1990, pp. 14–15.
28 John T. Koch, *Celtic Culture: A Historical Encyclopedia*, Vol. 2, ABC-CLIO, Santa Barbara, 2006, p. 461.
29 Julius Caesar, *Civil War* 1.34.4; Arnaldo Momigliano, *Alien Wisdom: The Limits of Hellenization*, Cambridge University Press, Cambridge, 1993, p. 55.
30 St Jerome, referencing the first century BCE writer Varro, *In Galatians* 2.426.
31 Alex Mullen, *Southern Gaul and the Mediterranean: Multilingualism and Multiple Identities in the Iron Age and Roman Periods*, Cambridge University Press, Cambridge, 2013, pp. 98–101.
32 U. Wilcken, 'Punt-Fahrten in der Ptolemäerzeit', *Zeitschrift für Ägyptische Sprache und Altertumskunde* 60 (1925): 86–102; Momigliano, *Alien Wisdom: The Limits of Hellenization*, p. 55; Michael Dietler, *Archaeologies of Colonialism: Consumption, Entanglement, and Violence in Ancient Mediterranean France*, University of California Press, Berkeley, 2010, p. 111.
33 Virgil, *Catalepton* 2; J. N. Adams, *Bilingualism and the Latin Language*, Cambridge University Press, Cambridge, 2003, p. 191.
34 Strabo, *Geography* 3.4.17, [adapted] translation from H. C. Hamilton, *The Geography of Strabo*, George Bell & Sons, London, 1903. A similar story is told by Diodorus, *Library of History* 4.20.2–3.

35 Athenaeus, *Deipnosophistae* 12.25.
36 Livy, *History of Rome* 38.17.12; Livy, *History of Rome* 37.54.21–2; Adolfo J. Domínguez, 'Greek Identity in the Phocaean Colonies', in *Greek Identity in the Western Mediterranean: Papers in Honour of Brian Shefton*, ed. Kathryn Lomas, Brill, Leiden, 2004, p. 451.
37 Justin, *Epitome of Pompeius Trogus' Philippic Histories* 43.5.3.
38 Diodorus, *Library of History* 14.93.3; Livy, *History of Rome* 5.21–23; Norman J. DeWitt, 'Massilia and Rome', *Transactions and Proceedings of the American Philological Association* 71 (1940): 609.
39 Justin, *Epitome of Pompeius Trogus' Philippic Histories* 43.5.8–10.
40 Sosylus, *Deeds of Hannibal*, *FrGH* 176, translation from 'Fragments of Greek Historians', Attalus, accessed 13 July 2023, http://www.attalus.org/translate/fgh.html#176.0
41 Livy, *Epitome* 60.2.
42 Strabo, *Geography* 4.1.8.
43 Cicero, *For Marcus Fonteius* 13.
44 Cassius Dio, *Roman History* 41.19, translation from Earnest Cary and Herbert B. Foster, *Cassius Dio Roman History*, Vol. 4, Harvard University Press, Cambridge, MA, 1916.
45 Lucan, *Civil War* 388–391, translation from Edward Ridley, *M. Annaeus Lucanus: Pharsalia*, Longmans, Green, and Co., London, 1905.
46 S. T. Loseby, 'Marseille: A Late Antique Success Story?', *Journal of Roman Studies* 82 (1992): 171–2.

## 7 HADRIAN'S WALL, ENGLAND

1 *Tab. Vindol.* 234, translation from 'Tab.Vindol. 234. Correspondence of Flavius Cerialis', Roman Inscriptions of Britain, last modified 11 October 2022, https://romaninscriptionsofbritain.org/inscriptions/TabVindol234
2 Plutarch, *Julius Caesar* 23.3, translation from C. Pelling, *Plutarch, Caesar: Translated with an Introduction and Commentary*, Oxford University Press, Oxford, 2011.
3 Strabo, *Geography* 2.5.8.
4 Horace, *Odes* 1.35.29–30.
5 His first invasion lasted approximately three weeks, while his second invasion began in late July and had ended by late September: Richard

Hingley, *Conquering the Ocean: The Roman Invasion of Britain*, Oxford University Press, New York, 2022, pp. 21–37.

6 Cassius Dio mentions three separate invasions planned by Augustus: *Roman History* 49.38; 53.22; 53.25.

7 Suetonius, *Gaius* 46.

8 Tacitus, *Agricola* 30.

9 Tacitus, *Histories* 1.2.

10 Historia Augusta, *Life of Hadrian* 1.5.1–3, translation from David Magie, revised by David Rohrbacher, *Historia Augusta*, Vol. I, Harvard University Press, Cambridge, MA, 2022.

11 Ibid.

12 Cassius Dio, *Roman History* 77.12.

13 My thanks to Dr Jo Ball for this observation.

14 Roman Inscriptions of Britain 3364, https://romaninscriptionsofbritain.org/inscriptions/3364.

15 *Inscriptiones Latinae Selectae* 2726.

16 Anthony Birley, *Garrison Life at Vindolanda: A Band of Brothers*, The History Press, Stroud, 2010, pp. 72–5.

17 Plutarch, *Eumenes* 11.3–4; Peter Toohey, 'Some Ancient Notions of Boredom', *Illinois Classical Studies* 13, no. 1 (1988): 162.

18 Jo Ball, 'Board and dice games in the Roman military – A game of soldiers', *Ancient History Magazine* 34 (2021).

19 Fronto, *Letters to Lucius Verus* 2.1, translation from C. R. Haines, *Fronto: Correspondence*, Vol. 2, Harvard University Press, Cambridge, MA, 1920; Alexander Kyrychenko, *The Roman Army and the Expansion of the Gospel: The Role of the Centurion in Luke-Acts*, De Gruyter, Berlin, 2014, p. 81.

20 *Tab. Vindol.* 164.

21 *Tab. Vindol.* 346, translation from 'Tab.Vindol. 346. Ink writing tablet', Roman Inscriptions of Britain, last modified 11 October 2022, https://romaninscriptionsofbritain.org/inscriptions/TabVindol346

22 Cassius Dio, *Roman History* 73.8.2–3.

23 Ibid., 73.8.2–5.

24 Guy de la Bédoyère, *The Real Life of Roman Britain*, Yale University Press, New Haven, 2015, pp. 145–6.

25 'Child skeleton at Vindolanda fort "from Mediterranean" ', BBC News, last modified 28 August 2012, https://www.bbc.co.uk/news/uk-england-tyne-19399441; Trudi J. Buck, 'A Child in the Barracks: Murder on a Roman Fort' (forthcoming).

26 *RIB* 1791, translation from Peter Kruschwitz, *Undying Voices: The Poetry of Roman Britain*, Reading, 2015, [permalink: thepetrifiedmuse.wordpress.com/undying-voices].
27 Kruschwitz, *Undying Voices*, pp. 56–7.
28 *RIB* 1124, 1129.
29 *RIB* 1129, translation from Kruschwitz, *Undying Voices*.
30 Carly Silver, 'Bull-Killer, Sun Lord', Online Features, *Archaeology Magazine*, archived 24 August 2010, https://archive.archaeology.org/online/features/bull_killer
31 *Tab. Vindol.* 185, 190, 203.
32 *Tab. Vindol.* 118.
33 *Tab. Vindol.* 291, translation from 'Tab.Vindol. 291. Birthday Invitation of Sulpicia Lepidina', Roman Inscriptions of Britain, last modified 11 October 2022, https://romaninscriptionsofbritain.org/inscriptions/TabVindol291–
34 Our earliest attestation comes from Cassius Dio, *Roman History* 60.24.3; for an overview of our literary evidence see Sara Elise Phang, *The Marriage of Roman Soldiers (13 B.C.–A.D. 235): Law and Family in the Imperial Army*, Brill, Leiden, 2001, pp. 16–21.
35 Livy, *History of Rome* 43.3.1–2, translation Alfred C. Schlesinger, *Livy: History of Rome*, Vol. 13, Harvard University Press, Cambridge, MA, 1951.
36 For a breakdown of recent archaeological data regarding shoes found at Vindolanda see Elizabeth M. Greene, *Women and Families in the Auxiliary Military Communities of the Roman West in the First and Second Centuries AD* (PhD Thesis, University of North Carolina), Appendix 1.
37 For more about the diploma, and the life of Sestius Longinus, see Werner Eck, Paul Holder and Andreas Pangerl, 'A Diploma for the Army of Britain in 132 and Hadrian's Return to Rome from the East', *Zeitschrift für Papyrologie und Epigraphik* 174 (2010): 189–200, and Anthony R. Birley, 'The "Cohors I Hamiorum" in Britain', *Acta Classica* 55 (2012): 1–16.
38 Eutropius, *Abridgement of Roman History*, 21; Orosius, *Seven Books of History Against the Pagans*, 7.25.2–4.

## 8 VOLUBILIS, MOROCCO

1 This match was the subject of a large number of ancient writers, both Greek and Roman. Each tells slightly different versions of the same basic story; this account comes predominantly from Philostratus, *Imagines* 2.21.

2 Plutarch, *Life of Sertorius* 9.3, translation from Bernadotte Perrin, *Plutarch: Plutarch's Lives*, Vol. 8, Harvard University Press, Cambridge, MA, 1919.

3 Hanno the Navigator, *Periplus* 6, translation from 'Hanno the Navigator (2)', Livius.org, accessed 19 July 2024, https://www.livius.org/articles/person/hanno-1-the-navigator/hanno-1-the-navigator-2/.

4 Marlene C. Sigman, 'The Romans and the Indigenous Tribes of Mauritania Tingitana', *Historia: Zeitschrift für Alte Geschichte* 26, no. 4 (1977): 420.

5 Polybius, *Histories* 3.33, translation from Elizabeth Fentress, 'Romanizing the Berbers', *Past & Present* 190 (2006): 6.

6 Sallust, *Jugurthine War* 19, [adapted] translation from John Selby Watson, *Sallust: The Jugurthine War*, Harper & Brothers, New York, 1899.

7 Duane W. Roller, *The World of Juba II and Kleopatra Selene: Royal Scholarship on Rome's African Frontier*, Routledge, London, 2003, p. 56.

8 Plutarch, *Life of Caesar* 55.2, [adapted] translation from Perrin, *Plutarch: Plutarch's Lives*, Vol. 7.

9 Sidi Mohammed Alaioud, 'Review of Archaeological Researches on the Maure's Period in Volubilis', in *L'Africa Romana: Momenti di continuità e rottura: bilancio di trent'anni di convegni L'Africa Romana*, ed. Paola Ruggeri, Carocci Editore, Roma, 2015, pp. 1,023–34.

10 Pliny, *Natural History* 13.29; Jane Draycott, *Cleopatra's Daughter*, Head of Zeus, London, 2022, pp. 185–6.

11 Eric Varner, *Mutilation and Transformation: Damnatio Memoriae and Roman Imperial Portraiture*, Brill, Leiden, 2004, p. 103.

12 Ibid., p. 237.

13 Pausanias, *Description of Greece* 1.17.

14 Tacitus, *Annals* 4.26.

15 Suetonius, *Gaius* 35.1; Duncan Fishwood and Brent D. Shaw, 'Ptolemy of Mauretania and the Conspiracy of Gaetulicus', *Historia: Zeitschrift für Alte Geschichte* 25, no. 4 (1976): 491–4.
16 Scholia to Lucan, *Civil War* 8.287; Draycott, *Cleopatra's Daughter*, pp. 185–6.
17 Pliny, *Natural History* 5.1.
18 Anthony Barrett, *Caligula: The Abuse of Power*, 2nd edn, Routledge, London, 2015, p. 160.
19 *ILM* 116, [adapted] translation from B. H. Warmington and S. J. Miller, *Inscriptions of the Roman Empire AD 14–117*, 2nd edn, Vol. 8 of *LACTOR Sourcebooks in Ancient History*, Cambridge University Press, Cambridge, 2023, p. 25.
20 Leonard A. Curchin, 'Family Relations in Mauretania Tingara: An Analysis of the Epigraphic Evidence', *Gerion* 40, no. 1 (2022): 210.
21 Paul MacKendrick, *The North African Stones Speak*, University of North Carolina Press, Chapel Hill, NC, 1980, p. 300.
22 Inscriptions antiques du Maroc II.2 364 = *ILAfr* 611
23 Georges Vajda, 'Inscriptions hébraïques', *Études d'Antiquités africaines Année* 1 (1966): 137; S. Andreeva, A. Fedorchuk and M. Nosonovsky, 'Revisiting Epigraphic Evidence of the Oldest Synagogue in Morocco in Volubilis', *Arts* 8, no. 4 (2019): 127, https://doi.org/10.3390/arts8040127
24 Martin Blumenson, *The Patton Papers 1940–1945*, Houghton Mifflin, Boston, 1974, p. 149.
25 Marlene C. Sigman, 'The Romans and the Indigenous Tribes of Mauritania Tingitana', *Historia: Zeitschrift für Alte Geschichte* 26, no. 4 (1977): 430.
26 Edmon Frézouls, 'Les Baquates et la Province Romaine de Tingitane', *Bulletin d'archéologie marocaine* 2 (1957): 65–116; Sigman, 'The Romans and the Indigenous Tribes of Mauritania Tingitana': 431–2.
27 Sallust, *The Jugurthine War* 18.1–2, translation from Watson, *Sallust: The Jugurthine War*.
28 Elizabeth Fentress, 'Idris I and the Berbers', in *The Aghlabids and Their Neighbors: Art and Material Culture in Ninth-Century North Africa*, eds Glaire D. Anderson, Corisande Fenwick and Mariam Rosser-Owen, Brill, Leiden, 2018, pp. 516–17.

## 9 KARANIS, EGYPT

1 *P col* 4 66, translation adapted from 'p.col.4.66', Papyri.info, accessed 13 July 2023, http://papyri.info/ddbdp/p.col;4;66
2 *UPZ* I 8, [adapted] translation from Roger S. Bagnall and Peter Derow (eds), *Historical Sources in Translation: The Hellenistic Period*, Blackwell Publishing, Oxford, 2004, p. 232.
3 Herodotus, *Histories*, 3.91.
4 'Unearthing the Past: The Expeditions of the Kelsey Museum', *Research News* XIII, 5, Office of Research Administration, the University of Michigan, Ann Arbor, 1972, p. 9; Elaine K. Gazda (ed.), *Karanis, An Egyptian Town in Roman Times: Discoveries of the University of Michigan Expedition to Egypt (1924–1935)*, 2nd edn, Kelsey Museum of Archaeology, University of Michigan, Ann Arbor, 2004, p. 7.
5 *SB* 6 9636, translation from 'sb.6.9636', Papyri.info, accessed 13 July 2023, http://papyri.info/ddbdp/sb;6;9636
6 Richard Alston, *Soldier and Society in Roman Egypt: A Social History*, Routledge, London, 1995, p. 137.
7 *P mich.* 9 535, translation from 'p.mich.9.535', Papyri.info, accessed 13 July 2023, https://papyri.info/ddbdp/p.mich;9;535.
8 Ibid., p. 123.
9 *SB* 4 7362.
10 *BGU* I 180, [adapted] translation from Brian Campbell, *The Roman Army, 31 BC–AD 337: A Sourcebook*, Routledge, London, 1994, p. 339.
11 *SB* 5 7523, translation from Naphtali Lewis, *Life in Egypt Under Roman Rule*, Oxford University Press, Oxford, 1983, p. 24.
12 *Digest* 49.18.1–3; Ian Hayes, *Blood of the Provinces: The Roman Auxilia and the Making of Provincial Society from Augustus to the Severans*, Oxford University Press, Oxford, 2013, p. 346.
13 *P mich.* 8 465, translation from 'p.mich.8.465', Papyri.info, accessed 13 July 2023, http://papyri.info/ddbdp/p.mich;8;465.
14 April Pudsey, 'Death and the Family: Widows and Divorcées in Roman Egypt', in *Families in the Imperial and Late Antique World*, eds Mary Harlow and Lena Larsson Lovén, Bloomsbury, London, 2012, p. 158.
15 Ibid., pp. 165–6.
16 *sb.*18 13305.
17 Pudsey, 'Death and the Family: Widows and Divorcées in Roman Egypt', in *Families in the Imperial and Late Antique World*, p. 169.

18 Anna C. Kelley, 'Searching for Professional Women in the Mid to Late Roman Textile Industry', *Past & Present* 258, no. 1 (2023): 25.

19 *P. col* 7 173, [adapted] translation from 'p.col.7.173', Papyri.info, accessed 13 July 2023, http://papyri.info/ddbdp/p.col;7;173

20 *SB* 24 16002.

21 Bethany Lynn Simpson, *Neighbourhood Networks: Social and Spatial Organization of Domestic Architecture in Greco-Roman Karanis, Egypt*, University of California, Los Angeles, PhD Thesis, 2014, 182.

22 Ibid., 236–9.

23 Horst Beinlich, 'The Book of the Faiyum', in *Egypt's Mysterious Book of the Faiyum*, eds Horst Beinlich, Regine Schulz and Alfried Wieczorek, J. H. Röll Verlag, Dettelbach, 2013, pp. 53–4.

24 Strabo, *Geography* 17.1.38, translation from H. C. Hamilton, *The Geography of Strabo*, George Bell & Sons, London, 1903.

25 See for instance this oracular query to the god, not from Karanis: *W. Chr* 122.

26 E.g. *CPJ* 460, with Marius Heemstra, *The Fiscus Judaicys and the Parting of the Ways*, Mohr Siebeck, Tübingen, 2010, p. 20; Aryeh Kasher, *The Jews in Hellenistic and Roman Egypt*, Mohr Siebeck, Tübingen, 1985, p. 103.

27 Gazda (ed.), *Karanis, An Egyptian Town in Roman Times,* pp. 43–4.

28 *P. col* 7 171, [adapted] translation from 'p.col.7.171', Papyri.info, accessed 13 July 2023, http://papyri.info/ddbdp/p.col;7;171.

29 For a list of symptoms compiled from Galen's various works see R. J. Littman and M. L. Littman, 'Galen and the Antonine Plague', *American Journal of Philology* 94, no. 3 (1973): 246–8.

30 Dominic Rathbone, 'Villages, Land and Population in Graeco-Roman Egypt', *Proceedings of the Cambridge Philological Society* 36, no. 216 (1990): 103–42.

31 Peter van Minnen, 'Deserted Villages: Two Late Antique Town Sites in Egypt', *Bulletin of the American Society of Papyrologists* 32, no. 1/2 (1995): 49.

32 Roger S. Bagnall, 'Agricultural Productivity and Taxation in Later Roman Egypt', *Transactions of the American Philological Association* 115 (1985): 293; van Minnen, 'Deserted Villages: Two Late Antique Town Sites in Egypt': 49.

33 *P haun* 3 58.

34 P col 8 242, translation from van Minnen, 'Deserted Villages: Two Late Antique Town Sites in Egypt': 53.

## 10 BILSK, UKRAINE

1 Marina Daragan, 'Belsk: The Largest Hillfort in Europe', *Current World Archaeology* 101 (2020): 32.
2 Ibid.: 35.
3 Herodotus 4.21.
4 Herodotus 4.108.1–2, translation my own.
5 Iryna Shramko, 'Bilsk (Belsk) City Site – The Largest Fortified Settlement of Scythia', *Ancient West & East* 20 (2021): 178.
6 Daragan, 'Belsk: The Largest Hillfort in Europe', *Current World Archaeology* 101 (2020): 34.
7 Shramko, 'Bilsk (Belsk) City Site – The Largest Fortified Settlement of Scythia': 180.
8 Ibid.: 179–80.
9 Iryna Shramko and Stanislaw Zadnikov, 'The Bilsk fortified settlement and the Hallstatt world', *Śląskie Sprawozdania Archeologiczne* 63 (2021): 126.
10 Ibid.: 126–31.
11 Iryna Shramko and Mykola Tarasenko, 'Egyptian Imports of 6th Century BC in the Materials of Forest-Steppe Scythia', *Shodoznavstvo* 89 (2022): 139–80.
12 Shramko and Zadnikov, 'The Bilsk fortified settlement and the Hallstatt world': 134; Shramko, 'Bilsk (Belsk) City Site – The Largest Fortified Settlement of Scythia': 185.
13 A. R. Ventresca Miller et al., 'Mobility and diet in the Iron Age Pontic forest-steppe: A multi-isotopic study of urban populations at Bel'sk', *Archaeometry*, 61 (2019): 1,399–1,416; A. R. Ventresca Miller et al., 'Re-evaluating Scythian lifeways: Isotopic analysis of diet and mobility in Iron Age Ukraine', *PLoS One* 16, no. 3 (2021): e0245996.
14 Herodotus 4.109.1, translation my own.
15 Shramko, 'Bilsk (Belsk) City Site – The Largest Fortified Settlement of Scythia': 195.
16 Daragan, 'Belsk: The Largest Hillfort in Europe', *Current World Archaeology* 101 (2020): 36.
17 Ibid.: 38.
18 Ibid.: 37.
19 Herodotus, 4.123.1, translation my own.
20 Ctesias, *Persica* 21.

21 B. Shramko, *Belskoe gorodische skifskoi epokhi (gorod Gelon)*, Naukova dumka, Kyiv, 1987, p. 163; Shramko, Bilsk (Belsk) City Site – The Largest Fortified Settlement of Scythia': 201.

22 Y. N. Boiko, 'Khram goroda Gelona', *Sovetskaya etnografiya* 3 (1990): 52–65; Shramko, 'Bilsk (Belsk) City Site – The Largest Fortified Settlement of Scythia': 204.

23 Barry Cunliffe, *The Scythians: Nomad Warriors of the Steppe*, Oxford University Press, Oxford, 2019, pp. 161–2.

24 Renate Rolle, *The World of the Scythians*, translated by F. G. Walls, University of California Press, Berkeley, 1989, p. 83.

25 Herodotus, 4.65, translation my own.

26 Stephanie West, 'Scythians', in *Brill's Companion to Herodotus*, eds Egbert J. Bakker, Irene J. F. De Jong and Hans van Wees, Brill, Leiden, 2002, p. 454; Shramko, 'Bilsk (Belsk) City Site – The Largest Fortified Settlement of Scythia': 209.

## 11 TAXILA, PAKISTAN

1 This is a very lightly edited version of the translation given by Richard Salomon, *Indian Epigraphy: A Guide to the Study of Inscriptions in Sanskrit, Prakrit, and the Other Indo-Aryan Languages*, Oxford University Press, Oxford, 1998, pp. 265–7.

2 Burjor Avari, *India: The Ancient Past, A History of the Indian Subcontinent from c. 7000 BCE to CE 1200*, 2nd edn, Routledge, London, 2016, pp. 166–7.

3 Plutarch, *Alexander* 59.1.

4 There are slightly different accounts about what the people of Taxila offered Alexander, and there is no reason to discount any of them as they are each within the realm of plausibility: Arrian, *Anabasis* 4.22.6, 5.3.5–6; Diodorus, *Library* 17.87; Plutarch, *Alexander* 59; Curtius Rufus, *History of Alexander* 8.12.11.

5 Plutarch, *Alexander* 59.3, translation my own.

6 Burjor Avari, *India: The Ancient Past*, pp. 158–62.

7 Herodotus, *Histories* 3.94–95.

8 Search for 'India', in R. T. Hallock, *Persepolis Fortification Texts*, Oriental Institute Publication 92, University of Chicago Press, Chicago, 1967.

9 *The Jakata*, 1. 55.

10 *Mahavagga*, 8.1.30–33; Kenneth G. Zysk, *Asceticism and Healing in Ancient India: Medicine in the Buddhist Monastery*, Motilal Banarsidass Publishers, Delhi, 1998, p. 124.

11 John Kadvany, 'Pāṇini's Grammar and Modern Computation', *History and Philosophy of Logic* 37, no. 4 (2016): 325–46.

12 Leonard Bloomfield, *Language*, Henry Holt Company, New York, 1933, p. 11; George Cardona,*Pāṇini: A Survey of Research*, Motilal Banarsidass Publishers, Delhi, 1997, reprint, p. 243.

13 Richard Stoneman, 'Naked Philosophers: The Brahmans in the Alexander Historians and the Alexander Romance',*Journal of Hellenic Studies* 115 (1995): 99–114.

14 Strabo, *Geography* 15.1.63, translation from H. C. Hamilton, *The Geography of Strabo*, George Bell & Sons, London, 1903.

15 Plutarch, *Alexander* 62.4, translation my own.

16 Radha Kumud Mookerji, *Chandragupta Maurya and His Times*, 4th edn reprint, Motilal Banarsidass Publishers, Delhi, 1988, pp. 15–17.

17 For an overview of the various terms used in both the Greek and Indian literature, see Mookerji, *Chandragupta Maurya and His Times*, pp. 22–4.

18 *Parisistaparvan*, 8.294–6; Hemacandra, *The Lives of the Jain Elders*, translated by R. C. C. Fynes, Oxford University Press, Oxford, 1998, p. 176.

19 Ahmad Hasan Dani, *The Historic City of Taxila*, Unesco, Paris, 1986, p. 49; A. B. Bosworth, 'The Historical Setting of Megasthenes' *Indica*', *Classical Philology* 91, no. 2 (1996): 113–27.

20 Plutarch, *Alexander* 62.2.

21 Strabo, *Geography* 15.2.9; Plutarch, *Alexander* 62.2.

22 For the laws forbidding it, see *Manusmriti* III 51; Stoneman, 'Naked Philosophers: The Brahmans in the Alexander Historians and the Alexander Romance': 107.

23 Strabo, *Geography* 15.1.62, translation from Hamilton, *The Geography of Strabo*.

24 John S. Strong, *The Legend of Asoka: A Study and Translation of the Asokavadana*, Motilal Banarsidass Publishers, Delhi, 1989, p. 208.

25 Richard Salomon, *Buddhist Literature of Ancient Gandhara: An Introduction with Selected Translations*, Cambridge University Press, Cambridge, 2018, p. 1.

26 *Anguttara Nikaya* as preserved in *Taisho Tripitaka*, 2:657–64; translation from Robert DeCaroli, *Image Problems: The Origin and Development of the Buddha's Image in Early South Asia*, University

of Washington Press, Seattle, 2015, p. 29. For a full analysis of the various traditions and debates see pp. 29–50.

27 Clement of Alexandria, *Stromata* 1.15.71.

28 Andrzej Szotek, 'Buddha statue found at Berenike (Egypt)', Polish Centre of Mediterranean Archaeology, University of Warsaw, last modified 27 April 2023, https://pcma.uw.edu.pl/en/2023/04/27/buddha-statue-found-at-berenike-egypt/

29 Strabo, *Geography* 15.1.73, [adapted] translation from Hamilton, *The Geography of Strabo*.

30 Rong Xinjiang, 'Land Route or Sea Route? Commentary on the Study of the Paths of Transmission and Areas in which Buddhism Was Disseminated during the Han Period', translated by Xiuqin Zhou, *Sino-Platonic Papers* 144 (2004), 20.

31 Faxian, *A Record of Buddhist Kingdoms* 9, translation from James Legge, *A Record of Buddhistic Kingdoms Being an Account by the Chinese Monk Fa-Hien of His Travels in India and Ceylon (A.D. 399–414) in Search of the Buddhist Books of Discipline*, Clarendon Press, Oxford, 1886, p. 32.

## 12 CO LOA, VIETNAM

1 There are a wide variety of traditions regarding Thuc Phan and not all consider him to be an outsider, as indeed there are many different interpretations about the origin of the ancient Viet kingdom. The one recounted here is one of the most commonly told, but it is not ubiquitous. My thanks go to Dr Nam C. Kim for this important reminder.

2 This reconstruction relies heavily on the excellent work of Marilynn Larew, 'Thục Phán, Cao Tông, and the Transfer of Military Technology in Third Century Việt Nam', *East Asian Science, Technology, and Medicine* 21, Special Issue: Forays into the Field of Vietnamese Military Technology (2003): 29–30.

3 Quoted in Keith Taylor, *The Birth of Vietnam*, University of California Press, Berkeley, 1983, p. 25.

4 Ibid., p. 22.

5 Larew, 'Thục Phán, Cao Tông, and the Transfer of Military Technology in Third Century Việt Nam': 32.

6 For an overview of the defences see Lại Văn Tới, 'Cổ Loa: the Capital of the Âu Lạc Kingdom in the 3rd and 2nd Centuries BCE (Cổ

Loa: Kinh thành của nhà nước Âu Lạc vào thế kỷ 3-2 tr. CN)', in *Perspectives on the Archaeology of Vietnam: International Colloquium, Hanoi 29th February–2nd March 2012/Toàn cảnh khảo cổ học Việt Nam: Hội thảo quốc tế, từ 29/2 đến 02/3/2012, tại Hà Nội*, ed. Andreas Reinecke, German Archaeological Institute, Bonn, 2015, pp. 149–50.

7 Nam C. Kim, *The Origins of Ancient Vietnam*, Oxford University Press, Oxford, 2015, pp. 210–13.

8 Charles F. W. Higham, 'Đông Sơn Chiefdom/ Lãnh địa Đông Sơn', in *Perspectives on the Archaeology of Vietnam*, pp. 93–4; Ben Kiernan, *Viet Nam: A History from Earliest Times to the Present*, Oxford University Press, Oxford, 2017, p. 30.

9 Higham, 'Đông Sơn Chiefdom/ Lãnh địa Đông Sơn', pp. 91–3; Kiernan, *Viet Nam: A History from Earliest Times to the Present*, pp. 31–5.

10 C. Michele Thompson, 'Scripts, Signs, and Swords: the Việt Peoples and the Origins of Nôm', *Sino-Platonic Papers* 101 (2000): 48–9.

11 The complexity of Yue identities is too much to address here; for an illuminating study see Erica Fox Brindley, *Ancient China and the Yue: Perceptions and Identities on the Southern Frontier, c. 400 BCE–50 CE*, Cambridge University Press, Cambridge, 2015.

12 Quoted in Charles Holocombe, *The Genesis of East Asia, 221 B.C.–A.D. 907*, University of Hawai'i Press, Honolulu, 2001, p. 148.

13 Kiernan, *Viet Nam: A History from Earliest Times to the Present*, p. 71.

14 Ibid.

15 Nguyen Dang Thuc, *The Origins of the Vietnamese People*, 'Vietnamese Culture' series no. 10, Saigon Directorate of Cultural Affairs, Ministry of State, In Charge of Cultural Affairs, p. 14

16 Quoted in Mark Lewis, *The Early Chinese Empires: Qin and Han*, Harvard University Press, Cambridge, MA, 2007, p. 13.

17 Kiernan, *Viet Nam: A History from Earliest Times to the Present*, pp. 76–7.

18 This account of the rebellion draws equally from the excellent works of Stephen O'Harrow, 'From Co-loa to the Trung Sisters' Revolt: Viet-Nam as the Chinese Found it', *Asian Perspectives* 22, no. 2 (1979): 158–61; Taylor, *The Birth of Vietnam*, pp. 37–41; Sarah Womack, 'The Remakings of a Legend: Women and Patriotism in the Hagiography of the Tru'ng Sisters', *An Interdisciplinary Journal of*

*Southeast Asian Studies* 9, no. 2 (1995): 31–50; Kiernan, *Viet Nam: A History from Earliest Times to the Present*, pp. 78–83.

19 Dang Thanh Le, 'Van hoc co voi nu anh hung Trung Trac', *Tap chi van hoc* 5 (1969): 42–5, cited in Taylor, *The Birth of Vietnam*, p. 334.

20 *Hou Han shu*, 24.13 a–b, translation from Taylor, *The Birth of Vietnam*, p. 40.

21 Taylor, *The Birth of Vietnam*, p. 40, n. 184.

22 Taylor, *The Birth of Vietnam*, p. 334; Womack, 'The Remakings of a Legend: Women and Patriotism in the Hagiography of the Tru'ng Sisters', *An Interdisciplinary Journal of Southeast Asian Studies* 9, no. 2 (1995): 35.

23 Nam C. Kim, 'Cultural Landscapes of War and Political Regeneration', *Asian Perspectives* 52, no. 2 (2013): p. 256.

24 Nam C. Kim, *The Origins of Ancient Vietnam*, Oxford University Press, Oxford, 2015, pp. 62–5.

25 Of course, linguistic family trees are never quite this straightforward. For an analysis of the languages that would have been spoken in northern Vietnam at this time see Mark Alves, 'The Đông Sơn Speech Community: Evidence for Vietic', *Crossroads: An Interdisciplinary Journal of Asian Interactions* 19 (2020): 138–74.

26 Bùi Văn Liêm, 'The Đông Sơn Culture in the Red River Delta and its Relations with Adjacent Cultures/Văn hóa Đông Sơn vùng châu thổ sông Hồng và mối quan hệ của nó với các văn hóa vùng lân cận', in *Perspectives on the Archaeology of Vietnam*, p. 121.

27 John N. Miksic, *Singapore & the Silk Road of the Sea, 1300–1800*, NUS Press, Singapore, 2013, pp. 26–27. The drums only formed part of a much larger bronze trade in the region; see Andrew Sherrat, 'The Trans-Eurasian Exchange: The Prehistory of Chinese Relations with the West', in *Contact and Exchange in the Ancient World*, ed. Victor H. Mair, University of Hawai'i Press, Honolulu, 2006, p. 51; Nicholas Tarling (ed.), *The Cambridge History of Southeast Asia*, Vol. One, *From Early Times to c. 1500*, Cambridge University Press, Cambridge, 1999, p. 129.

28 Kiernan, *Viet Nam: A History from Earliest Times to the Present*, pp. 32–3.

29 This has not been true in the academy for many decades, but public history books still resign these links to mere footnotes to their narratives, if they are mentioned at all.

30 Pliny the Elder, *The Natural History* 6.20.

31 Florus, *Epitome* II.34.

32 National Library of Australia, *Mapping Our World: Terra Incognita to Australia*, National Library of Australia, Canberra, 2003, p. 38.

33 Matthew P. Fitzpatrick, 'Provincializing Rome: The Indian Ocean Trade Network and Roman Imperialism', *Journal of World History* 22, no. 1 (2011): 49–50; Steven E. Sidebotham and Steven Sidebotham, 'Late Roman Berenike', *Journal of the American Research Center in Egypt* 39 (2002): 234.

34 John E. Hill, *The Western Regions according to the* Hou Hanshu, *the* Xiyu juan *'Chapter on the Western Regions' from* Hou Hanshu *88*, 2nd edn (Online: 2003), accessed 13 July 2023, https://depts.washington.edu/silkroad/texts/hhshu/hou_han_shu.html#sec12

35 Translation from Friedrich Hirth, *China and the Roman Orient: Researches Into Their Ancient and Medieval Relations as Represented in Old Chinese Records*, George Hirth, Leipsic and Munich: 1885, p. 82; Joshua R. Hall, 'Marcus Aurelius and a mysterious embassy to China', *Ancient World Magazine*, last modified 9 May 2018, https://web.archive.org/web/20210922012744/https://www.ancientworldmagazine.com/articles/marcus-aurelius-mysterious-embassy-china

36 Peter F. Bang, 'Commanding and Consuming the World: Empire, Tribute and Trade in Roman and Chinese History', in *Rome and China: Comparative Perspectives on Ancient World Empires*, ed. Walter Scheidel, Oxford University Press, Oxford, 2009, p. 120.

37 Raoul McLaughlin, *Rome and the Distant East: Trade Routes to the Ancient Lands of Arabia, India and China*, Continuum, London, 2010, p. 58.

38 Rebecca C. Redfern et al., 'Going south of the river: A multidisciplinary analysis of ancestry, mobility and diet in a population from Roman Southwark, London', *Journal of Archaeological Science* 74 (2016): 11–22.

39 T. L. Prowse, J. L.Barta, T. E. von Hunnius and A. M. Small, 'Stable isotope and mtDNA evidence for geographic origins at the site of Vagnari, South Italy', in *Diasporas in the Roman World, Journal of Roman Archaeology*, Supplement 78, ed. H. Eckardt (2010): 175–98.

## 13 AKSUM, ETHIOPIA AND ERITREA

1 His name's allusion to his travels in India are a little misleading. In the ancient and medieval worlds of Europe in particular, India was

often used as a catch-all term which equally covered the lands of Africa to the east of the Nile, as well as Arabia. David W. Phillipson, *Foundations of an African Civilisation: Aksum & the Northern Horn 1000 BC–AD 1300*, Addis Ababa University Press/James Currey, Woodbridge, 2014, p. 92.

2 Maja Kominko, *The World of Kosmas: Illustrated Byzantine Codices of the Christian Topography*, Cambridge University Press, Cambridge, 2013, p. 13.

3 Cosmas covers this at various points within his book, but the main thesis is laid out in book 1. Winston Black, *The Middle Ages: Facts and Fictions*, ABC-CLIO, Santa Barbara, 2019, p. 32.

4 Pliny, *Natural History* 6.34.

5 Cosmas Indicopleustes, *The Christian Topography* 2.140–1; [adapted] translation from J. W. McCrindle, *The Christian Topography of Cosmas, an Egyptian Monk*, Hakluyt Society, London, 1897.

6 Ibid.

7 Procopius, *History of the Wars* 1.20.9–13; Photius, *Biblioteca* 3; G. W. Bowersock, *The Throne of Adulis: Red Sea Wars on the Eve of Islam*, Oxford University Press, Oxford, 2013, pp. 107–9.

8 Habtamu Tegegne and Wendy Laura Belcher, 'The Solomonic Christian Kingdom of Ethiopia', in John Parker (ed.), *Great Kingdoms of Africa*, Thames & Hudson, London, 2023, p. 89.

9 Edward Gibbon, *The History of the Decline and Fall of the Roman Empire*, Vol. 3, J. J. Harper, New York, 1831, p. 281.

10 *Periplus of the Erythraean Sea*, 4.

11 W. Wolska-Conus (ed.), *Cosmas Indicopleustes: Topographie Chrétienne* (I: Sources Chrétiennes 141), Éditions du Cerf, Paris, 1968, pp. 360–1.

12 J. E. G. Sutton, 'Aksum: goldfield or vineyards?', *Azania: Journal of the British Institute in Eastern Africa* 43, no. 1 (2008): 18.

13 Stuart Munro-Hay, 'Aksumite Overseas Interests', *Northeast African Studies* 13, no. 2/3 (1991): 131.

14 Cosmas Indicopleustes, *The Christian Topography* 2.142.

15 *Periplus of the Erythraean Sea*, 6.

16 Munro-Hay, 'Aksumite Overseas Interests', *Northeast African Studies* 13, no. 2/3 (1991): 138.

17 Rodolfo Fattovich, 'From Community to State: The Development of the Aksumite Polity (Northern Ethiopia and Eritrea), c. 400 BC–AD 800', *Journal of Archaeological Research* 27 (2019): 273.

18 Ibid.: 257–9; Phillipson, *Foundations of an African Civilisation*, pp. 119–20.

19 Andrea Manzo, 'The Great Aksumite Decorated Stelae: Architectural Characteristics, Functions, and Meanings', *Aethiopica* 23 (2020): 8; David W. Phillipson, *Archaeology at Aksum, Ethiopia, 1993–7*, II, Memoir of the British Institute in Eastern Africa, 17, Reports of the Research Committee of the Society of Antiquaries of London, 65, British Institute in Eastern Africa, London, 2000, p. 476; Phillipson, *Foundations of an African Civilisation: Aksum & the Northern Horn 1000 BC–AD 1300*, pp. 139–47.

20 *Ch'ien Han shu*, as quoted in Brian Colless, 'Han and Shen-tu China's Ancient Relations with South Asia', *East and West* 30, no. 1/4 (1980): 164.

21 Phillipson, *Archaeology at Aksum, Ethiopia, 1993–7*, II, p. 114; Niall Finneran, 'Ethiopian Christian material culture: the international context. Aksum, the Mediterranean and the Syriac worlds in the fifth to seventh centuries', *Reading Medieval Studies* 32 (2006): 76–7; Munro-Hay, 'Aksumite Overseas Interests': 139.

22 F. A. Chami, 'The Early Iron Age on Mafia island and its relationship with the mainland', *Azania: Archaeological Research in* Africa, Vol. 34, no. 1 (1999): 1–10.

23 Katie A. Hemer, Hugh Willmott, Jane E. Evans and Michael Buckley, 'Ivory from early Anglo-Saxon burials in Lincolnshire – A biomolecular study', *Journal of Archaeological Science: Reports* 49 (2023), https://doi.org/10.1016/j.jasrep.2023.103943

24 *Periplus of the Erythraean Sea*, 5, translation from Wilfred H. Schoff, *The Periplus of the Erythraean Sea: Travel and Trade in the Indian Ocean by a Merchant of the First Century*, Longmans, Green and Co., New York, 1912.

25 Phillipson, *Foundations of an African Civilisation*, pp. 54–5.

26 Ibid., pp. 54–5, 187.

27 It is not within the scope of this book to take sides in what is a long-standing and highly technical debate. For two strong assertions, one on either side of the debate, and further historiography, see Gizachew Tiruneh, 'The Kebra Nagast', *International Journal of Ethiopian Studies* 8, no. 1 & 2 (2014): 51–72, and Stuart Munro-Hay, 'A Sixth Century Kebra Nagast?', *Annales d'Éthiopie Année* 17 (2001): 43–58.

For an overview, see Phillipson, *Foundations of an African Civilisation*, pp. 66–8.

28 Rufinus, *Historia Ecclesiastica* 10.9–10.

29 *RIE* 271, translation from Phillipson, *Foundations of an African Civilisation*, p. 96.

30 H. S. Sergew, *Ancient and Medieval Ethiopian History to 1270*, United Printers, Addis Ababa, 1972, p. 104; Phillipson, *Foundations of an African Civilisation*, p. 97.

31 Fattovich, 'From Community to State: The Development of the Aksumite Polity (Northern Ethiopia and Eritrea), c. 400 BC–AD 800': 274; Rugare Rukuni, 'Negus Ezana: Revisiting the Christianisation of Aksum', *Verbum et Ecclesia* 42, no. 1 (2021): 3.

32 Judith S. McKenzie and Francis Watson, *The Garima Gospels: Early Illuminated Gospel Books from Ethiopia*, Manar al-Athar, Oxford, 2016, pp. 1–4.

33 Qur'an 105.

34 G. R. D. King, 'The Paintings of the Pre-Islamic Ka'ba', *Muqarnas* 21 (2004): 219.

35 Ibn Ishaq, *Sīratu Rasūlillāh Allāh* 220; Munro-Hay, 'Aksumite Overseas Interests', *Northeast African Studies* 13, no. 2/3 (1991): 134.

36 Ibn Rushd, *Bidāyat al-Mujtahid wa Nihāyat al-Muqtasid* 10.1.2; Majid Khadduri, *War and Peace in the Law of Islam*, AMS Press, New York, 1400 AH/1979 AC, pp. 256–8.

## CONCLUSION

1 Ovid, *Ex Ponto* 4.14.13–16.

2 Ibid., 4.13.18–22, translation from Arthur Leslie Wheeler, *Ovid: Tristia, Ex Ponto*, Harvard University Press, Cambridge, MA, 1939.

# ACKNOWLEDGEMENTS

Planning the research for this book came with all the best intentions. A global itinerary was drawn up and I was on track to become a jet-setting historian, travelling across Europe, Africa and Asia to really immerse myself in the heritage of so many amazing historical societies. Unfortunately, the COVID-19 pandemic quickly scuppered most of those plans. That was okay, I thought, I can move quickly when lockdowns and travel restrictions were lifted. I would stay within Europe and around the Mediterranean, focusing on places I had not been to before. The first on my list: Ukraine. But the images of Russian forces marching into Ukraine on the television soon told me that my plan had some inherent flaws. While I did manage to see many of the sites for myself, suffice it to say, this book relies heavily on the generosity and ample support of historians and scholars from around the world.

For information, clarification and advice, I could not have wished for a more welcoming response from all over the world. I have not even met many of the people who have fed into this book, but the shared passion and desire to broaden the scope of ancient history was enough for so many great historians and archaeologists to answer my emails and indulge my speculations. In particular, I would like to thank Solange Ashby, Arianna Sacco, Josho Brouwers, Rebecca Futo Kennedy, Mai Musié and Kyle Lewis Jordan. Jo Ball, April Pudsey, Nam C. Kim, Andrew

Crome, Tilman Frasch and Gali Jaffe all read sections of this book and offered vital feedback and corrections along the way. We did not always agree on interpretations and emphasis, but the book is in far better shape as a result of all of their observations and thoughts.

This journey began with an innocuous conversation with Catherine Fletcher, who gave me a crash course in a very different way of looking at history writing. The book itself would not have been possible without the support and guidance of my agent Catherine Clarke and the amazing team at Felicity Bryan Associates. They took a chance on a new writer and I am forever grateful. Michele Topham in particular deserves special mention for handling all of my repetitive and I have no doubt tedious questions with the patience of a saint.

Equally, this book has been shaped by a tireless team at Bloomsbury who I should thank; guided by an amazing editor in Jasmine Horsey, who has made this entire process seem effortless when I have no doubt it was anything but. Gurdip Ahluwalia was my go to for all of my queries and updates and became a regular contributor to my email inbox throughout. Lauren Whybrow has been a godsend, from everything to coordinating proofreaders, to sorting out the images and maps. It sent my head spinning at times, but she was always a voice of calm and order that dragged me through. Richard Collins read through this manuscript numerous times and offered important suggestions on how the book could be improved, I really enjoyed our back and forth. Catherine Best did a fantastic job as proofreader, spotting problems I never noticed. The exquisite maps were produced by Michael Athanson.

Above all else, I am thankful for the unwavering support of my wife Carly who always pushed me to be better than I ever imagined, and my two children Matilda and Henry who have offered their unique perspectives on the topics at hand, as well as their company during the long periods of writing and editing. Matilda also served as my dedicated research assistant at many of the sites, taking photos as well as making notes of important details while I guided us through. It is to my family that I dedicate this book.

# INDEX

# IMAGE CREDITS

Items discovered in graves at Lake Turkana: PNAS journal, courtesy of Carla E. Klehm; world map in spherical projection published in Nicolaus Germanus' edition of Ptolemy's *Cosmographia*, 1482: National Library of Sweden/Universal Art Archive/Alamy Stock Photo; Remaining walls of Buhen Fort: Courtesy of The Egypt Exploration Society; Pillars being transported before the site was flooded: Courtesy of The Egypt Exploration Society; Relief of Thutmose killing Canaanite captives after the Battle of Megiddo: Richard Baker/Getty Images; Carving of a Canaanite woman, Megiddo: © Zev Radovan/Bridgeman Images; Winged creature ivory panel, Megiddo: © Zev Radovan/Bridgeman Images; Horn-shaped flask, Megiddo: Israel Museum, Jerusalem/Collection the Israel Antiquities Authority/Bridgeman Images; Site of Olbia: Multipedia/Alamy Stock Photo; Dolphin bronze coin: © The Trustees of the British Museum; Alabastron: Sepia Times/Universal Images Group via Getty Images; Earrings: © The Trustees of the British Museum; Bracelet: © The Walters Art Museum, shared under a Creative Commons CC0 1.0 Universal licence; 'A Buried City in Egypt': Look and Learn/Illustrated Papers Collection/Bridgeman Images; Ground Plan of the Town of Naukratis, as explored by Mr Petrie: Look and Learn/Illustrated Papers Collection/Bridgeman Images; Hadrian's Wall: James Hartshorn/Getty Images; Reconstruction of

Roman Town at Hadrian's Wall: English Heritage/Heritage Images/Getty Images; Staffordshire bowl showing forts on Hadrian's Wall: © The Trustees of the British Museum; Gallic imitation of a Massalian coin: TCx3/Alamy Stock Photo; Basse-Yutz Flagon: © The Trustees of the British Museum; Vindolanda tablet from Hadrian's Wall: © The Trustees of the British Museum; Hercules mosaic from Volubilis: Vito Arcomano/Alamy Stock Photo; Volubilis, Morocco: Giovanni Mereghetti/UCG/Universal Images Group via Getty Images; Karanis, Egypt: Emad Aljumah/Getty Images; Alexander fighting Porus: © The British Library, shared under a Creative Commons CC0 1.0 Universal licence; An Duong Vuong temple in Co Loa: Robert Wyatt/Alamy Stock Photo; The Trung Sisters: CPA Media Pte Ltd/Alamy Stock Photo; Obelisk at Aksum: John Elk/Getty Images; The Garima Gospels (top): The Picture Art Collection/Alamy Stock Photo; The Garima Gospels (bottom): History and Art Collection/Alamy Stock Photo.

# A NOTE ON THE AUTHOR

Owen Rees is a classical historian. Having previously held a Leverhulme Early Career Fellowship at the University of Nottingham, he is now a lecturer in Applied Humanities at Birmingham Newman University. He is the founder of the website BadAncient.com, which brings together a growing network of specialists to fact-check common claims made about the ancient world. He lives in Manchester.

# A NOTE ON THE TYPE

The text of this book is set in Fournier. Fournier is derived from the *romain du roi*, which was created towards the end of the seventeenth century from designs made by a committee of the Académie of Sciences for the exclusive use of the Imprimerie Royale. The original Fournier types were cut by the famous Paris founder Pierre Simon Fournier in about 1742. These types were some of the most influential designs of the eight and are counted among the earliest examples of the 'transitional' style of typeface. This Monotype version dates from 1924. Fournier is a light, clear face whose distinctive features are capital letters that are quite tall and bold in relation to the lower-case letters, and *decorative italics, which show the influence of the calligraphy of Fournier's time.*